# Death, Ritual and Belief

# Death, Ritual and Belief

## The Rhetoric of Funerary Rites

Douglas J. Davies

CASSELL 1997

London and Washington

Cassell
Wellington House
125 Strand
London WC2R 0BB

PO Box 605
Herndon, VA 20172

First published 1997

**British Library Cataloguing-in-Publication Data**
A catalogue record for this book is available from the British Library.

**Library of Congress Cataloging-in-Publication Data**
Davies, Douglas James.
    Death, ritual, and belief: the rhetoric of funerary rites /
Douglas J. Davies.
        p.   cm
    Includes bibliographical references and index.
    ISBN 0-304-33821-4. – ISBN 0-304-33822-2 (pbk.)
    1. Death – Religious aspects – Comparative studies.   2. Funeral rites
and ceremonies.   I. Title
BL504.D39   1997
291.3'8–dc21                                                    97-19557
                                                                    CIP

ISBN   0-304-33821-4 (hardback)
       0-304-33822-2 (paperback)

Typeset by Ben Cracknell Studios
Printed and bound in Great Britain by Biddles Ltd, Guildford and King's Lynn

# Contents

# Acknowledgements

Some of the empirical information contained in this book originated in the Rural Church Project funded by the Leverhulme Trust and the Cremation Research Project funded, initially, by the University of Nottingham and, additionally, by The Cremation Society of Great Britain.

Permission to reprint on p. 62 excerpts from Dylan Thomas, *Poems of Dylan Thomas*, copyright 1952 by Dylan Thomas, is given by New Directions Publishing, New York, and David Higham Associates, London. Permission to quote on p. 62 from Stevie Smith's 'Not Waving but Drowning' from the *Collected Poems of Stevie Smith* (Penguin Twentieth Century Classics) is given by James MacGibbon. Permission to use on p. 123 an extract from the hymn 'O My Father' is given by the Church of Jesus Christ of Latter-day Saints, Salt Lake City, Utah, USA.

I thank Cassell for efficient assistance in producing this volume and would also like to thank colleagues at the University of Nottingham for many discussions on aspects of mortality and for much support in my death studies. I do this, in particular, after many happy and profitable years at the Department of Theology and shortly before leaving Nottingham for the College of St Hild and St Bede, and for the Department of Theology, at the University of Durham.

Douglas J. Davies
Department of Theology
University of Nottingham
April 1997

# Introduction

This book concerns what might be called the rhetoric of death. Summarized in the phrase, 'words against death', which serves as a recurrent motif throughout the following chapters, this rhetoric constitutes the human response to death in many cultures over many eras. It takes the form of prayers and theologies, of songs and philosophies, as well as more concrete profiles in memorial architecture. Our task is to see how human self-consciousness not only copes with death, but uses funerary rites and their strong verbal component as a means of gaining a higher sense of identity and purpose through them.

In this sense funerary rites are taken to be symbolic of human nature, expressing the way people transform the given facts of biological life into values and goals of humanity. This kind of argument, inevitably, involves generalization and some real speculation. In so doing it lays itself open to proper criticism. But this is a risk well worth taking at a time when the study of death is ever increasing in volume and detail but not, necessarily, in theoretical interest.

The key topics of the book are self-consciousness, the use of language in ritual, along with human identity and its change to a higher order through mortuary rites. An element of cultural evolution underpins my speculation over the development of funeral ritual, with a hint that some religious traditions and local customs are better than others in using death for positive ends. This implicit, sociological, judgement is also open to criticism. The recent anthropological work of Maurice Bloch on the theme of rebounding conquest has been particularly influential on my thinking (1992).

It is quite impossible for a small book to provide an encyclopaedic description of the detail of death rites in all cultures, and this is not my prime intention. While there are descriptions of some basic variations in the disposal of bodies, especially in Chapter 2, and in Chapters 5 to 10, more attention is given to theoretical issues. So, Chapters 1 and 2 deal with anthropology and sociology, and the explanations of death rites they offer in terms of human identity and social status. Chapter 3 considers the social nature of grief, while Chapter 11 takes up the apparently odd case of the death of pets to show how a kind of human status is accorded to them when they die. Chapter 12 looks at the way death is used as a symbol of other life activities while the final chapter considers death in the context of secular and technological societies.

Because few books deal with death in this way it is possible that this volume may be read by a variety of people: some simply curious about death in general, and wanting a broad account of funerals and beliefs, while others, especially scholars interested in theology, philosophy, anthropology, sociology and history, may well be interested in particular details. At the outset I must say that it is impossible to satisfy all these perspectives, not least because of the limits of my own experience and knowledge. With that in mind it is important to say that my academic background in the study of religion lies in both social anthropology and theology, facts which will, inevitably, colour the way death is approached. Even so I have tried, whenever possible, to pin-point particular theories or interesting ideas from varied sources to encourage scholars from one area to be alert to issues which preoccupy others. At the same time I try to outline these issues in ways which the general reader might find appealing and wish to pursue through the references provided.

Finally we must agree that how we interpret death depends, to a great extent, upon our religious and philosophical outlook, as well as upon personal circumstances and experience. So, for example, in an unusual way, for a scholar of religion, the eminent historian of religion Bruce Lincoln prefaced his insightful set of essays entitled *Death, War and Sacrifice* with an observation on the way his own exploration of the mythical themes of Paradise and the Lord of the Dead reflected his own 'search for meaning and consolation in the face of death', not least in the light of a personal bereavement (1991: xiii). He tells how 'hope, reassurance, and consolation ... proved difficult to sustain' and expresses his realization that even academic discourse can 'never be perfectly neutral and disinterested' (1991: xvii). This serves as a reminder of the unusual fact that, unlike most other aspects of life, death is a framing inevitability for everyone who reads this book, or engages in the potentially transforming discussion of mortality.

# 1 Interpreting Death Rites

Death stands highly documented as the twentieth century ends and the new millennium dawns. Archaeologists describe the prehistory of death rites, historians compare and contrast the mortuary rites of more recent eras, and anthropologists describe contemporary patterns of dealing with the dead. Around these scholarly volumes clusters an ever growing number of biographies, booklets and pamphlets describing how individuals have coped with their own loss, with psychologists providing more technical accounts of grief. This book not only draws from many of these studies but also seeks to extend them through an additional theory of death rites summarized in the phrase 'words against death'.

## Introducing the theory

This expression encapsulates a theory which views death rites as an adaptation to the fact of death, an adaptation underlying not only the major world religions but also local religious practice. Although as formal theologies and philosophies these 'words against death' are expressed in books and lectures, they also pass into the public domain through the verbal form of prayer, blessing, invocation, eulogies and orations. Allied to music they gain great power in liturgical hymns while, as architectural memorials, they assume a durable public profile.

Human beings are animals and die. But they are, more importantly, also self-conscious. Adding these facts together we argue, from an evolutionary perspective, that death is part of the environment to which the human animal needed to adapt. Accordingly, mortuary ritual is viewed as the human adaptive response to death, with ritual language singled out as its crucial form of response. It is precisely because language is the very medium through which human beings obtain their sense of self-consciousness that it can serve so well as the basis of reaction to the awareness of death. We then argue that, having encountered and overcome this experience, both the individual and society are transformed and gain a sense of power which motivates ongoing life.

To state this same argument in a series of propositions we may say that: (1) humans are self-conscious; (2) language is the key medium of self-consciousness; (3) death is perceived as a challenge to self-consciousness;

(4) language is used as the crucial response to this challenge; (5) funerary rites frame this verbal response, relating it to other behavioural features of music, movement, place, myth and history; (6) having encountered and survived bereavement through funerary rites and associated behaviour, human beings are transformed in ways which make them better adapted for their own and for their society's survival in the world.

These assumptions constitute the speculative theory underlying this book and in subsequent chapters they are related to a wide variety of funerary rituals drawn from many societies and periods of history. As will be argued below, Maurice Bloch's anthropological development of the notion of rebounding conquest has been particularly influential in framing this argument (1992).

## Variety and caution

Mortuary rites are sometimes extensive and sometimes cursory. This variation is daunting for anyone seeking to describe, let alone to explain, funerary rites. So, even if we accept that one of the fundamental and universal problems of humanity is 'the consciousness of the possibility of death and having to cope with that finality in terms of after-death beliefs and mortuary rites and cults of the dead', we still need reminding that 'mankind's cultural constructions have been so profusely rich and varied that we are well advised to be circumspect about the prospect of isolating worthwhile generalities beyond the superficial' (Tambiah, 1970: 114). This caution is clearly important in that the theory of 'words against death' certainly does belong to the realm of generalities. It is my hope, nevertheless, that as an interpretation of human ritual response to the perception of mortality it will take us beyond the superficial.

## Rites of destiny

The great majority of cultures not only talk of a destiny beyond that of a single lifetime but also provide funerary ritual to convey the deceased from the land of the living to whatever lies ahead. Even in secular contexts, rites are performed to locate the dead firmly in the past and in memory. Accordingly, this chapter adopts a strong sociological emphasis to show how death rites transform the status of the living into one appropriate for the dead. Part of this sociological concern embraces the ritual function of language which, itself, raises additional philosophical and theological issues. Finally, these complex reflections on life and death demand some, brief, psychological comments on identity and death.

Just as language is a major characteristic of the human species so, we argue, it must be given its proper place in the dynamics of funerary rites, not only in coping with death but even in triumphing over it. Societies differ at this point. Some, indeed, seem just able to cope with corpses, while others appear to use funerary rites as the very basis for gaining cultural energy to motivate ongoing life. The difference between pygmies simply pulling down a hut over a corpse and wandering elsewhere in the forest is different from their village neighbours' more elaborate rites, and is far removed from elaborate city funerals entombing the dead under monumental architecture (Turnbull, 1965: 74). It would even be possible to provide a rough classification of cultures in terms, for example, of the degree of energy put into death rites or the extent to which the rites are used as a positive cultural resource. Though that task lies beyond the immediate scope of this book it is worth suggesting that part of the success of certain religions lies in the benefit they confer upon members by turning death to advantage. This combined emphasis on the verbal nature of death rites and the sense of triumph over death through mortuary rites comprises the distinctive feature of this book and will run throughout subsequent chapters. Through describing funerary rites, their attendant beliefs and verbal form, we will see how human cultures assert the ongoing power of human existence despite death's ravages. In particular we will see how death rites influence and change human identity as that self-consciousness, challenged by mortality, responds in its own defence through literal and metaphorical 'words against death'.

## Identity and death

At death, identity and social status undergo major changes. These cannot be ignored despite the fact that identity is an extremely difficult word to define, raising significant anthropological and philosophical questions concerning degrees of self-awareness and group membership in different cultures (Mauss, 1979: 57ff.; Carrithers, Collins and Lukes, 1985; Morris, 1991; Schweder and Bourne, 1991: 113). I take identity to refer to the way people understand themselves in relation to other persons, to the world around them and to supernatural realms. Identity is a consequence of self-consciousness within particular social networks embedded within a particular language. Throughout life, the relationships which grow between individual men, women and children, as members of families and society, help foster that sense of who they are and of their purpose in the world. Here identity and destiny become intimately combined.

Historians have done much to document and relate changing patterns of death rites, social attitudes and ideas of identity. Philippe Ariès has provided one magisterial interpretation of the way death has been perceived and experienced over a thousand years of European history, drawing extensively from literary and theological sources (1991). He not only emphasized human awareness but also saw death rites as a 'defence of society against untamed nature' and concluded that 'the ritualization of death is a special aspect of the total strategy of man against nature' (1991: 603, 604).

This 'strategy of man against nature' resembles my own focus on 'words against death' except that Ariès followed the French trend of setting human culture against animal nature in too stark a form. Despite a great appreciation of his cultural analysis of Western European life, my own argument does not work on the basis of this opposition between culture and nature, one which led Ariès (1991: 392) into the more Freudian association of death with sex, an alliance which may be far too culturally specific to be of real use in a comparative study.

I reject this type of argument, focused on what anthropologists call the binary opposition of culture and nature, because it reflects, too much, a particular preoccupation with categorizing things in pairs, something not all societies do (Needham, 1980: 41ff.). Rather, I see death rites as an inevitable consequence of human self-awareness. The idea of 'words against death' can reflect self-consciousness in a wide variety of ways, from asserting belief in an immortal soul to emphasizing the continuity of identity through heirs and successors. This is an important point because, for example, we do not wish to argue that some fear of death inevitably pushed humanity into generating a belief in an immortal soul. While it can be argued philosophically that self-consciousness cannot entertain the idea of its own cessation individuals can still think of their own absence from society as they ponder the death and removal of others. This is why the philosopher Jean-Paul Sartre is, I believe, correct in saying that 'death is always beyond my subjectivity'. 'Death', he wrote, 'is in no way an ontological structure of my being ... it is the *Other* who is mortal in his being' (1957: 546).

Self-consciousness is intimately linked with a sense of identity. It could even be said that identity is self-consciousness expressed in the public sphere. Some religious experiences, especially conversion, mysticism and possession, help generate a sense of identity while some rites actively confer identity, as in baptism or Islamic pilgrimage. Indeed some sociologists think that the sense of personal identity can become so important to individuals that they, in turn, invest the source of their identity with great significance, even seeing it as divine in some sense (Mol, 1976). At death identity is altered not only through the loss of figures who have served as sources of identity but also by the new responsibilities which the living must take upon themselves.

Grief is that human emotion which expresses death's rupturing of relationships. But, as a form of self-reflection, it also reflects the depth of human life itself. Life, not as some abstract idea but as the very physical experience of ourselves and of those with whom we live and work. The closer the living is bound to the deceased the greater is the sense of loss at death. Even the death of a national leader or some stage, screen or sports star can affect an individual's outlook on life. This book explores the ways people from different countries, times and places have responded to death and the changes in identity which follow funerals, whether transforming wives into widows or husbands into ancestors.

In the major religions of the world, as in small tribal groups, the living manipulate human remains to effect these new statuses for themselves and for the dead. Cumpsty has classified what he calls 'the modelling of survival after death' into the three neat groups of 'Nature Religion' in which the dead become ancestors, 'Withdrawal Religion' where they are reincarnated, and 'Secular World Affirming Religion' where they go to a distinct heaven (1991: 207). In a more theoretically useful way, Chidester's excellent study of death explored 'four characteristic ways of symbolizing the transcendence of death' as *ancestral, experiential, cultural* and *mythic* patterns of trans-cendence (1990: 14ff.). His discussion, along with that of John Bowker (1991), furnishes two of the more significant reflections on death rites in contemporary literature considered at the end of this chapter.

## Doubting death

Perhaps the most interesting fact about death is that human beliefs seem to contradict what meets the eye. Despite the obvious fact that an actively self-motivated agent becomes a passive corpse subjected to decay, human cultures have universally asserted that something of the individual continues after death; even the smell of decay can symbolize the process of transition (Howes, 1991: 135ff.). Sharp contrasts are drawn between the physical body and some other sort of dynamic element which may be called the soul, the life-force, the social status, or some other vital phenomenon. In many respects it is quite easy to see such beliefs as a wish-fulfilment on the part of grieving relatives and to make death rites extremely individual in purpose, but closer analysis shows that a post-mortem identity of the dead also relates to the ongoing social life of a community. Death rites are as much concerned with issues of identity and social continuity as with the very practical fact that human bodies decay and become offensive to the sight and smell of the living.

## Confronting death

The fact that practically all human societies possess some formalized death rites, alongside the otherwise practical task of disposing of a body, suggests that funerary ritual possesses some very positive function in human life. In evolutionary terms, it is likely that they have a positive adaptive significance for if they possessed no such benefit they would have been abandoned long ago. Throughout this book the major assumption is that death rites are a means of encouraging a commitment to life despite the fact of death. While this is certainly not a unique suggestion, as accounts of several scholars will show, the distinctive element in this book emerges in the power of verbal rites to expressing human triumph over death.

## Words and humanity

A strong sense of self-awareness combined with a powerful linguistic ability stand as prime features of humanity. As death challenges human self-awareness, threatening to terminate the identity it confers, so humanity deploys its most powerful weapon of language in rising to defy death. Archaeology suggests that burial was an early human activity and, certainly, the historic religions have given much attention to the ritual disposal of the dead. Though Laughlin and McManus emphasize the speculative nature of their suggestion they would not be surprised if ritual activity had not arisen very early amongst pre-human hominids who had developed brains enabling them to picture issues beyond their immediate sense experience. They felt it not inappropriate, for example, to 'consider that *Australopithecus* might have directed conceptualized ritual at such problems as ... the death of fellow group members' (1979: 110).

In evolutionary terms language has become the symbol of human self-consciousness and the means by which people become aware of themselves and relate to each other (Tambiah, 1990: 81ff.). I assume that death has been widely seen to challenge human identity and besiege social destiny. Accordingly, I regard death rites as serving to repulse this negative feature of death and, precisely because of this, I speak of death rites as 'words against death'. In symbolic terms words represent the ongoing and positive nature of human identity and of society as the cradle of identity, while corpses represent the negative domain of physical existence which is short-lived in each individual. Funerary rites and the language of death thus mark the divide between the paradox of social eternity and physical mortality. In this, funerals symbolize society.

It is this kind of argument which will be used to interpret the significance of the rites described in the following chapters. While I will certainly not ignore non-verbal forms of communication within funerary rites, I do wish to emphasize these linguistic factors. I am well aware of the significance of non-verbal aspects of human life and, in an earlier book, stressed the importance of emotional aspects of behaviour within the overall drive for meaning expressed as salvation (D. J. Davies, 1984). Though the following chapters do not deal with such religious themes as salvation they are, in terms of the sociology of knowledge – and of my own earlier studies just mentioned – closely related to that sense of plausibility underlying human destiny as discussed by Peter Berger, who spoke of death rites as one means of keeping members of society 'reality-orientated' (1967: 33).

This highlights the fact that, in terms of death rites, it is difficult to draw distinctions between the well-known salvation religions of the world and the traditional religions of small ethnic groups. All show a concern with death and most societies set about ritual performances which help make sense of the ending of a life by reconstructing the identity of the dead within some wider framework of significance. In all this the power of language assumes a dramatic, though often ignored, part in accompanying other ritual acts in emphasizing human belief in the triumph of humanity over death and in asserting the plausibility of existence.

## Performative utterances and death

Language influences human beings to a dramatic extent, not only helping to structure thought, but also directing emotion and mood, especially during critical moments in life, as when vows are taken at marriage or in courts of law. At times of death language can assume significant proportions as sympathy is expressed to comfort the bereaved and as eulogies reflect the life of the dead. Philosophers and Christian theologians have made much of the special nature of religious language in general (Ramsey, 1957), have shown how language operates both within liturgy and in secular contexts (Fenn, 1982) and have explored ways in which Christianity's emphasis upon verbal truth has influenced Western cultures (Fenn, 1987). While they have also discussed the issue of death (MacKinnon, 1957: 261; Cohn-Sherbok and Lewis, 1995), they have rarely pursued the debate into the area of death rites.

One concept which Christian theologians have found very useful is that of the 'performative utterance' introduced in what was a direct, and even humorous, paper by the philosopher J. L. Austin (1961: 220). He used it to describe statements of the kind 'I name this ship' or 'I pronounce them man and wife', which acted rather like actions within appropriate contexts and given what Austin called a certain kind of 'force'. Though explored in terms of prayer and other religious utterances, this idea still awaits serious consideration in the context of funerary rites. In Britain, for example, we can see how the traditional statement 'we commit his body to the ground, earth to earth, ashes to ashes, dust to dust' constitutes a clear performative utterance. Also accompanied by an act, that of throwing soil on the coffin, the utterance marks the ritual moment of burial, even though it follows the lowering of the coffin into the grave. In cremation services the words 'we commit his body to be consumed by fire' are, similarly, usually accompanied by the removal of the coffin or the drawing of curtains around the coffin. The words and the action conjoin in the performative utterance achieving its goal. This, then, affords a good example of 'words against death', in this context of performative utterances against death.

## Words and hugs

Such utterances relate to Donovan Ochs and his description of the death of an individual as 'bringing into existence a rhetorical situation' (1993: 21). Rhetoric, as a process of employing speech to persuade people of some particular point, embraces all that is said about the dead and the bereaved in an attempt to encourage them and give them strength and hope during their trials. This is worth emphasizing because of the contemporary British trend of down-playing words in an attempt to stress behavioural aspects of life. Some individuals emphasize the importance of simply being with the bereaved, giving physical comfort through touch or by hugging them, rather than in placing much significance upon words. Part of the reason for this is that people often comment that they do not know what to say. This sense of inadequacy may come from not having experienced personal bereavement, a situation true for many British adults under the age of 40, or it may derive from not possessing any shared belief in life after death. All this tends to play down the power of words in situations of grief and is the outcome of a very particular social world of urban, cosmopolitan and weakly secularized contexts, in which people do not share ultimate values in implicit ways. Indeed it is this which makes it hard for some people to 'find the right words' to speak to someone who has been bereaved. We should not assume that this is true for other contexts nor indeed for much of human history, nor even that it is increasingly inevitable in a secular world. As we will see, other words may well come to fill the partial vacuum.

Traditionally, however, many people have been and are called upon to speak, to sing laments or perform traditional ritual at times of death, and their words can assume particular importance for those involved. The power of words to trigger and direct emotion is great, not least when they are combined with music in song or chant. It is probably no accident that what are called life-directed funerals are increasingly popular, most especially in Australia. Highlighting the life of the deceased, professionals other than clergy are employed to engage in what is, effectively, a rhetoric of bereavement. Such rhetoric has long held a place in the funerals or memorial services for famous people but, increasingly, this applies to ordinary members of society as a way of beginning to cope with grief. It is often a rhetoric of the past, a reflection in memory rather than a depiction of future destiny. But, alongside professional leadership, it is also increasingly common, certainly in Britain, for various family members to take part in funerals and, even more so, in memorial services which may be held some time after the funeral. In situations of group tragedies where, for example, schoolchildren have died or been killed, other pupils or friends may speak or play music to involve them in the corporate event. Here 'words against death' may even be all the more powerful coming from the young yet, still, within the frame of ritual.

## Sociological and anthropological explanations

So it is that we turn to sketch major social scientific theories on the nature of mortuary ritual, ritual which assists the living through the stress of death, helps reform social networks broken by the loss of a group member and confers new identity on those passing from the land of the living into a new community of ancestors, saints or memory. Such mortuary ritual has been interpreted by an influential group of past and present social scientists especially Hertz, Durkheim, Malinowski, Van Gennep, Douglas, Bauman and Bloch, whose basic ideas we will now outline in a description which interlinks their contribution.

### The process of transforming corpses

Robert Hertz (1882–1915), student of the influential sociologist Émile Durkheim, died as a 33-year-old second lieutenant leading his troops in battle in April 1915. In a classic anthropological essay entitled 'The collective representation of death', which has influenced many subsequent studies of mortuary rites, he sketched the idea that society has a close relationship with the physical bodies of its constituent members:

Society imparts its own character of permanence to the individuals who compose it: because it feels itself immortal and wants to be so, it cannot normally believe that its members ... in whom it incarnates itself should die. (Hertz, 1960: 77)

Marcel Mauss, friend and collaborator of Hertz, also saw the powerful relationship between society and the death of its members (1979) while Mary Douglas, in her more recent anthropological work, has provided a similar theoretically abstract approach to the human body which she sees as a microcosm of society (1970: 93). If we assume with Hertz and Douglas that the human body may be regarded as a model expressing social values then, theoretically, we can see how the life and health of flourishing bodies may depict the dynamics and values of social life. Similarly, the illness and particularly the death of a body may be expected to involve a kind of challenge to society.

### Human body as microcosm

The idea that the human body may be viewed as a microcosm of society needs some explanation for those unfamiliar with this kind of anthropological perspective. In what sense is a body a microcosm of society? We can answer this question by acknowledging that, on the one hand we have bodies and on the other we are members of a society. If we pressed these points to an extreme position we would, in the most literal sense, have the biological body studied by anatomists on the one hand, while on the other would lie a much more metaphorical way of speaking about the 'social body' or 'society' studied by sociologists. The social body represents men and women, boys and girls, all together as parts of their community and wider society. 'Society', in this sense, is an abstract term used as a shorthand word to embrace a great mass of people with their values, beliefs, and customs.

In other words, the physical body is a very material entity while society is an abstract idea. This distinction raises the question of how these two realms may be linked. One easy answer is to say that people acting for society write down its laws and beliefs which can then be read and learned by each individual member. As the human baby grows it is, as it were, nurtured in such a way that it passes from being simply a biological body to becoming human. And part of this nurturing involves learning to read and then learning the laws and rules of its society.

There is much truth in this picture, especially in literate societies, but there is another dimension of even greater significance. For, as the baby grows through childhood and into adulthood, it acquires a tremendous amount of information about its world by imitating other people, by learning how to walk and talk in particular ways, by simply learning how to behave. A great deal of this kind of learning is implicit and not taught in any formal way. If, following the anthropologist Dan Sperber, we draw a distinction between factual or encyclopaedic knowledge on the one hand, and implicit or symbolic knowledge on the other, we could say that encyclopaedic knowledge is learned while symbolic knowledge is acquired (1975). Some scholars see this sort of distinction as expressing the way the brain operates through its two cerebral hemispheres. The left cerebral hemisphere is much concerned with language and rational aspects of knowledge while the right hemisphere deals with non-verbal aspects of knowing (Blakeslee, 1980). It is as though individuals have social values 'packed' into them through the way they learn how to behave. In a figurative sense the rule book of society comes to be 'written' into their deportment and carriage, each person being a little representation of the society at large, each body a microcosm of society (Blacking, 1977). The African Tallensi people offer a good example where the sense of the individual is tied up with various kinship relationships only some of which change after death. 'What dies is the matrilineal person or the individual', associated with the soft parts of the body and corpse, while the patrilineal 'person' continues in the form of hard bones and as a continuing identity within the kinship group (M. Bloch, 1988: 19).

This brief background helps explain the idea of a body as the microcosm of society. For the greater part of history the majority of humans have been pre-literate or illiterate. Laws, beliefs and customs have been acquired through oral tradition, often implicitly rather than explicitly. Accordingly, the power and authority present in society are, in a sense, 'written' on the body of individuals. In Mary Douglas' argument, the kind of control a society exerted over its members was expressed and reflected in the way individuals controlled their own bodies (1966, 1970). In some religious groups, for example, the tight social control over members is reflected in their dress, hair-style and demeanour. Where control is lax or hardly existent, the individual reflects this in personal free-expression of dress, hair and general behaviour. Within social life itself the body tends to be more fully controlled the more 'social' an occasion is: civic functions usually involve careful grooming with bodily movements and speech being highly stylized. If we picture social life as a series of concentric circles then the closer people are, on a particular occasion, to the very centre the greater will be their bodily control. The further they are from that centre so their control over themselves will decrease.

Within British culture we find that in religious worship or in courts of law, dress, speech and movement are all highly controlled and we interpret this as being because these are moments when individuals are closest to their central beliefs and values. These two examples are important because they remind us that in most societies central beliefs and values are often identified with the bodies of particular persons. Judges and bishops, for example, embody law and faith. In the same way the body of the monarch is clearly made to bear in a literal sense the marks of state at the coronation. The very breast of the monarch is anointed with oil, just as her head wears the crown and her hands carry the orb and sceptre. In accord with this perspective highly symbolic people, such as monarchs or archbishops, cannot simply put on and put off their symbols of office because their very body becomes the symbol. Their body and its behaviour is a microcosm of the whole world they represent. This is what is meant by consecration as the whole life is committed to a set of beliefs and values. It is also the reason why the distinction between private and public morality becomes hard to sustain. It is an issue which is also, probably, reflected in the bodies of actors and sport celebrities.

## Death of a microcosm

This idea of the body as a microcosm of society inevitably raises the theoretical question of what we might call the death of a microcosm. If the human body is a kind of model of society it is, obviously, much more than a mere physical body. As a symbol of society a body participates in that which it represents. In this sense, for example, spouses, parents, children, friends or pop stars are symbols of marriage, kinship, friendship or fame so that when an individual dies these very ideas are attacked or impugned in some way. It is against that background that I speak of the death of a microcosm. It is as though society is challenged when one of its 'expressions' within an individual dies. So, for example, parenthood is challenged when a child dies, or friendship with the death of a good friend. Similarly, there is something tragic when the actor Christopher Reeve is reduced by an accident to a wheelchair instead of playing his accustomed role as Superman.

This perspective places great weight on the human body as the vehicle and bearer of social values and beliefs. It is insufficient to speak only of roles or role models when dealing with the depths of human life and relationships. This is an important point which can easily be ignored by people unfamiliar with the social sciences, especially since the phrase 'role-model' flourishes in popular speech despite the fact that some sociologists like Anthony Giddens have cast serious doubts on its usefulness in sociology (1979: 117). In this book I largely avoid talking about roles and prefer to speak of embodiment or of social status and identity. Embodiment, in particular, has become an increasingly important theoretical idea in recent anthropology and is an attempt at dealing with the wide range of experience, mood and gesture which provides the context and medium of human life (Howes, 1991). The death of the body, as a microcosm, shows that death is not simply some problem of a philosophical or rational kind but reaches deep into the biological and social nature of human beings.

## Identity and embodiment

We have already referred to the fact that it is hard to define the idea of identity. Everyone knows what it is as far as general conversation is concerned but it is extremely hard to define and establish agreement from experts in different fields (Mol, 1976: 55ff.). Repeating what we have already said, this book takes a broad view of identity holding it to be the sense individuals have of who they are and of what makes them what they are. This includes the beliefs and values people hold, as well as the awareness they have of their own bodies and sensations. It embraces relationships with those people, things and places which give a framework of significance to our lives, and for religious individuals, it probably includes an awareness of God. And all of this sense of who we are is set within our personal history and the history of our family, society and religious tradition. Our identity and destiny are combined.

## Hertz and the two phases of death-identity

With this in mind we return to Hertz's analysis of death rites as involving a two-phased process. The first affected the dead body shortly after death and the second the remains of that body at some later date. The first set of rites deal with the corruptible flesh, with what Hertz called the 'wet' medium of the body. The second set of rites deal with the bony remains or ashes and constitute the 'dry' medium of the body. The first phase, whether involving interment, cremation or storage, was a time for the bones to dry, whether slowly through decay or rapidly through fire. This means that, for example, he describes cremation in a very distinctive way: 'This is precisely the meaning of cremation: far from destroying the body of the deceased, it recreates it and makes it capable of entering into new life' (1960: 43).

Symbolically speaking this clarifies what we earlier called the death of a microcosm. Insofar as the body represents society, and as such is an important symbolic entity, the death of the body might be thought to devalue that society which it symbolizes. The death of a microcosm issuing, as it were, a challenge to the integrity of the continuing cosmos. But, if Hertz is right, funerary rites rise to the challenge and turn the negative face of death into a positive image of some transcending reality. The identity of the body is not extinguished, it is simply transformed and revealed in its new state. The first rite removes the dead from the realm of daily social life while the second places the dead into the supernatural world of the ancestors. This is precisely why Hertz's comparative material led him to say that: 'As for cremation, it is usually neither a final act, nor sufficient in itself; it calls for a later and complementary rite' (1960: 42).

Hertz devoted his analysis to primitive Indonesian cultures with only passing comments on Europe. He was, after all, writing at a time when there was practically no cremation in Western European countries and when burial rites were still dominant and often elaborate, not least in France where, for example, in the mid-nineteenth century there were at least ten types of horsedrawn hearses available in Paris depending upon cost (Kselman, 1993: 241). But Hertz, I believe, discovered a principle of the dual-focused process of funerary rites, applicable not only to cremation and burial but also to other forms of funerary ritual and significantly illuminating several other theories now to be outlined in the rest of this chapter. Together they provide a powerful basis for interpreting the rites described in the remainder of this book.

### Durkheim: mourning a loss

Hertz's teacher, Émile Durkheim, in his influential book *The Elementary Forms of the Religious Life* (1915) established one sociological tradition for interpreting religion which drew heavily from the theologian W. Robertson Smith's *Religion of the Semites* (1894). Smith had stressed the power sensed by those engaged in corporate worship and played much upon the distinction between the holy and the common as categories of human experience. Durkheim expanded these ideas in his theory that social ritual yielded a sense of transcendence which was, in effect, the human experience of 'society'. He also focused extensively on the category distinction between what he called the sacred and the profane.

In both authors there is brief yet germinal acknowledgement of the positive function of death rites. Robertson Smith acknowledges the 'great range of funeral rites' which exist, but beneath this variety he sees them as being 'all directed to make sure that the corpse is properly disposed of, and can no longer be a source of danger to the living, but rather of blessing' (1894: 370). This additional identification of blessing is important for it shows how Smith saw death rites taken beyond the level of utilitarianism in corpse disposal into a more positive domain which has to do with the flourishing of a community.

In terms of basic ritual Durkheim talks in a strongly positive way of the 'increased courage and ardour' with which people re-enter into the profane world once they have acquitted themselves of their ritual duties (1915: 382). For him the sense of transcendence which might accompany ritual was directly derived from the effect of group activity. When it came to death rites Durkheim stressed the role of mourning rituals as serving social ends even more than they served the private needs of the bereaved. 'Mourning is not the spontaneous expression of individual emotions ... it is a duty imposed by the group' (1915: 397). And the duty is imposed because 'the foundation of mourning is the impression of a loss which the group feels when it loses one of its members' (1915: 401).

Durkheim the sociologist sees the sense of loss in mourning more in terms of a weakening of group membership than of individual grief, with emotions being 'intensified and affirmed' when they are shared collectively. In fact, he cautiously suggests that the origin of belief in the soul emerges from funeral rites and from the expression of both loss and a degree of fear occasioned by the social disruption of death (1915: 400). All this makes sociological sense for Durkheim's commitment to the idea that society exists before us and will exist after us, and must be maintained through all periods of potential fragmentation, including loss of members through death. While this kind of sociological argument may be acceptable as a fairly abstract discussion on the nature of society it can easily be criticized for ignoring individuals and their personal experience of grief even though it was not Durkheim's intention to discuss individuals.

## Malinowski: ritualizing optimism

Durkheim's abstract sociological emphasis on society met an appropriate challenge in the work of the anthropologist Bronislaw Malinowski. Unlike Durkheim, who always lived in France as a professor, Malinowski had prolonged and intimate experience of life in pre-literate societies. For him 'savages' or 'primitives' were real people especially in the case of the Trobriand Islanders, whose language he spoke and whose life he had shared.

Malinowski explicitly rejected Durkheim's ignoring of individual emotional experience (1974: 59) and speaks of death as touching deeply the private lives of people. He tells his European readers that the Trobriand response to death is 'more akin to our own, than is usually assumed' (1974: 47). He speaks of the mixed emotions of longing, fear and disgust associated with the dead and focuses on the 'double-edged play of hope and fear which sets in always in the face of death' (1974: 51). Religion, for him, helped people choose and emphasize the sense of hope in life rather than the sense of fear; religion gives them a conviction of continuing life and not of despair. The whole of mortuary ritual must, he thinks, serve some 'biological function of religion' (1974: 53), one that 'saves man from surrender to death and destruction', and reinforces 'the desire for life' (1974: 51). So it is that funerary rites help and assist individuals over the period of their distress as well as expressing the social loss of a member of society. In fact Malinowski adds, in a simple yet telling way, that to lose somebody in a society made up of a relatively small number of people is an obvious problem. His view of funerary rites as a desire for life is echoed by another early though often ignored anthropologist, A. M. Hocart, who placed great emphasis on ritual as something that helped people in 'securing life' or in 'promoting life' (1935: 46, 47).

These ideas of life-promoting ritual or of acts ritualizing man's optimism provide a basis for seeing humanity as social animals possessing a shared hope of survival, at once complex and fascinating. When extended into the past this hope can constitute history or myth, for people have been extremely creative in constructing interpretations of past events and in filling those events with a significance that transcends the simple event itself. Similarly, groups look into the future, filling it with plans and optimism to bring a sense of meaning to what, in the present, is still quite unformed. So it is that hope, as a basic human emotion, comprises one aspect of self-conscious social nature and becomes particularly apparent in contexts of strong patriotism and nationalism as well as in the intense social groups of some churches. When human emotions become strained by grief and when sadness threatens to overwhelm those who have lost those they love or to whom they are closely bound, death rites come to their aid. Through death ritual the afflicted feel the support of others, many of whom are not so directly affected by the death, until such time as they gain a sense of their own ability to cope. Communal support overcomes the sense of hopelessness of the individual who might otherwise have to stand alone.

## *Bauman: hiding death*

The contemporary sociologist Zygmunt Bauman follows Malinowski in seeing death as such a profound problem that it may swamp human beings and their will to live (1992a). For him the various institutions of society actively hide the reality of death from its members by giving the impression that death is under control, not least through religious ritual. While the reality of death cannot be totally eliminated, death rites do their best to keep its impact to a minimum. Bauman's view is strongly of the opinion that ordinary social life might well be seriously damaged if the fact of death was allowed a free hand to strike at people.

Even though in some societies, such as that of contemporary Britain, the work of hospitals and undertakers can easily mask death it is still easy for individuals to dwell upon the death of family or friends and come to feel that life is not worth living. Bereaved people sometimes say that life has lost its meaning for them, or that it seems so hard to find a purpose in life. This response to bereavement is perfectly understandable when key individuals have died, leaving a fragmented social world behind them. Bauman stresses that death is such an unanswerable problem that people would lose the motive to live if they had to dwell upon it for too long. If he is right death ritual serves the purpose of removing the dead from the world of the living so as to enable the survivors to give their minds to life issues as soon as is possible. It is obvious that human societies could not survive if death came to anaesthetize the living, making them feel a permanent sense of hopelessness.

Those who possess a religious belief will, very likely, think that Bauman goes too far in interpreting religions as themselves part of the social deception. Others may well agree with him and see religion as yet another means of preventing people from facing the stark fact that in the end we quite simply die and that is the end of life's endeavour. It could even be argued that in modern societies, where social rituals are reduced in their scope and where individuals are left much more to their own privacy, without the support of extensive networks of kin, the loss of death strikes home particularly hard. It may well be that individuals need a fairly extensive group to help survive grief or to perform adequately as a grief-stricken person. In terms of 'words against death' many relatively isolated individuals may simply not belong to a suitable speech community able to voice powerful ritual words. This is precisely where the established funeral professions move into action and provide various sets of traditional 'words against death', whether derived from the churches, the funeral-directing world or from death counsellors.

The argument that hospitals and funeral directors often seem to take over the processes of death and funerals, alienating the bereaved from the dead body, needs judicious consideration in this context. While there may be some truth in this alienation model of contemporary trends in modern urban societies, it should not be allowed to obliterate other possible factors such as the density of kinship relationships available to people at times of stress. It could be that a bereaved person living alone or with one child would find it much more difficult having the corpse in the home prior to the funeral in comparison with an extended family of four or more persons along with neighbours prepared to be closely involved with the bereaved. At least these are important questions when discussing death rites for, as we see throughout the subsequent chapters, death is often a time when members of a community are triggered into community action. But that always assumes that a community exists which can be activated and, in many modern urban contexts, this is not often the case.

## Rites of passage

The community context of death rites is one of the most important features of many of the following chapters. The individual's response to death is framed by the social group whether composed of kin, friends, neighbours or just of paid professionals. One of the most common concepts used to interpret death ritual in its social context is described by the term 'rites of passage'. This is one of the best known ideas from anthropology that has passed into popular use. 'Rites of passage' is a term first used by the Dutch anthropologist Arnold Van Gennep in 1908 to describe the way people passed from one social status to another (1960). His focus was on changes in status which he likened to moving from one room to another through passages or across thresholds within a house. Such changes in social status were brought about, Van Gennep believed, through a three-staged process given the overall name of 'rites of passage'. These rites consisted in a separation from the old status, a period of transition to help in learning aspects of the new identity and, finally, a reincorporation into new status. So the rite might begin with someone being a boy or girl and end with them being a man or a woman. Similarly they might begin as a single person and end as married, or begin as a lay person and end as a priest. He argued that one of these stages of separation, transition and reincorporation would be stressed above the other two depending on the final purpose of the rites of passage. Using the Latin word *limen*, or threshold, to describe these phases he spoke of pre-liminal (separation), liminal (transition) and post-liminal (reincorporation) stages of rites of passage. Though these terms are very useful when interpreting death rites great care is needed in using them. For example, the main focus for the bereaved relative may be separation from the dead while for the dead person the main ritual emphasis may be on reincorporation into the society of the ancestors or of the heavenly community.

Van Gennep thought that his idea of rites of passage had uncovered something of a universal phenomenon. Certainly it has received wide acceptance and extensive use, not only by successive generations of anthropologists but even amongst the general public. But his analysis of changes in social status through a ritual process has also been developed in other important ways. Two anthropologists stand out for the way they have taken germinal ideas from Van Gennep and developed them in very creative ways. Victor Turner (1969) focused on the liminal period and explored the dynamics of what happened to people when thrown together in periods of stress and change of identity, and thence developed the concept of *communitas* to describe this shared fellow-feeling (we will explore this in Chapter 3). The other major development, one involving a greater degree of criticism of Van Gennep, comes from the anthropologist Maurice Bloch (1992) whose ideas of 'rebounding violence' or 'rebounding conquest' are of particular importance in the study of death rites and to much of the rest of this book.

## Bloch: life to death and death to life

The natural facts of life which cannot be disputed are that people are born, grow old and die. They may reproduce themselves and achieve great or little things, but at the end of their life they die. While this is biologically obvious Bloch argues that world religions and many local traditions often turn these facts of life on their head by rituals of initiation which, symbolically, begin with 'death' and proceed into a higher order of 'life'. Though Bloch (1992) coined the terms 'rebounding violence' or 'rebounding conquest' primarily to describe such initiation rites, they are also extremely useful for interpreting death rituals and are of fundamental importance for my own theory of 'words against death'.

While Bloch accepts that there is much truth in Van Gennep's theory of rites of passage he thinks that Van Gennep did not go far enough in explaining the power of ritual in people's lives. Van Gennep focuses his attention on social statuses and on the shift of individuals from one social status to another. Bloch wants to add a new, existential, dimension to these rites because he thinks that through them individuals gain a sense of having encountered some sort of transcendent power or dimension. This sensation influences their lives, giving a sense of becoming different people in some way. Once possessing this new sense of power they are impelled to use it to demonstrate that they are now different people from what they were. Just as their own identity has changed through contact with the transcendent power, so they wish that power to conquer that same old identity present in others. This becomes especially clear when the language of ritual speaks of the individual's old nature being killed or transformed by a new nature. It is as though humanity interrupts the natural process of birth, growth and death, replacing it, in a symbolic way, with a process of ritual death and ritual rebirth.

In the Christian tradition, for example, there is a strong belief that because of sin and wickedness human life ends in death as a natural process. But, because of a divinely initiated salvation, it is now possible for people to become Christians and, accordingly, to overcome death. The symbolic language speaks of this in terms of baptism, through which the old nature of humanity – involving death and destruction – comes to an end as the baptized person is 'born again' in a spiritual sense. This new birth takes place here and now and means that when the physical body dies the baptized Christian will not ultimately die but will, by God's power, be caused to continue to live in an afterlife. In other words the new birth begins a new process which does not end in death, and this is achieved in close conjunction with a verbal formula of baptism. There can be no silent baptism – words are necessary just as they are for the central act in the Mass or Eucharist where words are directly linked to the bread which is to become the 'body' of Christ. Here, once again, we encounter the performative utterance at the heart of Christian ritual.

This inversion of the natural life cycle is repeated in several chapters in this book for a variety of other religious traditions. What it shows is that, in the history of human culture, men and women have been active in addressing themselves to the obvious fact of death by asserting that human life transcends death in some way, as in the case of the Dinka live-burial in Chapter 5. This reflects something of that tremendous dynamism, inherent in human nature, which drives social groups forward with a sense of real optimism and possibility. It is worth emphasizing Bloch's idea because it adds a new dimension to earlier anthropological interpretations of ritual and of human behaviour. Instead of simply agreeing with Durkheim, that funeral rites help to reintegrate society, or assenting to Malinowski's view that the bereaved need support through their period of bereavement, or even with Van Gennep that social changes need to be ritually performed, Bloch's perspective adds the new dimension of a power to leap forward. If it is permissible to extend this argument to embrace death rites we may suggest that death rites do not simply have the capacity to patch tears in the social or psychological fabric of life but actually add a new energy to those who are left as they set about the rest of their life in society. If this is true it makes it all the more important to study the death rites of the world because in them we have a powerhouse of energy which benefits society and adds to that human self-awareness and that power of identity with which we started this chapter.

## Psychological explanations

This anthropological perspective plays a much larger part in this book than do psychological ideas even though we will consider psychological issues of attachment between people and the way they are affected by death later in the book. One, more negative, psychological avenue involves thinkers like Feuerbach (1957) and Freud (1973) who see beliefs in the soul, God and an afterlife in terms of an illusion and as a projection of the human tendency to assert its survival. With Freud, as with some of the secular groups mentioned in Chapter 13, many will agree that such beliefs are really wish-fulfilments grounded only in illusion, one which humanity will need to give up if it is to become intellectually and emotionally mature. Others, especially devotees of the world religions, will radically disagree, arguing that without some aspect of continuing identity, life is relatively absurd and pointless. Though I agree with that majority of psychologists and anthropologists who give little credence to Freud, his theories need mentioning because they continue to influence some writers in the humanities and in the general study of cultures (Badcock, 1980; Obeyesekere, 1981). Walter Goldschmidt (1980), for example, refers to a Freudian perspective in exploring his own view that fear of the evil inherent in death lay at the heart of human attitudes to mortality. In his study of the African Sebei people he showed how their rites were called the 'driving away of death' and not of the dead. The Sebei paid scant attention to the body or indeed to the soul of the deceased, arguing that 'psychologically and metaphysically it is death that they feared and not the spirit of the deceased' (1980: 35). Similarly, in her description of how Jewish mothers responded to the sudden death of sons in the Yom Kippur War, Lea Barinbaum (1980: 121) drew heavily from Freud's idea of the three defence-mechanisms of the ego expressed as retreat, attack and the ability to cope.

It was rather late in his life, during the stresses of the First World War in 1919, that Freud began to distinguish between what he categorized as the ego-instincts and the sexual instincts in his small book *Beyond the Pleasure Principle*. He called the ego-instincts the death-instincts and identified them as negative forces seeking to reduce the human being to its original, lifeless state while the life-instincts were part of the sexual drive to perpetuate life (1922: 67). It was a speculative shift in outlook and one that only a few of his followers pursued (E. Jones, 1961: 406ff.). Freud had established a kind of battle in the self between the forces of life and of death, a battle which mirrored the world war surrounding him but one that possessed very little scientific validity as far as psychological life was concerned.

## Hope and survival

Still, these psychological explanations of death rites do entertain hope as an important human attribute helping to drive communities forward by providing an optimism for life. Kübler-Ross spoke of hope as a profoundly important part of her dying patients' outlook on life and, as she said, 'If a patient stops expressing hope, it is usually a sign of imminent death' (1973: 123). In fact several social and psychological scientists have identified hope as a significant topic of study (Stotland, 1969; E. Bloch, 1986; Holbrook, 1971; Desroche, 1979). Christian theologians have grounded hope not in simple membership of a society but in the very existence of God as a transcending fact of life. Accordingly, people may have hope because there actually exists something greater than them in the reality of God (Moltmann, 1969; Tutu, 1984).

It is, perhaps, either when a strong sense of religious belief or of a sense of community fades that some people find hope hard to grasp. And if that lack of belief coincides with minimal involvement in supportive social groups, as in late twentieth-century urban individualism, then the sense of hopelessness discussed by Bauman would be easily fostered. It would be in such circumstances that we might also expect to find a decrease in the sense of history as a significant dimension in life. Interestingly, however, the contemporary world of the media is not content to assert life as a meaningless mess of accidental events but is forever bringing experts to the screen to explain the problems of life. So, for example, while many recent catastrophes have thrown bereaved people into apparently hopeless conditions, government agencies set out to foster hope, not least through the media. They speak words against death and tragedy by setting up inquiries into the cause of death so that, as the phrase repeatedly expresses it, 'this will never happen again'. It sometimes seems as though this very expression functions as a performative utterance ensuring that death can be coped with if it is not seen as senseless and meaningless. If some lesson can be learned or some new procedure be put into place, then tragic deaths have not 'been in vain'. This shows how important hope and optimism are in motivating society. To have ritualized human optimism, expressing it in verbal form and dramatizing it in death ritual, was a major achievement of humanity.

## Death and transcendence

These issues of optimism and hope return us to the theme of transcendence raised earlier in connection with Durkheim and which is, broadly speaking, linked with my own focus on the adaptive significance of death rites through verbal ritual as explored in this book. Amongst more recent scholars John Bowker and David Chidester have also dealt with this topic and some comment is necessary to see how their arguments both resemble and differ from my own.

For John Bowker, writing from the perspective of Christian theology informed by phenomenology, death is best interpreted through the idea of sacrifice. Arguing keenly against evolutionist explanations of afterlife beliefs as a compensation for fear of death, he asserts that 'at the root of all major, continuing religions, earliest speculations about death did not produce belief that there is a desirable life with God beyond this life, after death' (1991: 29). Rather, he sees early death rites as a means of avoiding disruption and disorder and affirming value (1991: 38). Death is an inevitable part of the evolution of the universe and, in perceiving this, he thinks that believers should see their lives as a form of sacrifice, of 'life yielding for life' (1991: 41). Here Bowker borders on the creative social benefit of death ritual in general but ultimately, as a Christian theologian, he diverts to the Christian theological issue of the death and resurrection of Jesus to ponder the theme that runs through several of his books, namely that perhaps human beings and the universe are 'constructed in such a way that we are capable of entering into relationships not only with each other but (with) ... God?' Ultimately this is a matter of faith, grounded in the fact that one may 'know that our resistance to the tide of entropy establishes within us such miracles of relationship and grace and love that we know already that the fact of death is transcended' (1991: 228). In one sense Bowker's approach is strongly individual in terms of the intuition of faith rather than being sociological. Though he emphasizes the significance of liturgy and ritual, of music, architecture and poetry, he concludes that 'words are so much the currency of our consciousness that we sometimes rely on them when they cannot bear the weight'. He deplores 'people who talk at grief, instead of holding hands with grief' (1991: 42). By contrast with this particularly personal emphasis, my own stress both on the social context and on verbal ritual allows the dynamics of sacrifice to be explained a little more fully than in Bowker. This is possible with the help of Maurice Bloch in describing how a vitality is generated which feeds back into the resourcing of hope for the living.

A slightly similar case emerges with Chidester's most useful and wide-ranging analysis of death rites with its stress on transcendence expressed through his fourfold scheme of ancestral, experiential, cultural and mythic types. One problem lies in the fact that Chidester leaves the term transcendence largely undefined and seemingly referring simply to a human coping device, largely following James Frazer's approach to the history of religions as a 'catalogue of attempts to transcend death' (1990: 2). Once more the positive addition of value to society through death rites is not identified and the verbal power of the ritual is, similarly, taken for granted and not seen as a key feature in the process of benefiting from transcendence.

Both Bowker and Chidester show the importance which Maurice Bloch's work has brought to the analysis of death ritual, in that their work reaches a point beyond which it does not seem to pass. Some idea of transcendence is held but its essential feature of adding a dynamic to society to foster ongoing social life remains largely hidden. This means that much remains to be done, as the following chapters indicate.

# 2 Coping with Corpses

The corpse is the prime symbol of death. In its silence and decay it enshrines the radical changes inevitably brought by mortality, yet it challenges the living to respond. Although burial and cremation comprise the two major forms of response found throughout the world, particular care is taken to describe modern cremation in this chapter because it has received very little attention from social scientists.

## Burying, caves and cemeteries

There is archaeological evidence from the very early days of the human species to suggest that dead bodies were buried, often in the floor of caves. Certainly from the early part of the Old Stone Age there are cases of burial, with skeletons suggesting that the bodies had been laid in a foetal position or as in sleep and even with skulls arranged in apparently symbolic ways (Breuil and Lantier, 1965: 231ff.). This suggests that for at least some 30,000 years or more humanity has, occasionally at least, paid some attention to a special burial of the dead. In the upper period of the Old Stone Age, a time when cave art began to develop, bodies were often placed in graves, sometimes lying on layers of ash or set in thick layers of red ochre powder. Food and weapons were included with the body and, though it is a speculative interpretation, this may have been to aid the dead in passing to another world (Maringer, 1960: 1ff., 50ff.).

In the Neolithic or New Stone Age period, from some 10,000 or so years ago, there is extensive evidence of elaborate treatment of the dead which might have been part of a wider scheme of religious understanding. In South America, for example, there are several early finds of burials from north Peru dating from perhaps as early as 10,000 BC, while from as early as 5000 BC cases of artificial mummification begin to appear in Chile, as discussed in Chapter 9. At Chilca, near Lima in Peru, some skeletons dating to approximately 3000 BC showed marks of having been burnt (Arriaza, 1995: 54ff.)

Rather later, in the Mediterranean world, as in Malta, there are large stone structures which are often interpreted as being temples and perhaps memorials of some sort. These originate sometime between 2000 BC and 1500 BC, the same period reflected in the temples of Crete, especially at

Knossus, which many view as a royal palace but others regard as a temple to the dead. It has even been argued that Crete was important as a source of honey in the Mediterranean, honey that was used as part of the mummification process and was renowned for having been used to preserve the body of Alexander the Great. Cretan priests may well have been experts at embalming and may have plied their trade, and necessary products, across the Mediterranean to Egypt (Wunderlich, 1983: 184). Sometimes, as at Chania in Crete, *tholos* tombs were built, either of baked brick or stone. These domed, subterranean structures are rather like large beehives; the dead were buried beneath the floor, making the tombs appear rather like caves. Along with tombs placed in pits and tunnels all these examples show the care that human beings have taken when burying the dead. Exactly what they intended by these structures it is impossible to say. The only thing that can be said with certainty is that, for as long ago as archaeology can produce evidence, human beings have dealt ritually with their dead. Though all these sites stand silent today it is highly unlikely that the rites performed in them did not include some addressing either of the dead or of death itself, but that remains unrecorded.

## Funerals as two-phased rituals

Many funerals in widely differing parts of the world have two different parts to them, each related to the identity of the deceased. One often represents the process which removes a person's dead body from the realm of the living and the other gives it a status in the realm of the dead. In Chapter 1 we outlined Robert Hertz's theory of the two sets of rites involved in processing the identity of the dead person. He drew a distinction between the corpse and its later remains, whether as bones from burial or ashes from cremation, speaking symbolically of the corpse as representing the 'wet' medium of the body while the bones or ashes were the body's 'dry' medium with different rites for each symbolic form.

His study focused mainly on Indonesia where a great variety of ritual was employed to dry out the corpse before its final mortuary ceremony. He interpreted the first set of rites as embracing the period of death. His sociological approach explored the social processes of death alongside what we might call the biological aspects of death. He argued that 'death is not completed in one instantaneous act ... it involves a lasting procedure ... which is terminated only when the dissolution of the body has been completed' (1960: 48). And then, when all seems at an end, yet another process begins since, as he puts it, 'death is not a mere destruction but a transition'.

Many Indonesian practices involved placing the corpse in a container connected to a pot which collected the liquids draining from the decaying body, usually with some formal ceremony. Only when this 'wet' phase was ended was the 'dry' skeleton taken and finally buried. As one important part of this process of movement from the 'wet' to the 'dry' condition, Hertz stressed the shift of status of the deceased from the realm of living people to the realm of the ancestors. The dead person first entered into a period that seemed to be not quite that of the living and not quite that of the dead. The corpse might be kept in the house or in a specially prepared building where it was, in a sense, on the margins of human life. The corpse was, in a symbolic sense, lonely and isolated. Only after the period of decay had been completed did it go to join in the life of the ancestors placed in a special cave or building alongside the remains of other dead kinsfolk. This gives a clear example of the way in which identity is changed through the funerary processes associated with death.

## The double nature of burial

One of the best examples of the double aspect of burial may be found in some Mediterranean countries, especially Greece. There the body is buried for a period of several years, until it has decayed, when the skeleton is exhumed and placed in an ossuary, a special building for holding bones. (A full account of one such practice is given in Chapter 8 in the context of Greek Orthodox life in a contemporary Greek village.) Similar replacing of bones has been widespread in space and time. The storage of disinterred bones in charnel houses and other buildings close to churches was common in earlier centuries in Europe (Ariès, 1991: 59ff.), while extensive cemetery finds in southern Ecuador in South America, dating from about 6000 BC, contain remains indicating secondary burial where the bones of the decayed body were re-arranged and re-buried (Arriaza, 1995: 54).

When speaking of the contemporary Greek example of a double burial rite we are, really, referring only to what happens to the body and bones in a physical sense. In terms of religious belief it might be wise to speak not of a double but of a triple funerary process. For not only is the body buried and then the bones placed in an ossuary but there remains a strong belief in a final resurrection when the human remains will be transformed and given a new resurrection body. At that time the forgiven and purified soul of the dead will rejoin its purified and transformed body. The place of the soul in the total picture of death is discussed in Chapters 6 to 10. In Chapter 9 we also look at the case of traditional Maori life in New Zealand which involved a dual process of physical decay which matched the shift in identity of the dead from being one of the living to becoming one of the departed ancestors.

## Burning bodies

Not all funerals, however, took the form of burials for there is also early evidence of cremation. From archaeology we know that cremation was employed in parts of Greece from nearly 2000 BC, although there are periods within the same area when cremation and then burial predominate without any obvious reason for the alternation. Later, extensive accounts of cremation of warriors and heroic figures are found in classical literature and show that cremation could serve as a means of bringing remains home from military campaigns as well as a way of coping with corpses on the field of battle (Wunderlich, 1983: 228ff.). As we explore the topic of cremation it is worth remembering that cremation has taken several different forms, usually as a positive way of treating the dead though, occasionally, as a form of punishment. One very important aspect of cremation in general is that it is often only one part of a larger process of dealing with the dead body. For after cremation has taken place people are left with the cremated remains of the corpse and they usually think it necessary to do something with these ashes.

## The double nature of cremation

The dry cremated remains of people are, then, almost always subjected to a second ritual as stressed by Hertz, 'cremation ... calls for a later and complementary rite' (1960: 42). He wrote at the very beginning of the twentieth century when there was very little cremation taking place in Europe, despite early conferences on cremation at Padua in 1869 and Rome in 1871 under the influence of anti-clerical groups and Freemasons. In fact, although a crematorium was established in Paris in 1887, it was two years before anyone chose to be cremated there (Ragon, 1983: 285). Hertz dealt, primarily, with pre-literate groups employing various methods of turning the corpse into skeletal remains and transforming the identity of the dead into ancestral identities. Despite this emphasis upon pre-literate groups he discovered a widely applicable principle which is worth applying to modern cremation practices in many parts of the world.

## European cremation

We have already seen that cremation often involves a secondary rite when something is done with the cremated remains. It would, of course, be impossible to know of this in former cultures if ashes were simply scattered or thrown away, but where the remains were specifically deposited with some sort of memorial or in a fixed location they lie open to archaeological discovery. Indeed there are many known cases from Imperial Rome where cremated remains are found alongside buried remains, from periods when both practices were maintained at the same time (Nock, 1932: 328).

One interesting historical example of a double cremation rite in which cremation was followed by a special entombment of the ashes was discovered near London and exhibited at the British Museum under the name of its original site as the Welwyn Garden City Burial. Belonging to the period 55 BC–AD 43, this represents one of the richest Iron Age burials in the UK. The underground chamber contained a group of large Italian wine containers along with a silver drinking cup. The cremated remains were found in a neat pile to one side of the chamber and in front of them there is laid out a neat row of small bead-like objects which probably represent pieces used in a game. All this suggests a high status of individual who, after cremation, was given a tomb burial with wine and games provided for the afterlife. This is one of the clearest examples of cremation followed by a burial of remains which are treated as though they were the body itself.

## Modern cremation rites

Since cremation is, increasingly, employed in modern societies as the central funeral rite it is important to sketch its development and explore its social consequences. We do this in some detail for England since it is there that cremation has become most firmly established during the course of the twentieth century and because, until very recently, it has received very little sociological attention. Lahtinen has explored the slow emergence of cremation in Finland (1989), but Metcalf and Huntington's (1991) comparative study of mortuary ritual in the USA practically ignored cremation, simply noting its extremely low incidence in the population at large. They offer no analysis, for example, of the extreme contrast between the USA and the UK which, by 1992, was reflected in a cremation rate of 19 per cent in the USA and 69 per cent in the UK (*Pharos,* 1993: 157). In this chapter we can help correct this omission to some extent.

## Cremation in Britain

The growth of cremation in Britain was initially very slow indeed: three bodies were cremated in 1885, ten in 1886 and thirteen in 1887. In terms of percentage of the population it was not until the early 1930s that 1 per cent of the dead were cremated; this made 2 per cent by 1936, and 3 per cent by 1939. Growth then, increasingly, speeded up from 7 per cent in 1944 to nearly 15 per cent in 1948, and to some 31 per cent by 1958. But it was the decade of the 1960s that witnessed the balance between burial and cremation in the UK with 1967 marking the 50 per cent line. By the mid-1970s this touched 60 per cent of the population and by the mid-1980s something of a plateau was attained with some 70 per cent of the dead being cremated by 1993. This growth was obviously matched by a dramatic rise in the number of crematoria from, for example, 58 in 1950 to 148 in 1960, a number that subsequently expanded to 226 by 1993.

## The rites

While the obvious purpose of cremation is to reduce a corpse to ashes the actual act is practically never witnessed in Great Britain. As far as most kin and practically all members of wider friendship networks are concerned, a cremation rite involves a religious service in a crematorium chapel, with the act of cremation taking place 'behind the scenes' as a socially invisible act. The only general, though still indirect, indications that cremation occurs lie in the visual cue of smoke and the olfactory cue of smell. Both are viewed as socially unacceptable and crematorium technology and European legislation aim at their elimination as far as possible, hiding the fact of fire in the process. This contrasts, for example, with some European crematoria as in the Czech Republic and Hungary where crematorium architecture includes stands of burning flame – rather like those that hold the flame at the Olympic Games – outside and even inside crematoria. This reflects a long-standing cultural practice of using fire and torches at burials which was transferred to cremation rites when they were introduced.

After a British cremation, close kin are likely to know that the cremated remains have been placed in a garden of remembrance at the crematorium by its staff, but are not likely to have attended the event, one which is entirely utilitarian and devoid of any particular ritual.

More elaborate rites may be built around these basic features. In its fullest form the cremation funeral can involve an initial religious service at a church followed by a brief, and usually less public, rite at the crematorium chapel. A day or two later the cremated remains may be buried in a pre-existing grave by a priest or may be buried or scattered by family members through a private rite in a non-institutional location. Irrespective of mode of deposition of ashes there may be a final service of remembrance at a church on a later occasion.

A key feature of cremation focuses on the cremated remains and the options available for their deposition. As we just said, they may be scattered or interred by a crematorium official without any formal rite and in a basically practical way. They may, however, be interred by a priest with a rite resembling the burial of a corpse. Finally, they may be taken and used in a great variety of ways by the surviving kin. It is this last option which makes cremation a particularly interesting form of contemporary British funerary practice as traditional patterns of burial under priestly authority contrast with scattering as a totally private act. The first makes use of formal liturgies, the second often involves impromptu ritual in a radical invention of tradition. In a traditional burial, by contrast, nothing remains to be done after interment except to place a memorial stone over the grave and tend the site as time goes on. Cremation has introduced this optional rite where the single mourner takes the cremated remains of partner, child or friend and locates them wherever desired. This marks a new ritual process in the modern Western world, largely undocumented and difficult to assess in terms of frequency of occurrence and extremely difficult to study in terms of 'words against death'.

## Local practices

No uniform records have been kept by all British crematoria which could immediately show the proportion of ashes privately deposited. But many crematoria have information which can, indirectly, furnish some indication of this practice. Material drawn from some twelve crematoria from different parts of England and Scotland and representing older and newer, urban and more rural crematoria, shows that in 1993 some 41 per cent of cremated remains were taken away from crematoria. This figure cannot be taken to apply to the country at large because it reflects a tremendous variation depending on the age, region and location of crematoria. For example, Birmingham Crematorium as an older crematorium in a large city had 20 per cent of its remains removed, but also received the equivalent of 4 per cent of its annual cremations in remains from other crematoria in different parts of the country. Matching these exports and imports of cremated remains helps furnish a more realistic picture of the traffic of ashes in the country at large and also hints at the complexity of modern British death rites in relation to the place of residence, death and post-mortem interment of the dead. Social mobility seems to be reflected in the mobility of cremated remains. So on this reckoning of outgoing and incoming remains Birmingham had 16 per cent of its cremations removed and the urban South London Crematorium had 18 per cent removed.

These older crematoria reflect the tradition established during the first half of the twentieth century when cremated remains were nearly always deposited at the crematorium where a cremation took place. At its most formal, the early practice was to place cremated remains in urns and highly stylized containers which were located within a columbarium, a hall of niches at a crematorium bearing some resemblance to crypts except that they contain small urns rather than normal sized coffins and are not subterranean. Less formally, cremated remains are buried or scattered in gardens of remembrance at many crematoria. This became the dominant form of deposition of ashes from the 1940s and continues to be of major importance. Many people are probably still told that it is 'customary' for crematorium staff to deposit the remains without the kin being present. Even so, such depositions attract the remains of subsequent kinsfolk in growing family traditions; once one set of remains has been placed in a particular location others are likely to join them.

## Ashes as private memorials

More recently, private disposal of ashes in personalized significant spots has marked a shift away from public gardens of remembrance, especially in areas where crematoria have only made a relatively recent appearance. New crematoria show a quite different pattern with Bodmin, a rural crematorium in the extensively rural county of Devon, having a 67 per cent removal rate and practically a zero rate of reception of remains from elsewhere. What is evident is that the great majority of cremated remains are laid to rest without any formal religious ritual, whether at the hand of a crematorium official or privately by a family member. But there still remains a degree of freedom available to people in contemporary Britain when it comes to the final treatment of cremated remains of deceased family members. Neither religious professionals nor crematorium staff need have the last word or conduct the last ritual action. This situation differs from many other countries. Only in 1994 did it become possible to gain possession of cremated remains in Holland, for example, while the Swedes still retain public control over deposition of ashes in established cemeteries.

## Hertz and cremation

With this fact in mind we return to Hertz and to the three points of his argument already detailed in Chapter 1 and earlier in this chapter: (1) the abstract problem concerning the relation between society and the body of each of its constituent individuals; (2) the partial nature of cremation within a larger ritual process; (3) cremation as a form of initiation.

The challenge death brings to society is not devastating precisely because ritual processes are at hand to ensure that some kind of symbolic permanence ensues through a corrective act. The old identity is destroyed, and this challenges social stability, but a new identity is created. Although the body as a microcosm of society does die, the person associated with it does not cease to exist because his or her identity is transformed. In its transformed state that person continues to symbolize aspects of the total social world as an ancestor or as one of the Communion of Saints in Christianity.

Despite Metcalf and Huntington's extensive qualification of Hertz's scheme as far as America is concerned (1991: 79ff.), it still remains a useful model for approaching cremation in Britain. The first set of rites, dealing with the 'wet' symbolic medium of the body, consists of the funeral service either at a church or at the crematorium chapel. It is this rite which focuses on the past life, identity and social status of the deceased. The visible ritual object is the coffin with its contained body which is subject to decay. The second set of rites deals with the 'dry' symbolic medium of the cremated remains. Ritual practices connected with these remains have, since about the 1980s, begun to undergo a marked change. The direction of the change is, as shown above with data from some crematoria, from an institutional to a personal placing of the remains in a significant context, from public verbal utterances to subdued whispers or internalized thoughts.

The shift to a personal placing of remains involves the surviving kin taking the cremated remains and locating them in some spot already invested with significance in relation to the deceased's life. This is the case when, for example, ashes are buried or scattered on a racing track, cricket ground or favourite fishing river, all of which reflect pleasure gained through hobbies and leisure time. So, for example, approximately half a dozen sets of ashes have been buried annually over the last decade at the world-famous Trent Bridge cricket ground in Nottingham; these tend to be located in the soil near to a seat favoured by the person who has been cremated. A slightly different case comes from the even more frequent placing of ashes at places of natural beauty or within the garden of the deceased's house. Here the ashes may be interpreted as marking the married life of the dead, serving as a memorial of a relationship within the couple-companionate world of much modern urban life in Britain. This could be interpreted as a British form of 'fulfilment' of the social person within a retrospective view of their lives. It contrasts with Metcalf and Huntington's suggestion that in the USA it is the embalming and viewing of the dead as 'asleep' which reflects their fulfilment (1991: 210).

## Retrospective fulfilment of identity

In the British cases it would be possible to speak of this ritual of private placing of ashes in locations of relational significance as involving a retrospective fulfilment of identity of the dead rather than focusing fulfilment either in the symbolism of sleep or in the future-fulfilment expressed in Christian funerary rites, with their hope of a resurrection and life after death provided by God. Traditional Christian liturgy uses ashes as a kind of substitute corpse, symbolizing the body of the deceased in a rather direct way and with a preference for burying them. In this pattern of ritual they can easily fall into the more traditional Christian scheme of a burial that awaits a resurrection. As such it has been said that the Roman Catholic burial practice 'provides the imagination with a picture of permanence' (Dorsett, 1962: 21).

Another approach takes the cremated remains as symbolizing the body in a less direct way, as though the ashes are physical memories. This is where the private placing of ashes in a spot of personalized significance becomes significant. It is an act that does not require or utilize formal ecclesiastical liturgies, in fact people report simply scattering the ashes in silence or perhaps using a few words which come to them or which they considered beforehand, such as a favourite poem or song of the deceased. These locations are very seldom 'memorialized' in any concrete sense of inscribed markers or the like.

## Post-modern identities

By adopting Hertz's notion of cremation as a two-fold process of identity transformation we have shown how privatized rites reflect personal worlds of individualized meaning for couples, families or friends. This kind of world can easily be interpreted by the label of 'post-modern', referring to a way of life where there is little by way of extensively shared beliefs or ideologies and where identity consists in a small number of personal relationships that can be made part of memory through the private ritual act of placing ashes in significant places (Davies and Shaw, 1995: 102ff.). This contrasts with the traditional scheme in which dead individuals become part of an anticipated eternal heavenly cosmos through formal liturgical acts. Technological society produces crematoria which render the body into a ritually manipulable form which reinforces memory and can be set in a symbolic context of past events especially appropriate to a couple-companionate society. The identity of the dead is symbolically made to participate in a micro-history of small-scale sets of relationships by being located in places of past significance and not in a macro-history involving eternal dimensions through an ecclesiastical liturgy.

## Modern treatment of ashes

So it is that since the development of modern cremation from the late nineteenth century numerous things have been done with cremated remains. They have been buried in graves, as though they were a body. They have been placed in urns and deposited in special buildings called columbaria which were designed in imitation of classical Italian columbaria used by Romans (W. Robinson, 1880). One of the most interesting British examples is the columbarium at Golders Green Crematorium in London. This houses thousands of remains including a great number of famous individuals whose urns are often elaborate and quite distinctive including, for example, the remains of the psychologist Sigmund Freud. Though columbaria became relatively less used in Britain as the twentieth century went on, this is not the case elsewhere. In the USA, for example, a columbarium was established by an Episcopal church in New York in 1928 and, more recently, one was built into an active church at Bel Air, Maryland, next to the font to signify that life and death are both part of the Christian faith. Similarly a new columbarium was built at the Arlington National Cemetery in 1979 including 50,000 niches for cremated remains (Phipps, 1989: 69, 71).

In Chapter 13 we consider the Celestis Corporation which plans to send cremated remains into outer space. Here we can also mention the Neptune Society of California which has parallels elsewhere and which deposits remains at sea after casting them to the wind. In a much more traditional way the Royal Navy in Great Britain offers a service of 'burying' ashes at sea for those who had been members of the Royal Navy. Symbolically speaking there is something particularly appropriate about this kind of water dispersal of cremated remains, in that the natural elements of the body are returned to the natural medium of water in the most direct of ways. While this developed into a religious notion within Indian religious traditions, where both fire and water carried deep significance, in the West its significance is drawn more from an overarching sense of nature itself.

## The politics of burial and cremation

Death affords opportunity to use the identity of the deceased for a variety of political purposes (Barley, 1995: 114ff.). This is a significant fact reminding us that death is not simply a matter of personal grief for close family members.

In Revolutionary China in the 1950s it was initially decided that high party officials should be cremated so that neither grave sites nor mausolea should be raised to differentiate leaders from the mass of the people. Though this decision was motivated by what was seen as the unfortunate cult of Stalin in the then USSR, there was a twist in the direction of funerary rites when Chairman Mao ultimately died in China in 1976. Frederick Wakeman describes this problem of cremation versus preservation as the opposition between an egalitarianism of political party members on the one hand and the power and significance of the single party leader on the other (1988: 259). The preservation of the remains of a leader also opens the possibility of the desecration of the body if, at some time in the future, an opposing political party rises to power.

Cremation, by contrast, removes all possibility of that kind of personal destruction of an historical identity. But other political avenues are possible as far as such remains are concerned; so, for example, numerous Communist Party leaders in Hungary were cremated and had their remains placed in an immense columbarium in the form of a subterranean mausoleum in Budapest. After the collapse of the Communist regime practically no political leader would have their own cremated remains placed in that mausoleum, in which only a half or so of the available niches are occupied. It stands as a sharp reminder of the way Communism preferred cremation over the traditional Catholic burials of Hungary and of the end of that particular era. Communist commitments have not always led to sharp distinctions between funerary rites, at least not at village and local levels of community life. In Romania, for example, local Communist leaders at the village level did not always extend their ideology as far as death and would receive the last rites and end up being buried in the village cemetery which was reserved for those belonging to the Christian community of the Church (Kligman, 1988: 165).

A rather different problem, one associated with cremated remains, emerged in India in 1996 when some of Mahatma Gandhi's ashes were found to have been deposited in a bank in the state of Orissa. Portions of his remains had been sent to many states in India after his cremation to be placed in sacred rivers, according to Hindu custom and devotion, so that the discovery that some had not been so treated raised a slight political problem especially when no one seemed prepared to take responsibility for them. This is a good example of a case where 'words against death' could not finally be spoken, because of bureaucratic ineptitude. In this case, however, the situation was resolved in 1997 when the remaining ashes were placed in the Ganges.

## The evil politics of cremation

By complete contrast with the established cultural mode of cremation as the positively preferred form of funeral in India, cremation reached the height of negative value when used by the Nazis in the Second World War as a major means of disposing of very many Jews, and others regarded as unworthy of human life. Cremation as an immoral form of destruction has come to be symbolized by the camps of Auschwitz and Birkenau, now located in Poland.

For the first time in human history, thousands of individuals were subjected to mass, impersonal cremation. The fact that this destruction, especially of the Jews, has come to be called the Holocaust is particularly important since that was the word used for the burnt offering made as a sacrifice in the Old Testament. The inhumanity of this episode has been extensively documented, not least by survivors of the death-camps. One tells how one Sergeant Otto Moll was promoted to be Director of all crematoria at Auschwitz-Birkenau, camps separated by only a few miles, in May 1944. He is described as telling arriving prisoners that they would work at the camp after having a shower and being disinfected (Czech, 1990: 622). In fact many of them were killed and cremated. He is described as having pits dug alongside the crematoria into which excess bodies were placed to be incinerated. Accounts also exist of SS soldiers loading children into wheelbarrows and dumping them in these 'fiery ravines', where 'living children burned like torches'. Dr Sara Nomberg who gave that account of her own experience asked, rhetorically, how it was that she and others experiencing such things 'did not all go crazy?' (1985: 81). Her question expresses the sense of horror elicited at events which deemed human life so obviously worthless. This is a particularly important case as far as this book is concerned for it raises the theoretical observation that such mass destruction completely contradicts human 'words against death'. In fact the Holocaust becomes a blasphemy, whether in religious or secular terms, because it contradicts human purposes. Instead of words being set against death, death is actively pursued, and this runs counter to the nature of human culture.

This may be one way to begin a response to Palgi and Abramovitch's observation that 'anthropologists appear to have scrupulously avoided confrontation with ... the Nazi regime' and its death plan (1984: 408). This remains one of the first situations in human history in which the world at large has come to its own decision on the act of a group in one nation and set it apart as a type and example of inhumanity. Because of this, great controversy is caused by any attempt to minimize or even, in the extreme case, to deny the mass slaughter at places like Auschwitz (cf. Staeglich, 1986).

Many hundreds of thousands were killed in the Second World War, both in action and through disease, but these deaths are spoken of in patriotic language, in ways which often glorify war. They died 'For King and Country', or *Pro Patria*, for the fatherland. Drawing added validation from the biblical source of St John's Gospel, another key memorial-statement declares soldiers to have possessed that greater love which led them to lay down their life for others. They are said to have 'made the final sacrifice'. All these constitute 'words against death' and assert the importance of life lived according to a social morality.

## Air, earth and water disposal

Returning to non-war situations, and to other means of coping with corpses, mention must be made of disposal by exposure on platforms, in trees or in special enclosures as well as by being placed in water as discussed in Chapters 6, 7, 9 and 10. In terms of more ancient history it is also worth mentioning marshes because, occasionally, they served to preserve bodies which historians have been able to study. One of the most famous examples is that of the Lindow Man. This ancient Briton was discovered in a peat bog where it is possible he had been placed after having been killed. This remarkable case shows an individual whose neck still carried the garrotte by which he had been strangled and a knife wound, probably made after strangulation. The fact that his nails were well cared for suggested that he might have held a privileged status in early British society and some think that he might have been killed in some ritual way by the Druids of the ancient British and Roman period of history. What is sure is that his body ended up in a bog where the nature of the water and soil, and further deposits of peat, served to preserve the body to a remarkable extent.

## Enforced deaths

This case raises the issue of what might be called enforced social death. The very fact of funerary rites shows how most societies regard life in a positive light, highly valued and worthy of commemoration. Precisely because of this the greatest penalty which can be exacted of someone is to take away their life by force. The value of life, in a general way, is challenged by such things as murder, and explains why many societies see the death penalty as perfectly appropriate for the crime of murder, on the rule of an 'eye for an eye'. In a similar way, many cultures have viewed suicide as a crime or a sin because it may be seen as robbing society of one of its members, or because it seems to challenge the religious belief that God alone is the source of life, who alone has the responsibility to give it and to take it.

Enforced social deaths have taken many forms, whether in the ancient forms of administering poison by mouth, stoning, burning at the stake and impaling, or modern methods of hypodermic injection, beheading, hanging, the electric chair or the gas chamber. In all of these, death has been administered in a calculated and intentional way. Often the bodies of those killed officially have been treated with little formal ceremony or respect, whether by burial in unmarked graves or exposure to wild animals etc. The death and disposal display society's power over individuals and over their bodies. Their end is not generally attended by proud 'words against death'.

## Space for bodies

Just what a society does with dead bodies depends to a large extent both upon afterlife beliefs and also on attitudes towards death itself. Rapid dissolution of the body in cremation, with the scattering of ashes and no memorial plaque, can be viewed as the symbolic opposite of mummification, with the capping structure of a pyramid. In some senses this is perfectly correct so that we could agree with Michel Ragon that, in cremation, funerary architecture is negated. Unfortunately, his rather philosophical style leads to an overemphasis when he suggests that 'the space of death is no longer enclosed by a structured space. It is space, all space. And the immaterial body becomes as immaterial as the soul' (1983: 287). His study ignores the emergence of permanent crematoria as the major contribution of the twentieth century to the history of death in human cultures. Crematoria like those at Golders Green in London, the majestic arena designed by Asplund at Stockholm or the gigantic crematorium at Seoul in Korea are, to many modern cities, what the pyramids were to Egypt: they are the places of death ritual and can also be locations for memorializing the dead. At least they appear to be increasingly viewed as sacred places of some kind (D. J. Davies, 1996b). The preservation of the dead themselves, especially in mummification, has been moderately widespread and is discussed in detail in Chapter 9 for both the well known case of the Egyptians and the much earlier, but less familiar, culture of the ancient Chinchorro of Chile.

## Funeral parlours, mortuaries and the home

From ancient Egypt and Chile to the contemporary USA may seem an immense distance in time yet, in funerary terms, some real similarities exist, expressing the human need to oppose or transcend death. Until the twentieth century most families in Western Europe and the USA cared for their own family members while dying and for the body after death. From approximately the middle of the twentieth century, but with great regional variation, hospitals increasingly cared for the dying and funeral directors for the dead. In other words professionalism took over from domestic and community responsibilities (Howarth, 1996).

One consequence of this was the emergence of funeral parlours, premises owned by funeral directors, where the dead are usually embalmed and treated cosmetically before being laid out in their coffins for viewing by family and friends. Whereas in Great Britain the word 'mortuary' is largely restricted to a place, usually at a hospital, where bodies are kept in cold storage and perhaps undergo a post-mortem, in the USA the name is applied to the equivalent of the British funeral parlour where the body is fully prepared for the funeral and where the family and perhaps even more public viewing of the corpse takes place. Some of these mortuaries are very large and elegant buildings and may be found in prestigious parts of North American towns. One interesting feature of mortuaries is the sense they give of a domestic setting: they usually consist of larger and smaller rooms furnished with some items which would, normally, be found in people's homes. In this sense mortuaries provide a home beyond the home or a homely setting outside the home. There is, usually, opportunity and space for family members to meet and greet each other in such a way that, near to the deceased's body, the atmosphere is more restrained while at the other end of the room or just outside there may be a fair degree of conversation.

The extensive preparation of bodies in North America has led some commentators to criticize the practice because it appears to deny the reality of death. Bodies are regularly embalmed and treated to extensive cosmetic treatment to make the dead look as lifelike and healthy as possible. Set in their relatively expensive and elaborate caskets they look just as though they are asleep. Indeed the dressed and powdered corpse is often said by relatives to look peaceful or at sleep rather than being dead. This imitation of life in the dead has attracted much attention in the later part of the twentieth century and is taken by some to reflect an avoidance of the bare facts of death on the part of some North Americans. The provision of costly caskets and tombs, often built of brick with metal reinforcement below ground level, as well as of mausolea where coffins are placed in above-ground compartments, seems to imply a preservation of the body separated from the earth rather than simply providing an environment where decay may naturally take place.

Practically nothing is ever said of the fact that modern embalming is only a temporary and partial act, and that the sealed container will simply provide a context for the decay of the body without opportunity for the elements to return to the earth. While talk about a guaranteed tomb and casket can give the impression of some sort of guarantee on the state of the deceased it reflects the fact that the living tend to give but partial thought to what actually happens after death.

Though it has become fashionable to speak of permanent graves, costly caskets and the decoration of the death as a denial of death, some see it in the opposite light as a clear acknowledgement of death, which shows how important interpretations are when dealing with clearly observable facts. Dumont and Foss (1972) surveyed groups of clergy in the USA and found that they thought their congregations possessed a degree of openness about death. Indeed much depends upon context, a great deal depends upon geographical location and the cultural and religious background of people. For example, Garrity and Wyss (1980) studied death in Kentucky in the 1970s and argued that death rites were relatively open to the community, which suggests that a degree of caution is needed when making broad generalizations about death and society at large. It is always tempting for authors who lack an appropriate comparative dimension to generalize from their own narrow social experience.

Contemporary society involves a tremendous mix of attitudes, beliefs and opinions, not least as far as death is concerned. Now, probably more than at any time in the history of humanity, it is likely that amongst a group of neighbours some believe that there will be life after death, others do not, some will wish to be buried while others will opt for cremation. Similarly some will opt for practically impregnable concrete graves while a small but growing number of people, especially in the UK, are thinking more in terms of a cardboard coffin to be buried in a woodland grave. Such a burial would, ultimately, lead not to a large cemetery but to a small woodland and matches the mood of many urban Britons in the late twentieth century with their preferences for ecologically supportive procedures.

Still, in many parts of the UK and of the USA, funeral directors and their facilities have taken over from the home as the location of the dead immediately before their funeral. Though this might suggest that the identity of the dead moves relatively rapidly away from their prior domestic identity it should be understood that, in modern societies, where a great many services are provided beyond the home for people while they are alive, there is a sense in which death simply follows the pattern of other health care, of leisure and dining facilities. Still, it is true that the wider community, in which someone once lived, is decreasingly involved with death. In many parts of the world neighbours, or more distant kin, used to be involved in the whole period of sickness prior to death, in preparing the body or in visiting the bereaved and supporting them in their grief and in sharing words against death, but now, with the professionalization of death, this involvement has largely decreased and the range of words spoken has been reduced. Many see these changes as reflecting the growing privatization of life, especially in urban contexts but also in much more traditional areas, as for example in the North American Appalachian region including

Tennessee, Virginia, Kentucky, North Carolina and West Virginia (Crissman, 1994).

## Conclusion

In this chapter we have begun to see how corpses, the immediate outcome of death, are generally treated symbolically in a variety of ancient and modern cultures but especially in Britain and America. The identity of the dead and their network of links with the living have changed and the issue of death itself is addressed through what happens to the body. Subsequent chapters will furnish similar examples from other cultures and will extend the argument of the human response to the challenge of mortality. While this chapter has looked primarily at the deceased, the next shifts the focus more to those who are, themselves, bereaved.

# 3  Beyond Grief Survival

Given the evolutionary assumption behind my argument, that funerary rites are part of human adaptation to death, it is worth approaching the human experience of bereavement through the useful distinction between grief and mourning drawn in an early psychological paper by James Averill (1968). He, too, located grief within the biological and evolutionary framework of human life while setting mourning more within the social domain of human existence, then arguing that the nature of the combined act of grief and mourning was beneficial to society. His argument begins well but ends poorly. Biologically speaking, he sees the strong bonds that exist between individuals as necessary for ongoing human social life. The unfortunate consequence of these ties is that when they are broken through death or separation the individual suffers grief. He defines grief as a 'biological reaction the evolutionary function of which is to ensure a social form of existence ... necessary for survival. This is accomplished by making separation from the group, or from specific members of the group, an extremely stressful event both psychologically and physiologically' (1968: 729). In other words, grief is an inevitable negative consequence which has to be paid for the positive advantage of strong group attachment. I think this is an important contribution but one that needs to be pressed further. Averill discusses Freud and Bowlby's psychological theories of attachment to the mother or other significant persons, an attachment which causes grief when it is broken and leads to a search for the lost person before, finally, reaching a point of acceptance of the loss (Schulz, 1978: 142).

The one major failure in Averill's thesis is that while it can describe grief as the negative side of attachment, it fails to see funerary rites as leading to an advantage and, in some cases, even to a benefit from the fact of death. The implicit assumption of many theorists is that death involves a profound set-back for the individual, one that is inevitable for a social primate like *Homo sapiens*; the deprivation behaviour observed in some chimpanzees and other apes is even taken to reinforce this point (Averill, 1968: 71).

While I agree with the biological thrust of his argument I think that more can be said in connection with the social aspects of human nature and death rites. While human animals do grieve, because attachment to significant others is broken, as human beings they are not, normally, abandoned by society. This is precisely why funeral rites exist. It is because of grief's biological power, which Averill so clearly documents, that the human animal has seen to it that its prime mode of defence, intelligent self-consciousness expressed through language, has been directed at the source of dismay. In addition, the ritual setting for the use of these words itself adds power to their effect. Ritual performance through formal acts of many sorts, in movement, dance and music, conduces to a sense of achievement and purpose, indeed it has even been argued that 'ritual behaviour is one of the few mechanisms at man's disposal that can possibly solve the ultimate problems and paradoxes of human existence' (d'Aquili and Laughlin, 1979: 179). I think that the extremely widespread nature of death rites shows just how significant they have been in aiding human adaptation to the new verbal environment of self-consciousness and awareness of death.

## Ritual transcendence

Epstein, amongst many others, has spoken of grief as a 'serious problem for society', one posing the problem of how to 'assuage the anguish of the individuals concerned, and at the same time reawaken the interest that would restore them to group life' (1992: 185), echoing something of Bauman's position discussed in Chapter 1. While Epstein advances no single solution, in his description of the Tolai of New Guinea he sees one answer in the many opportunities provided when grief is revived and individuals recall their loss, occasions in which sorrow can end with 'festival and celebration'. Similarly, Gail Kligman's thorough study of Transylvanian villagers provides a detailed account of the use of many occasions when the living address the dead through mourning, festivals, dreams and religious rites, all as a response to the 'stark reality of mortality' (1988: 155).

This highlights the final part of my argument which emphasizes the transcendence of the realm of affront to consciousness by death achieved through mortuary rites and subsequent mourning activity. This reflects something of Maurice Bloch's powerful theory of rebounding vitality, already discussed in Chapter 1, and which describes that higher existential state conferred upon those who have undergone a ritual of rebounding conquest. Put simply, the power of funeral rituals lies in the fact that death is directly faced, addressed and, in one sense, is experienced as a kind of transcendence.

This unusual application of the idea of transcendence fits well with Bloch's notion that in certain rites people encounter something other than their usual level of awareness and are changed by it. Because the word transcendence practically always carries a powerfully positive connotation it is important, here, to stress its shadow-side. Indeed, it is through funerary rites that the shadow-side of existence is confronted and not ignored. The ritual words and songs press significance upon the participants who do not return to some prior 'normal' state of life. They may never even be 'happy' again, but they have touched 'the depths' and survived. It is, then, in the new strength of bereavement that they have the power to speak words of comfort to other people and, in so doing, speak words against death. Words invested with significance because of what they have experienced in the face of grief. It has been the genius of the human animal to turn a biological state of grief, with all its negative consequences, into a positive status of one who has survived to tell the tale. In terms of the sociology of knowledge a sense of meaning is not simply maintained through the funerary rites but is enhanced. It may well be that one major reason why religions became so pervasive in human cultures was precisely because they provided the vehicle for this adaptation to death. Those religions which became active world religions are particularly noteworthy in this very element.

## Implications

Having outlined this theoretical assumption we must, naturally, acknowledge that, even when social customs are strong, individuals may well respond in different ways (Epstein, 1992: 150ff.). In our own lives we know how people vary a great deal so that, even within a single family, responses to grief may take divergent paths. These are important cautions we bear in mind when we make generalizations about various cultures, especially since our emphasis will always tend to fall on the shared and traditional behaviour in a society rather than upon individual differences.

Behind all grief lie experiences shared with the one who now is dead. Walter Burkert in his important book on Greek mythology and death reflected something of Averill's argument when arguing that 'Man's neoteny, the long period of time he spends in the process of learning, forged a new relationship between young and old, above all between son and father, in which the catastrophe of death became especially disturbing and dangerous' (1983: 55).

Though we might want to broaden Burkert's stress on the relationship between son and father, it is likely that his speculation on the long period which children spend with their parents in the process of growing up and learning how to live does influence in a deep way their own reaction to the death of such influential parents. The long period of childhood and infancy guarantees that the identity of the child is suffused with elements of the identity of its parents. In a similar way, in modern urban society, spouses can live together for many years in deep dependence upon each other and relative independence from other members of society. When one of the partners dies the grief of the other can be as extensive as their mutual inter-dependence was great but the degree to which even such individuals can go on to live a fruitful life is the degree to which society proves itself worthwhile.

## Feeding grief

It would be easy to ignore one context in which society so proves itself, that of eating. One major response to death is food, in the form of a funerary meal. It often happens that after the main funeral rite of burial or cremation the participants join together in some sort of festivity involving food and drink. In classical literature Achilles, while he mourns the death of Patroklos, still lets his companions 'feast the heart-pleasing burial' (Burkert, 1983: 50). The practice of eating at graves was well known in ancient Greece and was also practised by early Christians in the Mediterranean world who not only, initially at least, buried their dead alongside pagan neighbours but held similar memorial banquets for their Christian dead (Colvin, 1991: 105ff.). In modern times, especially in Ireland, a wake was held at the death of a relative when the family members along with neighbours could drink and eat in an occasion which allowed sympathy to be expressed within a context of relatively high spirits. It is still widely the custom that people hold a gathering for something to eat and drink after a funeral and such traditions develop with changing circumstances.

If it is possible to generalize about such party events, especially following funerals, we might say that they are marked by a shift in mood. The funeral itself inevitably evokes the negative experiences of sadness, anxiety and some fear. The obvious act of finally parting from the one who is buried or cremated is a major emotional moment in the life of the family. But intense negative emotion cannot be sustained for long periods, nor is it good for society or individuals that it should be maintained; this is where the party as a time for the shifting of mood in a positive direction comes to be important (Yoder, 1986). While the negative mood is often focused on the site of the funeral, coming at the end of a negative period in the household of the deceased, the positive switch is often focused back in the house again. This reflects the fact that, as the well-worn English phrase expresses the idea, 'life must go on'. It is in the household that life must go on and this makes it all the more important that it is in the house that the party should occur. But this is not always the case as, for example, in contemporary Holland where a more public celebration may be held instead of, or in addition to, the domestic event. So, for example, at the main crematorium of Amsterdam there are large rooms or halls where the funeral party may eat and drink with wider family and friends after a cremation service, a facility which some British crematoria are also considering. In such a context the site of negative emotion can also be the same general locale as the place of festivity, it is a time of life affirmation. In many British households it is likely that if stories are told about the dead person they will reflect happy times, positive aspects of the deceased's life will be emphasized as part of life affirmation rather than, say, the period of suffering preceding death.

## Food against death

There is no better way of expressing the positive and ongoing nature of life than by sharing food together, expressing as it does the sustaining of life and working for the future, just as fasting or eating very little is a way of showing corporate discipline in the face of potentially destructive elements of life. When alcohol is drunk, as it often is at funerals in many parts of the world, it also conduces to an increased feeling of well-being. Parties are often accompanied by noise, by much talking and by general bustle as opposed to the restrained and silent house of mourning before the funeral. Sounds and noise are further signs of life just as silence, the deathly hush, is typically a sign of mortality.

But even more may be said than this. We described Maurice Bloch's theory of rebounding conquest in Chapter 1. By returning to it here and applying what he wrote to mortuary rites in general we can suggest that 'the consumptions which follow rebounding conquests ... may not be just a restoration of lost vitality. The recovery is triumphalist and outward directed' and 'may indeed lead to a legitimate increase in vitality' (1992: 37). Bloch saw the significance of powerful words in the particular case of Godfrey Lienhardt's classic study of the Sudanese Dinka (1961), but he did not raise this phenomenon of verbal formula to a general theoretical level. It is precisely that adoption of verbal formulae as a key part of the transcending of mortality which we take up in this book, not least as far as grief and public mourning are concerned.

## Performing grief

Not all cultures practise grief in the same way and it is important not to let our own experience dictate the way we think about the emotion of other people. Indeed the 'pageant of death', as Epstein has described some mortuary rites, is one in which certain basic human attributes such as 'vanity and egoism' may also play a part along with standardized conventions of mourning (1992: 172). There is a real sense in saying that a great deal of human activity is a performance of some kind. We learn how to behave in many different contexts and recognize that some individuals seem better able to realize and fulfil what is normally expected in a typical situation than are some other people (Schechner, 1988).

We should not, of course, confuse the idea of performance with the issue of sincerity. The degree to which people are aware of giving a performance in any explicit way will vary from society to society and perhaps even from one individual to another. What seems to be true is that differences can be observed amongst distinct groups. It is often the case in Britain, for example, that televised accounts of the funerals of people who have been killed in some sort of tragedy even show a difference between social classes. Many working-class women are often shown being supported quite literally by the physical contact of others lest they collapse under the weight of grief, while in more upper-class cases the female kin walk unaided in a firm display of controlled emotion.

One society in which the display of grief was very dramatic and required was that of the New Zealand Maori. Death for the Maori was, traditionally, a time of potential danger because it engendered high levels of *tapu* (taboo) which was a kind of spiritual power grounded in respect for a kind of supernatural authority and power (Schwimmer, 1966; Metge, 1976). The house in which a person might have died would be burned. The corpse would be dressed and then the kinsfolk would keep watch over it maintaining a continuous moaning sound. When a new relative arrived this moan would rise to a loud wailing sound. Relatives might cut themselves until they bled and, as Eric Schwimmer's detailed description outlines the scene, all kinsfolk would 'weep copiously and mucus would run out of their noses. Grief had to be totally unrestrained' (1966: 59).

## Tears, emotion and cremation's context

So it is that tears display ideals and reveal social values. Tears give clearer insight into what we so easily take for granted; they have an established place in a sociological understanding of ritual as well as in psychology (Prior, 1989: 133ff.). For simplicity's sake we may focus on two 'types' of tears, private and public. In this brief description I offer no more than a sketch as a reminder that phenomena we think we know well may yet have deeper significance.

Private tears will usually be shed when quite alone or with very close partners or friends. As tears of grief they speak of the loss that one self feels in the departure of another. From one side they are tears of pain for the one left behind, from the other side they are tears of sorrow for the one whose life has ended. It would be inhuman and morally aloof to speak of these tears for one's self as selfish, just as it would be insensitive to speak of tears shed for another as useless. Private tears are symbols in the profoundest sense, they participate in what they represent, an identity that was shared within a relationship that has now been broken.

Public tears will usually be shed in the presence of others, including more distant kin, friends and neighbours. Many people have the experience of sitting with a bereaved person or family with no one crying at all, despite the sadness of the occasion. Then as another person comes to the house or enters the circle of bereaved relatives, one or more of them greet the newcomer with tears and an upsurge of emotion, the newcomer acting as a trigger for emotion.

This is an important point and raises the often ignored question of emotion itself. What is emotion? How do we understand it in general and in the context of bereavement in particular? Emotion is one aspect of life which all cultures take for granted but treat differently. The apparent difference between English reserve and Italian effervescence is but the tip of an iceberg of human variation. Yet, within a society people are apt to think that the way they live and experience life is firm, concrete and absolute. In this chapter I follow a much more anthropological and comparative approach to emotion agreeing with Renato Rosaldo that 'feeling is ever given shape through thought and that thought is laden with emotional meaning. ... Emotions are thoughts somehow "felt" in flushes, pulses, "movements" of our livers, minds, hearts, stomach, skin. They are *embodied* thoughts' (1984: 143).

## Embodiment, soul and role

To approach life primarily through the theoretical perspective of embodiment, rather than through roles, is particularly fruitful in the case of bereavement and grief. To speak of embodiment is to talk of human beings as total and whole entities, not splitting them into souls or bodies, nor even into real selves and mere parts played in some social drama of existence. When it comes to understanding ourselves and other people the duality that lies behind the theological body–soul division is as unhelpful as the sociological division between role and performer.

Yet there is rarely smoke without fire, and the eager acceptance of role theory throughout the middle of the twentieth century in Western, urban societies tells its own tale of lives that are perceived as being lived between a private world of 'real self' and the public world of roles played. This model of division is only another version of the Freudian distinction between unconscious and conscious levels of life. Western culture has long been given to believing in some sort of distinction of this kind. Plato's doctrine of the divide between the body and the soul was one ancient foundation for this conviction that men and women are fundamentally not what they seem. In an odd sense this is a Western version of the Indian idea of illusion, the belief that what is seen is not the ultimate reality but simply a veil or covering of deceit for perception.

When it comes to emotion this idea of split-level life becomes apparent within the British context through what is called the Jamesian theory of emotion. Roughly speaking, this theory sees a person as a kind of container which gets filled with an emotion, a container not ordinarily visible to the outside world. In terms of bereavement the emotion which fills the inner container is grief. A healthy response to bereavement requires that the container be emptied or grief be released. According to this interpretation tears expelled through the act of crying afford the preferred mode of release. Tears bring the inner world to the outside. Tears are healthy.

This popular theory of emotion, of grief and healthy reactions is widespread and has assumed a status of truth, especially in English middle-class society, which itself is the source of many involved in death- and grief-counselling. And this view may not be true. Or at least it is not the whole truth, and in some cases may be positively misleading. Some who would like to help bereaved people are seldom happy until the bereaved person weeps, until they 'let it all out'. Perhaps they may even feel that they have failed in trying to help someone if that person does not end up crying, for crying can easily be taken as an index of a certain kind of relationship. Few would be so calculating or explicit in their thinking to see crying in this way – for them, crying is the sign of catharsis or, more properly speaking, crying is the symbol of catharsis, participating in what it represents. Of course there can be no doubt that for some people crying is a very necessary part of their life at moments of climactic joy or sorrow. But context is as important in the act of crying as is some deep lying emotion just waiting to escape.

The empirical research conducted in one important study of grief and bereavement – the Leiden Bereavement Project – shows, contrary to popular opinion, that excessive emotional behaviour, including crying, may not actually lead to better adaptation to bereavement, at least as far as some individuals are concerned. As Marc Cleiren, the Project Director, expressed it: 'A bereaved person showing strong emotional release and intense occupation with the event some months after the loss is, by the lay public, sometimes seen as evidencing adequate coping with the death. The opposite seems to be true' (1991: 257).

This suggests that those actively involved in grief-counselling should be aware of their own power in trying to influence the behaviour of others in ways they deem most suitable. In our society, as in some others, tears attest to social relationships as markers of degrees of affinity and friendship. In this sense they are also context dependent as certain moments and places demand a display while others do not. The cultural complexity of grief is, obviously, great and we are only beginning to understand its many levels. Several examples from European contexts will help show some of these complexities while, also, bringing to the surface some of the more implicit assumptions which normally lie unconsidered.

Beginning in the UK, one of my own studies shows how people react differently to emotion and funerals in different sorts of contexts. Some 62 individuals were interviewed as part of a survey of the general public in Nottinghamshire (D. J. Davies, 1990a). When interviewers asked which they found to be the more emotional occasion, burial or cremation, nobody said they had found cremation more emotional than burial. About half found burials and cremation equally emotional, while the rest found burial a more emotional event than cremation. The greatest distinction lay in those adults who had attended the funeral of at least one of their own parents. Of the 23 individuals in that category, 17 thought that in general terms burial was a more emotional rite than cremation and six thought there was no difference.

What is of additional interest is that a further question asked all 62 individuals if they felt there was some difference between the therapeutic capacity of burial and cremation. As far as those who had lost parents, spouses or children were concerned, they practically all felt there was no difference between the rite and the degree of therapy afforded them. Only two individuals felt there was a difference and in both cases cremation was viewed more positively than burial. The point worth stressing is that even those who thought burial was a more emotional occasion than cremation did not think that burial was any more therapeutic because of it. This example, drawn from an admittedly small sample of interviewed people, would seem to reinforce the idea that emotion may be as well interpreted in terms of a display within a context as a discharge of some sort of inner energy.

## Popular psychology of grief in Greece

Chapters 2 and 8 describe ways in which traditional Greek Orthodox villagers practised burial, exhumation and the final placing of bones. One feature of that entire process of bereavement includes popular attitudes to the emotions associated with grief. Danforth's study of Greek villagers speaks of the five or so year period between burial of the corpse and the exhumation of the bones as a time of accommodation to death. Though the final exhumation is marked by intense emotion it also tends to bring the period of grief to a close, expressing what he calls an 'indigenous theory of catharsis'. 'The result of this process is as complete an acceptance of the final and irreversible nature of death as is possible' (1982: 144).

This theory of catharsis reflects a belief that repeated talking about the death finally rids people of the intense emotion of death described as pain and anguish. But great caution is needed in understanding this issue for while the popular view is that singing and crying not only permit a 'knot' to leave the throat but also bring a 'lightening' and 'cooling' to a person there still remains a 'wound that will never heal', as Danforth entitles one of his chapters (1982: 117ff.). This suggests that while it is important for the grief-stricken to work some emotion out of their system, as we might explain it, this does not mean that the system 'returns to normal'; instead there is an expression of emotion which is important for coping with the immediate experiences of grief and for accommodating to bereavement over a period of time. But ultimately, the bereaved person is changed and altered and now lives with a degree of acceptance of death that was not there before. The acts and the words of the funerary rites have achieved their purpose.

Danforth even suggests that people attend the grave and go to the funerals of others in order to experience again their sense of pain as a way of remembering the dead and maintaining a relationship with them. He also discusses the ways in which women who have experienced what might be called ordinary grief, as with the death of aged parents, come to an acceptance of death which helps them bring a degree of acceptance to women whose bereavement is stark as in the loss of a young child or a young husband. Their more intense grief is, in a sense, moderated by the realism of the larger number of people.

## Grief, normality or illness

While this Greek case reflects our earlier discussion on the social distance of mourners in relation to grief it also raises the issue of 'normality' in relation to bereavement. Here sociological ideas of kinship distance are inevitably associated with psychological aspects of emotion. Given the complex interrelationships between social and psychological dimensions it is worth exploring one particular aspect of grief, namely, what might be called the medical model in which grief is viewed more as an illness than as a change in social or religious status.

A good place to begin is with the idea of normality, even though this may seem a strange concept to apply to bereavement, assuming as it does that there is some kind of level path in life from which the bereaved deviate and back to which they will come in time.

In many respects this outlook likens grief to illness, implying that when death comes to someone their relatives become 'ill' in some sense. They are 'wounded' and it will take some time for this wound to heal. This medical model of illness, as perhaps it might be called, has many levels of significance. Most deaths take place in hospital and many follow periods of illness associated with hospitalization. Though we do not normally discuss this kind of idea this fact may, in itself, lead to an association of death with hospitals and therefore with the idea of illness intrinsic to hospitals.

But there is also the fact that the death of someone is often said to come 'as a shock'. Even after long illness relatives quite often say that the actual event and its aftermath took them by surprise. This element of surprised shock can easily be perceived in terms of a medical condition, since in many Western societies most dramatic changes of mood are more likely to be interpreted medically than theologically, sociologically or philosophically.

A popular phrase reflecting this view of bereavement is that 'time is a healer'. To see how popular an idea this is we asked people, in the Nottinghamshire survey already mentioned, if in their experience they had found it to be true. For a large majority of 79 per cent of individuals it was indeed felt to be the case, but for 11 per cent it was not true. For them aspects of their bereavement remained significant in their continuing life. Some 10 per cent had no comment on this matter. Interestingly enough, those who did not think time was a healer tended to argue along very similar lines to those who did basically agree with this popular formula but placed a much stronger emphasis on memory. Many agreed that time healed but also stressed the place of memories which may or may not be painful ones. Whether or not memories ceased to be painful seemed to lie at the heart of agreeing that time could heal. The husbands who had lost their wives seemed particularly involved in memories, but it happened that in the small interviewed group their bereavement was within the prior two years.

The following quotations reflect something of that experience known by many when it comes to memory and time:

'I don't feel it so strongly now, but the loss stays with you.'

'Yes, time heals in one way, you get things in perspective, but missing somebody never goes away.'

'Time doesn't heal but it's not so vivid now' (two years after husband's death).

'Yes, but it is still fresh in my mind' (thirteen years after a sister's death).

One person, who had experienced a powerful religious conversion to Christianity from active atheism, also disagreed with the idea of time as a healer, not because changes had not taken place over time but because she wished to stress her belief that 'God is the healer'. She had, in fact, 'received prayers for healing the pain' and now felt that while the pain of bereavement for her father was still influential it was more distant from her. She described it in vivid terms as 'like labour pains in reverse'.

Another, more specific, question asked how long it took people to return to normal. The majority (45 per cent) reckoned it to have been days, for 23 per cent it was a matter of weeks, for 18 per cent months, and for 15 per cent years. This spread of time reflects the closeness of relationship between mourner and deceased. One woman said it had taken her 40 years to come to the point of being able to speak of her mother's death, while for quite distant relations or neighbours there is no real need to 'return to normal' since the ordinary ongoing nature of life has not, in any real sense, been altered. The sample presented here covers a wide variety of distance between the dead and the bereaved and reflects the much more detailed Dutch research of Marc Cleiren, who found that adaptation after bereavement varied significantly between people of different kinship relationships (1991).

Cleiren describes how parents continue to suffer the loss of a child for a considerable period of time; this was especially true as far as mothers were concerned. In his sample, some 35 per cent of mothers showed no sign of decreased attachment to their dead child fourteen months after its death. Cleiren also stressed the point that while fathers often appear less troubled than mothers shortly after being bereaved of a child, this may be because of the support they have to give to their wives, since fathers often come to show the strain months later. He also found that widowers adapted much less well to bereavement than did widows, and that sisters constituted a category of people who often suffered very much at the loss of a sibling. Cleiren called sisters a 'forgotten group' when it came to grief and bereavement. Adult sisters of a dead person are much less likely to receive support and attention than the surviving spouse or children. This is interesting in the light of the fact that the least troubled group in the long term are adult children, especially sons, of deceased parents.

These findings stress the fact that death often involves a varied group of people, each one of whom is caught up to a greater or lesser extent in the network of relationships focused on the dead person. It is important to stress this variation because it is too easy to focus only on the immediate kin of the deceased and to forget the others less centrally involved. This has often been the case in research pinpointing widows but, for example, ignoring sisters.

What these various studies show is that the idea of bereaved people 'getting back to normal' is potentially misguiding. For the majority of close family members there is no return to some former state as though nothing had happened. New experiences have been gained which change people in perpetuity. The idea of 'getting back to normal' refers more to the social world than to the realm of inner experience. During the immediate period of bereavement people may be perceived as in a special situation, they are given a status of their own which is, to a greater or lesser extent, separate from that of everyone else whose lives continue in an ordinary way. Getting back to normal refers to their return to an ordinary flow of life in everyday terms. Inner changes in experience, memory and outlook may give quite a different picture from that of mere appearance. Even so, for some, bereavement does change even the way they live once they are back in the ordinary flow of social life. So much depends on the way the deceased individual is related to the identity of the survivor and to the degree that social rites have made their impact.

Cleiren's studies give substance to the experience familiar to most of us, that personal identity is made up, in part, by the influence of others. It is no wonder that some mothers simply do not 'recover' after the death of a child; indeed, the very use of the word hides the significance of a child's death. To speak of recovering is to use illness as the model of bereavement. It speaks as though a mother has been ill with some unfortunate and inconveniencing malady but is now undergoing a recuperation which will, sooner or later, leave her normal again. Great care, then, is needed when speaking of grief as an illness just as when emotions in general are discussed as diseases (Averill, 1968: 743). Yet, this attitude was particularly obvious until quite recently in women who experienced the stillbirth of their babies. The work of my colleague Jane Robinson on perinatal deaths is particularly sensitive to the profound importance many mothers give to the birth of their child whether or not it is alive on delivery (1989). She rightly documents the unsympathetic situation where, after a spontaneous premature birth of a stillborn baby, the mother was not only told that since the event was classified as an abortion the hospital would arrange disposal, but was also further upset by being told that she was young and had plenty of time to have another child (1987: 17). Here the issue focuses on how the stillbirth is identified precisely because the way it is classified feeds into the way the woman relates to it, to him or to her, and also determines how others, including the medical profession, relate to the woman. The stark framework of possibilities of a non-human or certainly of a non-personal identification of a stillbirth is dramatically emphasized by Robinson when she quotes Lovell referring to the fact that 'If the baby is delivered before twenty-eight weeks legally it can be treated in the same way as gynaecological scrapings and incinerated. It is not treated as a dead person, it is a *thing*. Its potential identity is destroyed with its remains.'

Perspectives like this express an underlying medical model ignoring deep facts of existence, whether existential experiences lying at the heart of life, or religious experiences at the centre of faith. Some experiences influence human life so much that people are never the same again. They simply become different people through what has happened to them. To speak of recovery is to talk about a kind of backwards change, an undoing of what has been done, an unliving of part of life. And this is impossible. As far as many women are concerned the process of conceiving and carrying a child, of giving birth to a boy or girl, of nurturing them through years of helplessness into childhood and perhaps also into adulthood, takes up an enormous amount of personal attention, time and psychological energy as well as creatively producing a new dimension to the woman's life. The woman *becomes* a mother through this experience, so that if she is bereaved of her child it is the mother and not only a woman who is bereaved. In this sense motherhood is an existential fact of life and not simply a sociological description. This is a telling fact, even in terms of sociology, because in English a bereaved wife is called a widow while there is no word for a mother who has lost her child. It is both physiologically and psychologically true that a child is part of its mother in a different way than it is part of its father. This is not to deny the grief of fathers towards their children, not least in cultures in which the father–son link is very strong, but simply to indicate the obvious difference owing to facts of pregnancy.

The hopes, aspirations, longings and fears which parents may have for their children are all part of the identity of each parent, just as the relationship between parents is partly made up of shared anticipations. When these are crushed through death it is foolish, both philosophically and theologically, to speak of bereavement in terms more appropriate to physical illness. And, to a certain extent, this truth about mothers and children can also apply to other intimate relationships where people become 'part of each other'. This has been widely studied by anthropologists in terms of the social links and networks between people which are altered through death (Epstein, 1992; Vitebsky, 1993).

## Motherhood and loss of child

To some degree, then, human identity includes the identity of others. A mother is a mother because she has children. When she no longer has children her identity is radically altered. This is probably even more important in modern Britain where women tend to have very few children and where each child is invested with great significance often long before it is born. So, while death may be the annihilation of someone else's life the memory of that dead individual still forms part of the life and identity of the living. In strictly social terms this change is very clear as far as certain categories of people are concerned. So, as we have already said, a wife becomes a widow and a husband a widower on the death of their spouse. Similarly children become orphans on the death of their parents. But there is no name change for parents whose children have died. This may be taken to indicate that marriage changes social status in Britain more than does childbirth, but it should certainly not be read psychologically to mean that being a mother is less significant to the woman concerned than being a wife. This fact is increasingly important with the rise of single-parent families, where the identity of motherhood is more to the fore than is that of being a wife. Certainly it is important not to ignore the fact that motherhood is an existential fact of life and not simply a sociological description.

It may well be that descriptive terms are closely linked to the social benefit or lack of it derived from their use. The absence – in England – of a word for a mother who has lost her child may say much about traditional attitudes to childbearing and gender but such descriptive bareness is not the case in every culture. So, for example, in contemporary Israeli society not only is there a phrase, *ima shkula*, meaning a bereaved mother but there are similar terms for a bereaved father, *aba shkul*, and for bereaved parents, *horim shkulim*. Not only do these terms have a psychological significance in relation to bereavement, but they also carry powerful social and political significance in the context of Israel's military defence strategy. To have lost a son serving in the army, in defence of the country, is deemed an honourable sacrifice for the nation. The regular and extensive televising of military funerals in Israel reflects these values. This is a constant reminder to us of the need to be alert to the interplay of the rhetoric of power and sympathy, of politics and psychology, in human life. This is, perhaps, especially important when care and counselling have financial implications, and funding is often a political issue.

So it is that the medical model of bereavement as an illness, followed by stages of recuperation, is inappropriate. In some ways this idea that bereavement is an illness can be linked to Philippe Ariès' argument that in modern, Western Europe death itself has become a technical phenomenon focused on the hospital (1974: 88). But an existential model focused on issues of identity and change in identity is far more appropriate for matters of life and death than is the medical model, not least because it throws the individual into sharp focus rather than having the individual subject to imperious forces. So it is that Cleiren's important research showed that many mothers simply do not 'return to normal' after the death of a child. The loss of a child involves a partial loss of self which cannot be compensated for in any simple way, as Dennis Klass expressed it in his extensive study of bereaved parents: 'like amputation, parental bereavement is a permanent condition' (1993: 344). And certainly no simple stage-theory of grief can cope with this kind of bereavement, as several critiques of Elisabeth Kübler-Ross's (1973) stage-theory approach to bereavement increasingly make clear (Corr, 1993: 69–83).

Whatever view is taken of grief, however, this chapter has urged that the combined biological and social dimensions produce, in general terms, individuals who have been changed through the experience of bereavement. By means of funerary rites, not least the power of words, they have so overcome life's hardship as to affirm the social goal of their culture. The reason it is wrong to interpret grief as an illness is precisely because it implies that recovery returns someone to a normal state. The whole thrust of our argument is that the rituals of bereavement produce a different kind of person. While funeral rites do constitute a rite of passage in Van Gennep's sense of shifting an individual from one social status to another social status, they also need to be viewed in Maurice Bloch's terms as a process of rebounding conquest, through which a personal change occurs because of what has been encountered.

The public sign of this transformation is often that of formal memorials which stand as testimony not only of the one who has died but of those who consent to continue to live a social life. War memorials constitute a particularly good example of texts and architecture standing together as a witness of the way that death can be used as a vehicle to oppose evil and to foster the ongoing life of society (J. Davies, 1993: 112ff.). In terms of this book, memorials express the triumph of 'words against death' and are symbolic of that rebounding vitality which ensures society's continuation.

# 4 Book, Film and Building

The creativity of human imagination has not left death to itself, uncommented upon, unaddressed. Through literature, film, art and architecture death has been framed so as not to leave the last word with mortality. The following sketches of these fields seek only to illuminate this underlying venture of life-affirmation. In a sense the sacred books of world religions resemble the popular media of film and television in providing an objective focus for reflection on the fact of death. While there are obvious differences between the tradition of supernatural authority vested in sacred texts and the much more transient nature of modern media and popular culture, both foster public discussion of human worth in the face of death (Kearl, 1989: 379ff.).

Literature in the broadest sense has, certainly, addressed death both indirectly through novels and directly through criticisms of modern approaches to death (Scott, 1967; Weir, 1980). Evelyn Waugh's classic critique of the emerging American pattern of a cosmetic presentation of the dead as though they were simply asleep in *The Loved One,* written as early as 1948, and Jessica Mitford's later *The American Way of Death* (1963) both serve, in their own way, as a call to ensure that human responses to death may be more, rather than less, authentic. As these very titles demonstrate, some books may possess a degree of durability, but still it is in buildings that the most lasting statement is made about death, not least because such edifices attract depths of meaning and convey them from one generation to another. Needless to say, sacred buildings also gain a great deal of their power in the face of death from the very use of sacred texts recited within their walls (L. Jones, 1993; D. J. Davies, 1996b).

## Religious sources

The distinctive feature of world religions is that death becomes associated with their supernatural forces and with guidance on death and dying, provided as part of a total theory of life, especially of the moral life. While the deity may be thought to have overall control over life and death, some specific manifestation of deity or of a messenger is often particularly associated with death. So, in Hinduism, Kali, the great mother and consort of the god Shiva, himself both destroyer as well as a creator, is the symbolic expression both of judgement and of death. In Buddhism the figure of Mara plays a similar part. In the mystical tradition of Judaism the *Book of Splendour*, or *Zohar* in Hebrew, which originated in medieval Spain, dealt with matters of death. One tradition argued that Adam, the first man of all and the first sinner, appeared to those about to die, while other traditions argued that it was one's deceased relatives who appeared to the dying (Abramovitch, 1988: 182). The Tibetan Buddhist traditions of death have become particularly well known through the *Tibetan Book of The Dead*, discussed in Chapter 6.

Many branches of Christian theology also conceived of post-mortem worlds even though they did not end, as in Buddhism, with a belief in reincarnation but with a final entry into heaven. In some Christian folk traditions there is a belief in the dead welcoming those who are dying and even taking messages to them from the living (Kligman, 1988: 152ff.).

## Media sources

This idea of the dead being welcomed by people in the other world has become increasingly familiar in the late twentieth century not from specifically religious sources, nor even from a folk religion as such, but through television, newspaper and magazine articles on near-death experiences. Indeed, this very phrase, near-death experience, has come to be an established category with an increasing literature of both popular and more scholarly forms (Gallup, 1982; Greyson and Flynn, 1984). Many tell of a sense of passing down a tunnel towards its brightly illuminated end where a welcoming person stands awaiting the newcomer, perhaps telling the new arrival to return to earthly life once more. These are very largely, though not entirely, positive experiences and often foster a more intense spiritual outlook in the survivors (Basford, 1990). While the experience itself owes more to the basic technology of medical resuscitation than to religious practices, such as prayer or meditation, it is often told in ways which invest the memory with profound significance bordering the religious. In fact they afford a very significant form of 'words against death' not only because of the medical context in which the death was, as it were, certain and the recovery a form of scientific achievement but because of the deep sincerity and conviction with which this person now speaks.

These reports gain tremendous public coverage and are not insignificant because, in most contemporary societies, radio, television, films, plays, newspapers, magazines and books all contribute to furnishing a background of information to daily life, and what is produced in them can be quite uncritically accepted as true. These media have become increasingly important since about the 1950s in giving a public focus to many aspects of life, including death. This is not only true as television carries news-pictures of important funeral rites but also through documentaries and other features.

Although death makes its impact on individual lives in very private ways, the more public images of death, regularly represented by artistic media, provide a rich spectrum of resources for responding to bereavement and loss. While the more temporary forms of music or film may only last a moment, compared with the long duration of grave monuments or the immense timespan of the pyramids, this makes them none the less powerful for particular individuals and it is very likely that, in actual experience, both forms may feed upon each other as death becomes a pervasive cultural preoccupation.

## Television

Television has been, perhaps, the most significant medium for presenting issues of death to an extremely large number of viewers as both fictional and factual material has reached millions of people's homes. There have been deaths presented on soap operas and in films, as well as in news items and documentaries covering wars, natural disasters and epidemics. The most dramatic single example of actual death must be that of President Kennedy. His death and the subsequent funerary rites reached extensively into the lives of millions in the USA, with over half the population having wept, four out of five reporting that they felt the loss of someone dear to them, and nine out of ten saying they suffered some sense of physical discomfort (Manchester, 1967: 189). It has been argued that the funerary ritual did a great deal to 're-establish and reassure the national community' after the whole tragedy (Ochs, 1993: 26); even so, there is no guarantee that a televised rite will achieve a totally positive end, as in the case of the funeral of Martin Luther King, which was thought by some to have been something of a failure (D. L. Lewis, 1978).

## Music

Music is one of the profoundest means of expressing emotion between people and within the experience of each individual, not least in terms of death. Although cultures differ in their emphasis upon music, the place of songs, chants and laments at the time of death is well established, as shown in Chapters 3 and 8 for traditional Greek Orthodox society. There we find music not only in the form of the sung liturgy of the Orthodox Church, centred as it is on the human voice, but also in a wide variety of popular laments. These put into words the general human experience of grief and make it even more specific in terms of particular deaths. The words of many of these laments are, locally, well known and are constructed in such a way that some details of each particular death can be inserted into them to render them personal. With contemporary social change, many modern and urban Greeks are said to find such laments old fashioned and expect them to end in the atmosphere of contemporary life and it may well be that such songs

57

require a relatively close-knit traditional community in which to survive. It was neighbours and friends who sang these songs and not the inner circle of bereaved people; in urban contexts it is unlikely that such a background community will exist. Still, such songs reflect the importance of music in many communities over many centuries, if not millennia, in helping people cope with death. Examples could be drawn from hundreds of traditional societies, such as that of villages in Transylvania (Kligman, 1988), to illustrate this point. Singing is, fundamentally, a community activity which sets group hopes and power over those of the individual. It is as though the strength and insight of others help the bereaved when at their weakest.

## Hymns and music of death

In the Christian tradition there are two particularly important streams of music related to death: the requiem mass and popular hymns and laments. In Catholicism the major form is related to the music accompanying the ritual of the Requiem Mass. Especially since the sixteenth century, an entire musical form developed to which practically every major composer added another theme as with, for example, Mozart and the contemporary Andrew Lloyd Webber. These, and many more, have greatly added to the cultural life of many nations extending well beyond their European home.

Although in Protestantism the very idea of a requiem, along with prayers for the dead, is traditionally rejected, great music concerning death has come to be associated with the passion and death of Jesus Christ (Minear, 1987). Bach's *St Matthew Passion* is one of the finest examples of a musical reflection on death while Handel's *Messiah* is widely known with its focus on the passion and resurrection of Jesus. At a much more widespread and popular dimension, many Protestant congregational hymns on death have embraced both the death of Christ and also the death of individuals with a considerable emphasis on the journey to the heavenly city. The hymn 'Abide with me, fast falls the eventide' has come to be widely sung at a great variety of events, including football matches, and has made available the public sharing of emotion at times of death and tragedy within the UK. The Methodist Revival in Britain in the eighteenth century marked a vitally important change as hymns, alongside sermons, came to be the central means of expressing doctrine and faith, as in the first book, *Hymns and Sacred Poems,* published by John and Charles Wesley in 1739. Developing from metrical psalm-singing, hymns expressed the doctrines of new religious outlooks in language that could be deeply biblical but could also use non-biblical expressions to great effect. The freedom to use ordinary language to mirror and echo biblical turns of phrase was a powerful means of stimulating piety, not least in attitudes to death. It was in the Protestant tradition that hymn singing came to be a central and vitally important aspect of worship during the eighteenth and especially the nineteenth century with the publication, for example, of *Hymns Ancient and Modern* in 1861.

Another important folk tradition, that of the lament, saw Christian forms develop from even older funeral rites in which the dead were addressed while the deep emotion of the mourner was also given free expression (Alexiou, 1974; Kligman, 1988: 285ff.). Through the world of modern musical communication, many other forms of musical response to death can occur as, for example, in Nigel Osborne's opera *Hell's Angels* or John Corrigliano's First Symphony, both of which are more specifically directed at death through AIDS (D. J. Davies, 1996a: 18). Because, in such works, the international stage replaces the village they demonstrate with even greater force the human need not to remain silent in the face of death.

## Sculpture

Though music may last but a moment, sculpture lasts for ages. At the grandest level, pyramids and other mausolea reflect memorials to the dead long after the words of death-songs have been forgotten, while grave decoration of very many kinds provides a medium expressing attitudes to death. In Christian cultures the cross and crucifixes as grave markers unite the death of Christ with the death of believers. In countless churches, as well as in graveyards, there are works of art representing the dead, especially those who were influential while alive.

From the thousands of sculptures which depict death here we choose to describe only one, that of *Orpheus and Eurydice* by Auguste Rodin (1840–1917). This remarkable work, now found at New York's Metropolitan Museum of Art, was sculpted in about 1895 and depicts the youthfully virile Orpheus coming from the underworld with his lover Eurydice just behind him, almost as his shadow. He has been leading her out from her captivity in the underworld but has broken the golden rule and looked back; she must now return there, to death as it were, while Orpheus is left bereft. This dramatic depiction of human grief touches the heart of bereavement, not least as a representation of the close of the nineteenth century when disbelief in an afterlife began to assume new proportions for many Europeans. Orpheus is sculpted with great clarity and precision, he is a picture of clear individuality bearing the weight of human loss of love – he cannot and must not look back upon what he has lost. While they both seem to emerge from the marble she is caught up in it, she already returns into its formlessness. Her face lacks precise definition, her eyes closed and lost. Her left hand, clasped in a grip, is no longer open to touch or embrace. So too her right hand. His right hand holds his brow in grief, his left hand is open but does not reach back to touch her. His limbs are strongly toned while hers are already becoming flaccid. She loses her identity while his is powerful in bearing the consequence of consciousness in the pain of separation and grief.

The Orpheus myth has attracted the attention of several scholars from some quite varied academic fields interested in death. The Swedish historian of religion Åke Hultkrantz has rehearsed similar themes from North American Indian cultures in stories where a husband brings his wife back from the land of the dead but, accidentally, strikes her, despite a warning that such an action would lead to her having to return to the dead. Hultkrantz explains these myths as having their origin in 'the narrative of a shaman's ecstatic journey' which has become transformed by tradition (1957: 310). The anthropologist Walter Goldschmidt has also referred to 'the ancient symbol of Orpheus' and its taboo against looking back, to express 'the fear of evil inherent in death' rather than the fear of the deceased (1980: 35). He also cites the biblical theme of not looking back which he links with Job but, presumably, means to refer to Lot whose wife becomes a pillar of salt when she looks back during the pair's escape from Sodom as detailed in Genesis 19:26.

The Lot story is, explicitly, explored from a historical and theological point of view by Breitwieser who argued that the great Protestant reformer John Calvin used the Lot episode to expose 'grief's phenomenological movement' and to establish it as a model for grief in the Protestant tradition (1990: 72). The argument is that grief exhibits two contradictory tendencies, on the one hand involving a speedy sense of things sliding away while on the other it marks a lagging behind in a static experience.

## Exhibition and art

Art of various sorts has long furnished not only a major vehicle for human reflection on death but also an opposition to it, as human creativity engages with mortality through paint and sculpture. From the medieval portrayal of life as a dance, with death in the background, to more modern existential depictions of death through a wide variety of symbols of desolation artists speak against death for many (Holbein, *Dance of Death,* 1538; Gottlieb, 1959; Clarke, 1976; Camille, 1996).

Here I focus on one contemporary exhibition held in March and April 1996 in Amsterdam and organized by Harry Heyink and Walter Carpay (1996) around the theme 'In the Midst of Life We Are in Death'. It brought together a wide variety of material from some 60 artists and all dealt with facets of death. The five rooms of the exhibition began with modern costumes which could be used as clothes in which the dead might be dressed – one included a shroud with wings embroidered on the back. The second major room brought together a collection of coffins, beginning with a simple fabric which would soon disintegrate after burial. Such cloth may be the solution to contemporary ecological problems, as may the neighbouring wickerwork coffin and another very lightweight coffin furnished with strapping to enable it to be carried on an individual's back. Other coffins carried brightly coloured messages or were very natural in the sense that one was carved out of a tree-trunk.

The next room was extremely unusual, containing a dining table set for a meal. Thrown onto the white tablecloth was a shadowy outline of a human body, its head at one end of the table and its feet at the other. The significance of this shadow-presence was clarified through the extensive menu which set out a wide variety of dishes that might be produced from a human body. This reflection on a form of cannibalism was, perhaps, the most dramatic example of contemporary consideration of death and death rites. It was complemented in the next part of the exhibition where a video documented the possibility of destroying the human body by exploding it in a special chamber. The diagrams and plans presented for this method of disposing of bodies, as stark and innovative as it seems, resemble the late-nineteenth-century designs for crematoria and shows how an idea which seems nearly absurd in one era can become completely acceptable in another.

The largest room of the Heyink and Carpay exhibition was filled with an extremely wide variety of artefacts and designs for commemorating the dead. In pride of place was a bright metallic hearse with large wheels, shafts to enable it to be pulled by people and a central rugby-football shaped container to carry a coffin. Other objects included an hour-glass filled with cremated remains, and highly creative grave memorials, one featuring a metallic framework with gravestones hung from it rather like coats on coathangers and hinting at death as, perhaps, a change of clothing. Another memorial consisted of an automatic piano-accordion within a birdcage. The final room housed special headwear for mourners, extensive black structures of immense proportion, one of which stood on wheels. An aspidistra plant had words of remembrance written upon its leaves while some computer software made it possible to access information about dead people.

This entire exhibition dealt, artistically, with the seriousness and the humour often associated with death in contemporary societies, addressing death, as it were, but without the voice of traditional religion. The fact that very many people visited the exhibition, not least large numbers of younger adults, shows not only that death continues to be a topic of curious interest but one which people still wish to be creatively addressed. And as in the art of picture and sculpture so too in poetry.

## Poetic 'words against death'

Poets are first amongst those using words of self-awareness to express human emotions, not least those of love and death, and to refine the effect of memory upon experience (Simpson, 1977). This includes the secular message which emphasizes death as the end of life whilst endeavouring to place a strong value on the life lived (Lamont, 1952). Here, once more, we are able only to point out this capacity of poetry to be in the vanguard of words against death rather than to document the mass of poems which have set life against its mortal negation. Two poems must suffice, one by Dylan Thomas (1914–53) and the other by Stevie Smith (1902–71). The first expresses one of the most powerful sets of words against death ever voiced in an English language poem while the second lies at the opposite end of the spectrum, where words have failed and futility strives to be heard.

The very title and first line of Thomas's poem, 'Do not go gentle into that good night', command his dead father, and through him all the dead, not to accept death as a passive inevitability. 'Old age should burn and rave at close of day / Rage, rage against the dying of the light.' His poem combines those lines, 'Rage, rage against the dying of the light' with his titular line, 'Do not go gentle into that good night' to produce a powerful poetic barrage of opposition to death for those he addresses, successively, as 'wise, good, wild' and 'grave men near death' (1987: 432).

Stevie Smith, by contrast, in her extremely popular poem, 'Not Waving but Drowning', tells of a man at sea, thought by those on land to be waving a greeting while really he was indicating his distress as he drowned:

> It must have been too cold for him his heart gave way, They said.
> Oh, no no no, it was too cold always
> (Still the dead one lay moaning)
> I was much too far out all my life
> And not waving but drowning. (1987: 370)

This stanza is particularly important, indicating as it does, the opposite of 'words against death'. Here, words are reduced to the manual sign of a wave, a communication from a distance, and one misunderstood for its opposite. The individual man, the poem's subject and object, is socially distanced from others, an irrelevance – 'I was much too far out all my life'. So when it came to his death the insignificant others with their feet firmly on the ground could not differentiate between a wave of despair and one of greeting. This reflects the importance of a social network as the bastion against death, whether religious or secular, and demonstrates a sense of individualistic futility as far as both life and death are concerned.

How readers respond to these poems will depend much upon their own life experience and sense of group and community involvement. George Steiner, one of the most insightful intellectuals of the late twentieth century, represents one such poignant stream of response when saying that 'However inspired, no poem, no painting, no musical piece – though music comes closest – can make us at home with death, let alone "weep it from its purpose"' (1989: 141). In this he probably speaks for many, precisely because it is the active and creative mind, so much given to self-reflection, which finds the idea of the thoughtlessness of death so inconceivable and takes refuge in descriptive words. We cannot be at home in such a strange country.

Still, despite such intellectual reflections, the power of poetry to console and to elevate in funerary rites remains strong. One very clear and interesting example lies in a substantial and, perhaps, historically significant volume of 'Readings, Prayers and Music chosen for Memorial Services' entitled *Remembrance*, introduced by Ned Sherrin, the popular media presenter, and with a foreword by the Archbishop of Canterbury. Interestingly, neither of the above poems is included though Dylan Thomas's 'And death shall have no dominion' is there as one of many which could be regarded as secular poetry (Sherrin, 1996: 59). This collection was produced for the charity Cruse Bereavement Care and reflects the fact that death elicits collaboration from both secular and religious segments of society as the twentieth century draws to a close. The book sets biblical readings and traditional hymns alongside excerpts from novels and established classics and not only sets out the actual form of former memorial services for some distinguished people but also forms of services some of the well-known living have devised for themselves. A list of suitable musical pieces is also included. The eclecticism in the face of death is reflected by successive poems on one page where T. S. Eliot is followed by the great Bengali poet Rabindranath Tagore, the popular entertainer Joyce Grenfell and the Anglican mystical priest George Herbert (Sherrin, 1996: 40–1). What Sherrin's volume shows is that individuals increasingly wish to shape their own final words on their own life and their death and not, necessarily, accept those provided by traditional religion. What is obviously true is that words and music remain profoundly powerful and significant when it comes to planning a reflection upon a deceased life. Indirectly this collection also speaks of the importance of the locations within which some of the memorial services have taken place. Even the most secular of 'words against death' have found themselves spoken within the confines of ancient religious walls. Indeed, it is interesting to see that numerous studies devoted to aspects of grief often include some poetic words, as though clinical prose demands them before justice is done to the topic (Hill, 1986: 189). One of the sharpest examples is Kübler-Ross's deeply influential book *On Death and Dying* (1973), where each chapter begins with the poetry of Rabindranath Tagore. Her final section, 'The silence that goes beyond words', deals with the ultimate calm before death and also ends with another stanza from that most evocative of all Rabindranath Tagore's volumes, *Stray Birds* (CLXXVI):

The water in a vessel is sparkling:
the water in the sea is dark.

The small truth has words that are clear,
the great truth has great silence.

## Humane 'words against death'

It is not easy to locate poems by Tagore, nor indeed by many other poets, in the strict classification of sacred or secular. Even if we are certain about the specific religion of the author we can never know the way the poem is read and accepted by individuals. That profound problem of hermeneutics lies beyond the goal of this book. What must be said, however, is that the very form of poetry, especially when it addresses what many would perceive as the depth of life, speaks to the situation of death and to the condition of mortality. For this reason I speak here of humane words, not least because even words which are not explicitly religious may be accepted in a sentiment of emotion which would be hard to distinguish from some explicitly religious views.

This brief comment introduces the relatively new phenomenon, in Britain at least, of using popular songs at funerals as a distinctive way of framing mortuary ritual. The term 'popular' may be entirely accurate or may, occasionally, need to be extended to embrace classical music which is simply not explicitly part of the repertoire of sacred music. Be that as it may, increasing numbers of people are requesting that popular songs or tunes be played, usually in crematoria at the time of the funeral rite, as an appropriate way of recalling the deceased person's life and of bidding farewell. A list of the top ten funeral songs, published by the *Funeral Service Journal*, provides an extremely clear picture of non-traditionally religious sentiments chosen by significantly large groups of Britons in the 1990s (*Guardian*, 23 August 1996).

Whitney Houston's 'I Will Always Love You' came first followed by Frank Sinatra singing 'My Way', 'Unchained Melody' by the Righteous Brothers and 'Wind Beneath My Wings' by Bette Midler. Fifth came Barbra Streisand singing 'Memory' followed by John Lennon with 'Imagine', Glenn Miller's version of 'In The Mood', Aled Jones singing 'Walking in the Air', Louis Armstrong's 'Wonderful World' and, finally, The Platters' version of 'Smoke Gets in Your Eyes'. In these popular items, evocative words and music reflect something of life shared together and of the personality of the deceased. The very fact that they are used at all shows how accustomed most Britons are to having powerful words involved in funerals. Even if a funeral is specifically secular the use of music and favourite readings by friends and members of the family, rather than by a priest, brings a felt sense of significance to the rite. Kearl has shown, in a similar way, how some popular music has come to have associations with death in the USA (1989: 390). In my opinion this demonstrates the efficacy of 'words against death' and the historical success of Christianity in establishing death rites as the occasion when the human genius to oppose negativity and to seek to overcome adversity is manifested. We will return to this theme in the final chapter.

## Architecture of death

The human genius has, traditionally, even cast such sentiments in stone. Indeed, building against death has been one of the most expressive of all human endeavours so obviously manifest in the great burial chambers of pre-history, in Egypt's pyramids and in memorial buildings across the entire globe. They may speak of future realms in which the dead now live, as in ancient Egypt, or of the cultural contribution made by musicians, poets or scholars, as in the tombs of the famous at Westminster Abbey in London or Père Lachaise in Paris, or they may comprise that kind of the memorial space Richard Etlin has called 'the space of absence' (1993: 595–9). It is, perhaps, particularly appropriate that he should cite Gunnar Asplund's crematorium in Stockholm, built in the late 1930s, as an example of this type. Its appropriateness lies in the fact that cremation does, most effectively, create a literal absence of the body whilst leaving the need for a memorial site. Others have explored many aspects of the history of the architecture of death (Curl, 1972) as well as providing detailed accounts of, for example, particular cemeteries, as in Nicol's study of Adelaide's famous Centennial Park Cemetery (1994) or California's even better known Forest Lawn Cemetery where its founder, Hubert Eaton, sought to realize the dream of a park filled with beautiful plants, statues and art. On New Year's Day 1917 Eaton wrote 'The Builder's Creed' which combined Christian affirmations with statements of managerial practice:

I believe in a happy eternal life.

I believe ... in a Christ that smiles and loves you and me.

I therefore know the cemeteries of today are wrong because they depict an end, not a beginning ... unsightly stoneyards full of in-artistic symbols and depressing customs ...

I shall try to build at Forest Lawn a great park devoid of misshapen monuments and other customary signs of earthly death, but filled with towering trees, splashing fountains, singing birds, beautiful statuary ... redolent of the world's best history and romances.

Sculptured marble and pictorial glass shall be encouraged but controlled by acknowledged artists.

A place ... protected by an immense endowment care fund.

(Rubin, Carlton and Rubin, 1979: 24)

Given the criticism so often levelled against the Forest Lawn style of cemetery it is worth acknowledging the success of Hubert Eaton in taking over, in 1913, what had been the arid Tropicano cemetery and bringing to it not only a new water supply, making the lawns possible, but also setting about a cultural creation. After visiting the San Francisco Exposition of 1915 he was inspired by the ideal of a non-denominational Christianity as an essential foundation for the great American civilization. Eaton then sought to ensure that, as he saw it, key elements of the wider European Christian-inspired culture should take their place in Forest Lawn. So it was that he visited Europe and purchased copies and replicas of established works of art and enshrined them in churches and buildings on his site in which people might be married, as they were from 1920, or, as subsequently was the case, they could be baptized. As his biographers expressed his genius, he enabled middle-class Americans 'to buy minuscule shares in a version of the Memorial Impulse' (Rubin, Carlton and Rubin, 1979: 63).

This famous attempt at constructing an earthly paradise may be seen as setting the stage for the American treatment of corpses as sleeping relatives. Both acts serving an artistic framing of death in a dramatically hopeful way, despite the European criticism so often levelled against it. The extent to which individuals find their community given to building and maintaining monuments to the dead is a measure of the extent to which any particular society addresses itself to death. 'Words against death' have, traditionally, been shared by individual and society, but as individualization expands so they become increasingly private. Michel Vovelle, an eminent historian of death, has also written on the impact of contemporary funeral rites on cemeteries grounded in economic standardization which, nevertheless, runs along with a new sense of individualism (1993).

It remains to be seen whether private 'words against death', symbolized perhaps by an ink-written message on a bunch of flowers placed over a small pile of cremated remains, will serve as well as the shared inscriptions on public memorials in addressing death and asserting life. What is interesting is that even private memorials often stand in public cemeteries where a kind of impersonal publicity is gained through a memorial. Written memorials afford the capacity to share with others who, themselves, are unknown. In so doing people acknowledge the communal fact that death comes to all and that all may respond verbally to it. But few gravestones stand bare and silent.

## Death studies

Finally one should not ignore the fact that, complementing this architectural, literary and artistic creativity associated with death, one finds an increase of interest in death since about the 1950s in the academic fields of anthropology, history and sociology, with a considerable development in the therapeutic and pastoral professions as explored in many of the chapters in this book. All these fields constitute a cultural response to death, not least in the light of a decreased sense of broad religious certainty over the post-mortem realms of hell and heaven. Historians in particular not only saw death as a fact of life in need of documentation but as a cultural motif enabling them to compare different eras (Vovelle, 1993; Ariès, 1976, 1991; McManners, 1981).

Medical doctors, psychiatrists and therapists all came to devote increasing attention to the issues of grief and mourning. Their writings paralleled the growth both of the hospice movement and of self-help groups of individuals who had been bereaved in particular ways. The impact of individuals such as Elisabeth Kübler-Ross (1973), with her early stage-theory of grief, and Colin Murray Parkes (1972), in his study of bereaved people in their reaction to bereavement, was particularly influential. American journals such as *Death Studies* and *Omega* and the new, British-based, interdisciplinary journal *Mortality,* itself published from 1996, all attest to the explicit interest in death grounded in the broadly secular context of post-modernity. Courses in schools and colleges have also begun to address the issue of death.

## Contemporary adaptation

Together these sources show that death is no longer left within the domain of official religious institutions and to be interpreted theologically. 'Words against death' are only just, at the close of the twentieth century, passing from the realm of the sacred to that of the secular. While many traditional 'words against death' may still be theological they are now equally likely to be poetic or explicitly therapeutic. Through them, the whole process of adaptation and social evolution continues through expanding patterns of the rhetoric of death. The pool of potential orientations to death was once very deep in terms of traditional religion. In contemporary advanced societies that pool has become an entire series of pools. While the religious person may well regret the increased loss of committed religious interpretations of death and the afterlife, it is also possible to see the emergence of other approaches as providing a greater good for a greater number of persons.

Adaptability of response can be a characteristic feature of successful groups and individuals. The mix of traditional and innovative, of religious and secular, of artistic and idiosyncratic approaches to funerals which is now emerging in many contemporary developed societies can be interpreted not only as indicative of secularization but also of the human drive for significance. More than this, these innovative forms may well contribute to that sense of conquest which has been characteristic of the best of traditional funeral rites. In societies of traditional Christian culture, for example, it would be unwise only to think of funerary rites as representing some antiquarian human endeavour grounded in the past and slowly weakening in effect. Just as ritual has come to be adopted as a powerful tool by many groups, whether for therapy or drama, its possibilities in terms of secular ritual have not been ignored. The popularizing and secularizing of funerary rites is likely to be one of the major arenas of ritual development in the coming decade. If our argument is correct, then the rites which flourish will be those which cause the bereaved to flourish as they enhance the quest for life.

# 5 Sacrifice, Violence and Conquest

If ritual 'words against death' are as significant in human adaptation to existence as this book argues it is important to explore the social contexts which invest them with power. Every society and era establishes its own theory of life and death and frames its verbal rites of death. The historian Philippe Ariès, for example, has outlined his own view of death in Europe, passing from a sense of 'tame' death, natural and inevitable for all, through a change in the twelfth century or so, when death became more individual and people thought of their own death as crucial, to the eighteenth and nineteenth centuries when an ever growing sense of intimacy with others shifted the focus to a sense of concern at the death of others rather than with our own death. Finally, he talks of death in the twentieth century as something 'unnameable' and distant from everyday experience (1974: 1106). While there is, doubtless, some truth in these differences between broad trends across centuries and eras they should not, I think, be pressed too far by applying them to cultures beyond those of France which is, largely, Ariès's historical concern. For example, the generalizations he makes about cremation in Britain are highly questionable and in some ways misguiding (1974: 91, 101).

Still, some generalizations are inevitable. One which I think important in Western thought, throughout the twentieth century, focuses on the idea of control. Death involves a challenge to life and it is likely that the inevitability of death becomes more of a problem as members of a society become increasingly competent in mastering the natural world.

It has often been argued, following the sociologist Max Weber, that the process of secularization, by which religious institutions and beliefs lose influence over people's lives, increased in direct proportion to the increase of human rational mastery and control over the world (1930). Work in factories, for example, was much more under human control than work in fields; the weather was much less important for indoor workers. Just as the nineteenth century witnessed the rapid growth of modes of production governed and influenced by rational forms of control, the twentieth century added to this human capacity the significant capacity of medicine to control illness. Now, at the close of the twentieth century, people in Western societies have a dramatically greater access to the control of natural processes than ever before in the history of the world. But, and this is the significant point, no matter how influential medical control becomes in delaying the moment of death, that moment still arrives.

In other words, ultimately there is no control over death. In this sense death opposes modern human beings, especially those who are in their strength and prime of life and who may experience extensive powers of control in their daily life. They cannot avoid the fact that, as with everybody else, death controls the end of life; they fail to control death. Often this failure is set in the framework of medicine, especially of surgery, where doctors are said to regard death as a failure.

But, as this chapter will show, human beings do seek to control even death. Whether through their religious beliefs or through particular rituals, they act upon the lives of particular members of their society as though using life as a sort of tool to make a social or philosophical point. With this in mind one can say that, odd as it may seem, death by natural causes is rare. This is especially true in modern societies where doctors and hospitals play a major part in managing and controlling death. All deaths are accompanied by medical certificates stating the cause of death and these causes tend to belong to a relatively small range of options.

So it is possible, in a sense, to speak of the medicalization of death as a kind of control over death. Indeed, giving a reason for a death is itself a kind of control and many find a degree of comfort in having this named cause of death. It is as though a medical cause of death answers part of the human need to know why someone died. Though in a logical sense it is not persuasive it still remains true that some people see the cause of death as part of the reason for death. In cases of unexpected death, the moral question of why someone has died takes dramatic precedence over how they died. So in the case of a young child the parents will not see any sense in the loss of such a young life, irrespective of the cause, while the death of an aged parent seems more natural and inevitable though relatives still expect a cause of death to be given since in modern societies there is a general expectation that people will live until some illness carries them off in old age. These deaths by illness, accident or natural causes can all be contrasted with what we may call death by social causes. Though it is possible to dispute just which kinds of death may be classified as social causes here we place together execution, war, suicide and what might be called sacrificial deaths.

## Execution and personal freedom

Very many societies have, in the history of human cultures, regarded themselves as possessing the power of life and death over their members. In return for the benefits of protection and survival that come from belonging to a society, individuals are expected to act according to its social rules in helping to maintain the unity and integrity of a community. To break those rules is to expect a degree of retribution, whether minor or major. In other words individuals are expected to sacrifice part of their own freedom in order not to infringe the freedom of others. This is an intriguing issue, especially in modern societies where individual freedom is increasing to the point at which private pleasure seems to take pride of place above social duties and obligation.

Sigmund Freud was one, among many others, who addressed himself to this problem in his book *Civilisation and Its Discontents* (1930) where he explored the kinds of sacrifice of personal freedom that were necessary to live with other people and to derive benefit from membership in a protecting society. It is an issue which comes to sharp focus in the very modern expression we consider elsewhere that 'it's my body and I can do what I like with it'. Most societies in the history of human culture have not accepted that statement because many people have an interest in any particular human body. Parents, spouses and relatives, as well as agents of law enforcement or, indeed, of medicine have often had some interest in and power over an individual's body. This remains true, for example, in respect of dead bodies. In contemporary England, for example, a corpse does not belong, in a legal sense, to the person who once lived as that body, rather it is the next of kin who have certain rights of ownership (Smale, 1994: 46). So even if a person sincerely wanted, for example, to be buried, the next of kin could still opt to have that body cremated.

Execution takes this control of bodies one step further by taking away the very life of a person in an ultimate form of social control. The power and also the potential horror of execution lies precisely in the way a life is officially and, in a real sense, cold-bloodedly taken from someone. This ultimate sanction is often reserved for those who have wrongly taken the life of another person or who have acted against the welfare of the whole society in some profound way as, for example, in treason. It is one of the clearest examples of society using death to demonstrate that society itself is of the greatest value. Though executions normally occur in societies with an advanced system of law and of social hierarchy they can be found in a wide variety of social groups. The influential anthropologist of India, Christoph von Fürer-Haimendorf, tells of the execution of a man for continuous theft of cattle beyond the level of social acceptability among the Apa Tani peoples of northeast frontier India:

When the hour for execution came several prominent (leaders) told him he had to die for his thieving habits: it was his own fault and he should bear them no grudge. Then they cut off his hand 'with which he had stolen', slashed him over the eyes 'with which he had spied on other men's cattle', and over the mouth 'with which he had eaten stolen goods'. In a few moments he was dead. (1967: 76)

But the same anthropologist showed how some tribes of relatively simple organization would allow retribution to be made even for homicide without taking the life of the murderer.

One of the major differences between societies in the late twentieth century lies precisely in attitudes to execution. Those who are deeply influenced by

Western liberal thought tend to argue that the death penalty is uncivilized because, for example, it treats murderers in the same way that murderers treated their victims. In terms of anthropology, this kind of argument is perfectly intelligible in that the kind of society which allows people to hold liberal thoughts also treats criminals in less exacting ways. The extent to which the death penalty is imposed is the extent to which a society exerts strong pressure over its members. The degree of social power expressed in the death penalty matches the degree of social power used in ordinary social control within a society and, most probably, will reflect the extent to which that society has a widely shared set of moral values and also a firm sense of the boundary between that society and other, surrounding societies.

## Warfare and head-hunting

If execution reflects power inflicted upon a member of one's own society there remain two rather different forms of violence where the direction of force is outward rather than inward, namely war and head-hunting. Both of these involve death and situations where the killer is viewed in a positive rather than a negative way.

International warfare, as in the First and Second World Wars, furnishes a dramatically large-scale example of this positively valued human behaviour while head-hunting presents a relatively local and limited type of formal aggression between groups. One element of both activities lies in the official sanction on killing particular categories of people, usually defined as enemies. Indeed, to kill an enemy can be viewed as being as virtuous as killing a fellow citizen is wicked. This shows the power of society to define death in terms of bad and good behaviour and also of death itself as a phenomenon open to carry different loads of meaning.

### War and the war-dead

It is characteristic of wars to place a very low human value upon the enemy as human beings and to increase the status of one's own soldiers. The bodies of enemies may be mutilated or simply abandoned while victors treat their own dead heroically. The emergence of war memorials after both the First and Second World Wars demonstrates the significance invested in the war-dead (J. Davies, 1993). These memorials often exist at both local and national levels with perhaps only a few names on a village commemorative cross or plaque, while the national memorial may list thousands or else provide a statement concerning the greatness of the sacrifice made by the dead. In fact this is an interesting example of the use of sacrifice as a means of making sense of the countless deaths involved in twentieth-century warfare. Texts like that from St John's Gospel saying that 'Greater love hath no man for his friend than that he lay down his life for his brother' are common.

Many countries continue to give formal commemoration to their military dead as they rehearse these ideals of personal sacrifice. This can involve large scale events, such as on Remembrance Day annually in November in Great Britain when the monarch along with the Prime Minister and other senior politicians engage in a ceremony at the Cenotaph in London to lay wreaths memorializing the dead. As these rites are televised they reach many millions of people. So too, for example, in the USA when the President and other senior people attend formal rites at places such as the Arlington National Cemetery which is even administered by the Army. Locally many people visit their local cemeteries to place flowers on graves of their own dead, whether they belonged to the military or not.

The USA provides a further example of the status accorded to soldiers in that every person who has been honourably discharged from the armed forces is allowed a free grave when they die, a benefit also granted to the spouse and any minor children of the deceased. They may be buried in one of approximately 114 national cemeteries located across the country. This system was created by President Abraham Lincoln as long ago as 1862 to acknowledge the death of Union soldiers in the American Civil War. Something of the size of this programme can be gained by realizing that, for example, in 1995 there were 27 million veterans still alive who would be eligible for a state funeral even though only about 10 per cent apparently choose to accept this option, largely because national cemeteries do not often exist near to their place of residence (*Deseret News*, 28 May 1995).

## Head-hunting

On quite a different scale and with limited incidence in human history is head-hunting, a practice described in several cultures, often as a means of the hunter gaining status and prestige or to engage in retribution for earlier harm done to his own kinship group. And here we use the masculine gender because head-hunting, as in most warfare, is a male activity. Fürer-Haimendorf speaks of how an elderly Konyak Naga tribesman of North India 'expressed pity for a boy he and his fellow-clansmen had bought with the express purpose of cutting off his head' (1967: 114). In quite a different culture, that of the Ilongot of the Philippines, M. Rosaldo (1980) describes how young men learned how to control themselves and gain the bearing of adult males through the taking of heads. Here the life of an enemy, taken by stealth, was a means of gaining personal status. Though such head-hunting seems to exist on quite a different plane from the sombre funerals of Western suburban life they both deal with the issues of identity and death. Death is used as a vehicle for increased status and identity.

## Suicide

Suicide involves many complex questions and any full account would need to discuss its significance in the social context of the cultures where it occurs (Durkheim, 1952; Rosengren, 1988: 215). Putting aside Durkheim's idea of altruistic suicide, here we wish only to raise the idea that suicide is, in many respects, the opposite of a 'proper' death as far as the idea of death-transcendence is concerned. It inverts the ideal of triumph over death for suicide is often, though not always, interpreted as a kind of failure of an individual or the failure of society against the hardships of life. In this sense suicide is an expression of hopelessness or of the triumph of negative forces over positive social forces. Suicide does not present an opportunity for a society to speak 'words against death'.

The Cheyenne of North America traditionally spoke of suicide victims as individuals whose souls did not take the full journey to dwell alongside the Great Wise One; rather they were diverted when they arrived at the fork in the Milky Way and went on their way into nothingness. The one significant exception to this lay in the destiny of warriors who had taken a suicide vow to die in battle (Hoebel, 1978: 92). This example demonstrates the value placed on life and the way in which life is lost. To kill oneself is quite different from being killed, especially in a culture where great value is placed upon the dignity of the individual along with the duty owed to the wider community, not least as a community of warriors. This is also a culture in which certain men may decide to undergo considerable pain in the Sundance ritual when they have heavy symbolic objects suspended from ropes attached to wounds in their chest or face. Self-inflicted pain of this type is believed to bring advantage to the community and is a kind of self-sacrifice quite opposed to suicide and more expressive of the transcendence over fear and mortality. One unusual context of death and suicide was found amongst the traditional Kwakiutl people of British Columbia for whom accidents were said to constitute the 'principal cause of death', with drowning being the chief form of accident; some anthropologists suspected that 'some reputedly accidental drownings are not accidents at all' (Rohner and Rohner, 1970: 52).

## Sacrificial deaths

Unlike suicide, a socially useless death, several other forms of death may be classified together as socially positive sacrificial deaths. It is in sacrificial deaths that the value of life comes into prominence whether as a valued life that is being sacrificed or as a life which will, somehow, be preserved if a sacrificial offering is made for it. Some sorts of human or animal sacrifice, acts of valiant death in war and even some sorts of suicide may all constitute sacrificial deaths. It is with this in mind that it is worth looking at some specific forms of sacrifice connected with death.

Michael Bourdillon (1980: 19) spoke of the 'ritual control of death' when introducing Sir James Frazer's late Victorian and highly speculative theory of sacrifice. This was part of Frazer's romantic interpretation of ancient classical myths in which he reckoned that a failing priest-king, unsuccessful in achieving his goal of maintaining the prosperity of his people, would be sacrificed. By contrast with this speculative interpretation Bourdillon rehearses the well known and important anthropological account of the voluntary death of a ritual expert among the Dinka of the Sudan, as documented by Godfrey Lienhardt (1961). Lienhardt tells how the master of the fishing spear, a person invested with power and the capacity to bless the people, did not simply die, whether by illness, old age or natural causes, but was put to death in a voluntary act of being buried alive. This he did for the good of his people and, accordingly was not to be mourned, since his death brought benefit to them. In a symbolic sense this act of voluntary death left alive the ideal and image of the dynamism of life in the master of the fishing spear. There is a tremendous sense of awe and power underlying Lienhardt's account of this live burial. It seems to strike at the heart of life itself, showing that a person can have such a depth of commitment to the community that death itself can be embraced for the well-being of that society and expressed in the dying person's own final words against death.

### Sati

One practice which has also been interpreted as expressing a sense of commitment to social ideals is that of *sati* in India. This is sometimes called concremation and involved the joint cremation of a live widow on the cremation pyre of her dead husband. While it has, indeed, been interpreted as an act of devotion of the wife to her husband, *sati* has also been vigorously opposed as a cruel act of violence to women. Several different kinds of vested interest underlie the interpretations that have been given (Anand, 1989).

Much depends on how a few sacred Hindu texts are interpreted. The key text, from the Rig Veda (X, hymn 18, verse 8), describes a funeral rite in which a woman is presented lying on the pyre alongside her husband before being summoned to leave to be united with his living brother. Some traditionalists seem to stress the first half of this verse indicating that the wife should lie with her dead husband, as he is cremated, and so be cremated herself. Certain strictures were applied to prevent *sati* on the part of women who were pregnant, nursing small children, menstruating or drugged. This last item of drugs is relevant because in some parts of India bereaved people might be given medicines to assist them in their grief. Part of the religious tradition argued that when a woman gave herself to this death, 'she would follow her husband to another world and shall dwell in a region of glory for so many years as there are hairs on the human body, or 35,000,000' (Anand, 1989: 60). Others stress the second half of the text showing that she should leave her dead husband and be joined in marriage to her living brother-in-law to raise children to the name of her dead husband. Yet others argue that if she does not engage in such widow-remarriage she should live as an ascetic.

Numerous early political rulers in India and more contemporary reformers, especially Ram Mohan Roy, have campaigned against this practice of widow concremation. What often seems unclear is the precise motivation for the act, whether it is entirely voluntary on the part of a devoted and bereaved wife or whether there are degrees of coercion from family or community or from the context of death itself. One example from July 1979 illustrates this clearly. The husband of Jivatri, a 17-year-old, was shot dead along with his twin brother. Jivatri was grief-stricken. Her dead husband's family was said to blame her for bringing bad fortune on the family and she responded by saying that she would become *sati*, which she did. She is said to have sat smiling as she was cremated. Apparently the very pyre burst into flame of its own accord and the police failed to prevent the now illegal act and instead paid homage to Jivatri. Subsequently a temple has been built at the spot of cremation and is becoming a place of local pilgrimage which brings clear economic benefit to the family and community (Anand, 1989: 164ff.). Several similar and equally recent cases have also resulted in temples as sites of local devotion.

But these examples should not give the impression that widow concremation is widespread and very common in India: it is not. In a brief but important essay on the sociology of *sati*, Ashish Nandy distinguished between occasional occurrence and regular custom. Nandy found three periods in Indian history when it became more customary than spasmodic and all three were periods of political conquest and social change, including the medieval period when Rajput kingdoms were under attack and the eighteenth and nineteenth centuries when the British were establishing themselves over India. Nandy also found that *sati* occurred amongst upper castes or in castes that sought upward mobility, especially under British rule and that it took place more in Westernized and urban sectors of the population; almost no *sati* took place in villages not exposed to colonialism. Over a four-year period some 1500 cases were found in Calcutta and these represented two-thirds of all recorded cases. Nandy argued that 'in all known cases direct or indirect coercion was used' (1989: 158). His conclusion is slightly mixed, arguing that death by concremation asserted the value of self-sacrifice at periods when it sounded hypocritical and that concremation was a means to economic success. What is obvious from this brief account is that such deaths are open to several kinds of meaning and emphasis depending upon the standpoint of the interpreter. Similar problems involving the interpretation of sacred texts surrounds the question of whether human sacrifice was ever practised in ancient India (Chakrabarti, 1974: 221).

## Aztec human sacrifice

On the other side of the world, in Mexico, human sacrifice was practised in the Aztec culture as recently as the fifteenth and sixteenth centuries, until the Spanish conquest. This offering of human life was part of a religion which saw close relationships between the deities, nature and society within a mythical system, reckoning that the sun was kept on its daily cycle by the power of blood. Slaves or other captives were laid out on altars high on the sacred pyramids before having their hearts cut out by the sacrificing priests. The victims were also flayed and their skins worn as part of the total ritual.

The heart was called the 'precious eagle-cactus fruit' in a reference to one of the key myths of the culture which said that the people should settle where they found an eagle perched on a cactus killing a snake. One interpretation of these rites sees the gods as living on 'the transfigured energy of human hearts torn from the living body in solemn sacrifice' (Sanday, 1986: 173, 177). This example illustrates the idea of power or vitality emerging from death and contributing to a higher level of life in the form of the sun-deity in its daily rising. In the ancient Mayan civilization, a similar myth urged the necessity of using human sacrificial blood to strengthen the sun after its daily crossing of the heavens. The many human sacrifices of the ancient Mayans are said to have been followed by cannibalistic meals as well as by a dance in which the priest wore the flayed skin of the sacrificed human, usually a prisoner of war (Hultkrantz, 1979: 237).

## Conquering death

Here, once more, we may draw from Maurice Bloch's theory (1992) of rebounding violence or rebounding conquest to interpret the power of these funerary rites. He suggests that the ordinary biological facts of life as a picture of birth, reproduction and death are often negated by particular societies which introduce a social ritual in which someone is said to die and to be born again as a new kind of person over whom death has lost control. So the social facts of life involve natural birth, a ritual and social death and a ritual rebirth. For Christianity people are said to die to self through baptism and to be reborn by the power of the Holy Spirit and, thereby, to share in the resurrection of Jesus Christ. I have, elsewhere, developed this theme in terms of the Acts of the Apostles in the New Testament. This Christian case is of particular importance because it came to influence emergent Christianity in the most powerful of ways and, I suspect, fostered Christianity as a world religion (D. J. Davies, 1995).

My interpretation of the coming of the Spirit to the early Christians was derived, in part, from Bloch's account of ritual processes in which, symbolically speaking, life is transformed into death prior to death being transformed into a higher form of life. Just as the anthropologist Victor

Turner (1969) took the liminal stage of Van Gennep's scheme of rites of passage and elaborated it in his own study of *communitas*, which represented a sense of unity and empathy between people undergoing ritual events together, so, in effect, Bloch focused on the post-liminal phase to argue that, for example, initiates do not simply leave 'one form of existence behind with such panache simply to return to it', instead they attain a new level of existence, 'achieving a combination of the sacred and the profane', at least in Durkheim's terms (1992: 15).

'Rebounding violence', as an idiom, resonates with earlier Marxist, Freudian and post-Freudian arguments grounded in the belief that violence is intrinsic to human culture, whether in the conflict between social classes or in the dynamics of individual psyches. Both Freud (1960) and Girard (1977) strike obvious notes while Lienhardt's study of the Dinka (1961) affords a classic and more substantial study of the relationship between weakness and strength within cultural classifications of humanity.

In death the human body comes to the end of its capabilities. Even the power of medicine in its ideal hospital environment ultimately proves to be weak before the power of disease and accident. Here the process of cremation may, itself, come to serve a positive end. Even though most Britons place their dead in coffins, and in that sense may seek to overcome the ravages of the earthen grave, there is little sense of any ultimate triumph over death, except for those who adhere to traditional Christian belief in eternal life. In many parts of the USA the sense of triumph over death may well have more to do with the cosmetic presentation of the dead in their extremely durable caskets which are, in turn, placed in reinforced concrete graves ignoring the fact that the only purpose served is to contain the rottenness of human decay and preventing it being absorbed by the earth in a more natural process of decay.

Cremation, by contrast, offers the symbolic possibility of taking the process of decay into human hands through the speeded up process of cremation where society is more in control of the body-microcosm in cremation than in burial. We show how true this is for cremation in Hinduism in the next chapter. Cremation is not simply an act of incineration. The ultimate product, cremated remains, or cremains as they are termed in the USA, is invested with a high value, representing the person who once existed. The rebounding violence factor involves taking the dead body and instead of leaving it to decay through biological processes, works a transformation upon it. The ashes which result from the process represent the element of rebounding violence, they mark the transfer of the deceased to a new symbolic existence as one who can be rooted in memory and enter into a new, though abstract, relation with the living.

## Cremation and rebounding violence

It is through this speculative interpretation that cremation can be seen to involve violence done to the dead. Though the violence is largely impersonal, unseen and part of the technological ritual of cremation, it lies at the heart of the conquest of death. And conquest is, for Bloch, practically synonymous with violence in his understanding of the ritual process of the transformation of initiates. In the British context people know that bodies are burnt but do not see or talk of them as being burnt. As already mentioned the sight and smell of cremation attract highly negative valuation in British society. It is only specifically Indian cultural groups within British society who desire to see some smoke rise from the chimney as a reminiscent symbol of traditional Hindu cremation rites – which come with their own appropriate mythology of the cremation as a kind of an offering to deity.

In the USA, as in parts of Sweden, the funeral service may take place in a mortuary funeral home or in a church, with the cremation being a quite separate act attended by very few or no family members at all. The cremation comes to be absolutely distinct from the social rites performed by the living. Traditional American and British culture has no positive mythical or theological value for the act of cremation itself. Instead there is either a borrowing of symbolic meaning from burial or else, instead of myth, there is an ideological silence, offset only by utilitarian ideas of hygiene or the saving of space. Even so the deceased's body is not, ultimately, destroyed by cremation because the cremated remains offer a new symbolic medium, Hertz's dry medium, which can be interpreted through Bloch's idiom of rebounding violence or conquest. As the relatives take the cremated remains to place them in sites of private significance they, in a sense, engage in a transcending of death. The dead transcend the fact of death, the deposition of ashes invests a site with a significance it did not possess before.

To focus specifically on the idea of cremation and violence is not an easy thing to do because there is a great deal of silence surrounding the idea of burning the dead in most Western societies. The European culture history of crematoria, through the experience of the Holocaust, is as much negative as positive. In fact the Holocaust is interesting here because it seems to furnish an example of non-ritualistic incineration rather than of a ritual cremation. This, perhaps, is a significant factor which has not been sufficiently explored and may explain how devastating a cultural image is presented through the marked utilitarian and technological device of mass incineration of human beings. For here we have the rare phenomenon of an act which 'should' be a ritual performance involving dead persons but which, instead, is a mechanical destruction of bodies. Here there could be no 'rebounding violence' or 'conquest' of death precisely because those conducting the act specifically sought to eliminate the very social identity of those they had killed. In the most speculative sense the modern state of

Israel is the rebounding violence response to the Holocaust; it is probably no accident that cremation is not practised in Israel.

Returning to contemporary Britain we have already mentioned the fact that smoke from crematorium chimneys is not socially acceptable, reflecting an avoidance of the reality of fire in association with cremation. Similarly the mid-European examples where open flames are burned on symbolic stands outside and inside some crematoria would not, for whatever complex reasons, be architecturally or socially countenanced in Britain. It may be that part of the reason for this reticence lies precisely in an awareness that the living are, in some way, destroying their dead. When, for example, the Catholic Truth Society (McDonald, 1966: 2) explained how cremation came to be accepted by the Roman Catholic Church, it spoke very directly of 'violently destroying the corpse by fire' and of the 'violent destruction by fire'. Because people seldom voice this idea it is difficult to be sure whether the idea itself informs people's thinking at some unvoiced level or whether it is an idea that does not actually present itself to Britons. This is, obviously, a real problem for interpretation but, if only for theoretical reasons and as a basis for future research, it is worth posing the question in relation to Bloch's theme of rebounding violence.

In this context it is also worth observing that Bloch's notion bears a certain family resemblance to Tambiah's important notion of 'ethical vitality' used to interpret bodily control in the creation of merit in specific Buddhist ritual contexts (1968: 105). Both 'rebounding violence' and 'ethical vitality' deal with symbolic mastery and control of bodies in relation to highly prized social values focused on life and on the relation between life and death. It is precisely because these terms engage with life and death that they have an obvious appeal when it comes to interpreting the ritual of cremation.

We have already suggested that cremation in Britain involves a kind of social control over bodies resulting in a socially beneficial goal. To this we may add the hypothesis that when cremated remains are taken and used to give positive reinforcement to former relationships they may be viewed as conferring value on these contexts. They bring merit to a past life and to the continuing relationship of the living with the memory of the dead and in so doing imply that death has not finally triumphed.

The fact remains that opportunity is increasingly taken in Britain to take and use cremated remains idiosyncratically. Theoretically speaking, this might be interpreted as involving an awareness of having done something positive for the person against whom one has, earlier, engaged in the negative act of cremation. Though it would be improper to use the language of sacrifice for this process in the British context it might be possible to speak of the process of cremation as a process of symbolic change in such a way as to reflect Bloch's notion of rebounding violence as a means of achieving transcendence over death.

One interesting application of this theory can be made to Garrity and Wyss's account of North American death ritual in the particular context of Kentucky in the 1970s (1980: 105). They gave an account of the way in which these strongly Christian communities used funerals as an occasion for evangelistic preaching by several noted ministers. Singing and preaching were combined until, as often happened, someone 'came forward' to be 'saved' from their sin. In terms of Bloch's theory, we might argue that the occasion of death was transcended by the example of a person undergoing a ritual or symbolic death at the graveside to be 'born again' as a Christian. Spiritual newness of life came to stand, symbolically, over against the physical death of a member of that community. In this case the gospel message constituted 'words against death' just as they promised spiritual life for the new convert.

## Euthanasia

As a final example I want to suggest that euthanasia, as currently being developed in parts of the Western world, is a clear example of an attempt at conquering death. As a conquest it gains added power from the medical world in which it is most likely to take place. It is often said in contemporary society that many people are not afraid of death but are afraid of the process of dying and of the pain they may suffer at the end of an illness. The word so often used is 'dignity', as when people speak of wanting to die 'with dignity'. This can be interpreted to mean that they wish to retain that status and sense of identity which they had developed throughout their life. They do not wish to be reduced to some sort of suffering individual, lacking all control and increasingly devoid of their sense of self-worth. In this context medicine gains a great power, both as the context in which terminal illness finds its normal definition and as the source of control available for this last phase of life. An active process of euthanasia, in which the dying individual decides on the moment of death, allows for final communications in relationships with other people while also, in a sense, not letting the destructive power of illness have the last word. Here the rhetoric of death draws jointly upon medicine and personal autonomy. In symbolic terms, euthanasia employs medicine in a conquest of death through illness; it uses medicine against the enemy of medicine, terminal illness.

# 6 Indian and Persian Souls

Until very recently most civilizations have speculated about a life after death, expressing discontent with the everyday world of mortality and describing alternative environments into which they believe people pass when they die. The idea of the soul, already explored in Chapter 1 (cf. Sullivan, 1987), has been the most constant explanation of how this transition occurs whether in the Indian traditions, discussed in this chapter, or in the Jewish and Christian religions considered in Chapter 8 and in the traditional ethnic beliefs of Chapter 9. Rituals surrounding death are, usually, closely related to basic views of human nature and destiny including the way in which human identity is composed, especially in the link between the material body and some energizing spirit.

Western religions set human identity within a historical framework beginning with creation, involving some sort of prophetic revelation and the emergence of specific churches, before going on to talk about a future period when the world comes to an end and some sort of divine paradise is established. The great Eastern religions, emerging from India, speak much more mythologically and less historically about the passage of time, preferring to emphasize human consciousness and various processes of meditation which can be the source of salvation. Similarly the Christian idea of salvation provided by God on the basis of God's loving generosity and grace differs to a marked extent from most of the Eastern traditions which locate salvation within a scheme of reincarnation operating under the system of *karma* by which individuals receive the precise outcome of their own personal actions (Sharpe and Hinnells, 1973). But even here it is hard to generalize because there are Eastern traditions, reflected in Sikhism as well as in some mainstream Hindu traditions, which also emphasize the love relationship between the divine and the devotee and give an opportunity for grace to flourish between them (McLeod, 1968: 204).

But despite these great differences in the content of belief, the underlying notion of a soul or life-force passing from a dead person remains very similar in both East and West. In fact the notion of the soul is one of the most enduring of all human concepts and although there have been sceptics and rationalists both in ancient and modern societies and in Eastern and Western hemispheres, it is only since the emergence of the biological sciences in the mid-nineteenth century that serious and widespread disbelief in souls has emerged. However, it is still true that a considerable proportion of modern societies still gives some credence to ideas that a soul underlies human life.

## Indian death rites

In the broad tradition of religion in India, several ideas are held in common. These include a belief in the transmigration of souls, that process by which the life-force passes through many existences in striving to obey universal principles yielding increased benefits and resulting in an improved form of transmigration at its next cycle. This process of reincarnation or trans-migration is often called *samsara*, while the moral advantages or disadvantages accruing from the way life is lived is often called *karma*. Samsara and karma provide the basic dynamics behind the traditional Indian caste system into which people are born and whose rules should be followed during life so that in the next life a better state may be achieved. This general perspective lies behind Hinduism, Buddhism and Sikhism and gives a distinctive perspective to human identity, one that has far reaching consequences for death ritual (cf. Holm with Bowker, 1994). The strong belief in a life following on from the death of a human being is, in the broad Indian tradition, expressed through the funeral rites of cremation. These have developed over thousands of years and possess extensive interpretations providing death with a significance which helps to make sense of both death and life.

A general picture of Hindu death rites has been very well documented, for example, in Jonathan Parry's excellent study of death rituals at the sacred city of Benares on the sacred river Ganges (1994). The basic pattern of death ritual is, at one level, quite simple. Dying persons should be laid on the ground with prayers chanted to help them focus on the name of God as they die. After death, the body is washed, dressed and carried from the home for cremation. During the cremation the skull is cracked by the eldest surviving son (emphasizing the importance of producing sons); after the cremation the remains are thrown into the river. Subsequent rites are performed to ensure that the spirit of the deceased passes on its proper journey.

Behind these direct and visible actions there lies a tremendously rich tapestry of symbolic messages interpreting what constitutes human nature, how we come into being and how we pass on into a variety of new identities after death. An individual is composed of flesh, which is believed to come from the mother's menstrual blood, and of bones, which originate in the father's semen. The foetus, growing in the womb, is nourished by the 'heat' that comes from the mother and the food that she eats. At about the fifth month of pregnancy the spirit or life-force is believed to come to the child and enters it through the cranial suture in its head. Those who attend the mother at birth are drawn from very low caste group people.

Death, symbolically speaking, parallels this pattern of birth for just as the maternal heat helps produce the foetus so the heat of the cremation fire destroys the flesh, leaving the bones behind. It is as though the elements derived from the female are destroyed, along with the sin of the individual, which is symbolically associated with body hair, itself also destroyed by fire. The remaining bones are placed in the river which is associated with the female principle of existence and thereby, in a symbolic sense, becomes a fertilizing agent. One of the popular interpretations of cremation cited by Parry refers to the corpse as rising from the pyre as smoke which becomes transformed into clouds and into rain which in turn produces vegetables as food; this, in due course, becomes male semen (1994: 179).

Death thus becomes transformed into something positive. In addition, just as the spirit came to the baby in the womb through its skull so now it departs, through the skull, as the skull is cracked during cremation. Parry goes so far as to say that 'at death it is men who give birth' (1994: 152) in the sense that they take charge of the ritual action which brings about the shift in identity of the deceased. The rites which follow cremation involve making offerings of rice balls and of food and gifts to particular funeral priests. These are believed to assist the transformation of the deceased from a ghost-like status into the status of an ancestor.

This may at first appear strange against the idea of reincarnation which is so often taken to be the key Hindu belief about life after death. Here Parry draws out the important fact that several ideas are held together in Hindu attitudes towards life and death. The deceased is said to become an ancestor, to return to earth in the life of someone else, especially a grandchild, or even to assume some other form of life. But the significant fact is that each belief serves its purpose as far as some particular issue is concerned with ideas of reincarnation and rebirth being used, perhaps, 'to explain the present and the idea of heaven, hell and salvation to visualise the future' (1994: 209). This quotation from Parry needs to be emphasized because, in an important respect, it contradicts what is often written in formal textbooks on Hinduism, stressing as they do the belief in the transmigration or reincarnation of souls. Parry is drawing attention to the fact that in terms of practical religion people seem to be speaking about two rather different ways of thinking about life. On the one hand when they talk about their own present existence they do so by using the idea of transmigration and see themselves as a reincarnation. When talking about the future condition of those they cremate, however, they speak more in terms of a heaven and a hell. This is a reminder of the complexity of human beliefs and shows how different idioms or pictures of existence can be drawn upon for particular purposes.

Yet another aspect of this process of living and dying in Hinduism draws out greater detail from the idea of spirit or life-force which, so far, we have used only in a broad sense. In general terms Parry speaks of the individual Indian as possessing two sorts of animating power: one concerns the obvious signs of life in an individual while the other deals with the underlying existence of the individual. The first sort of breath, or life-force, leaves the body at what might ordinarily be called the time of death. This is one reason why it is a good thing for the dying person to be placed in the open air, so that the breath might more easily take itself away. But the second, body-pervading, breath is not so easily released. In fact it is only released at the point in the cremation ritual at which the skull is cracked.

There are some interesting consequences associated with this distinction between the two sorts of 'breath'. In the simplest terms, for example, a woman is not said to be a widow until the breaking of her dead husband's skull; until then there is a sense in which her husband is still 'alive'. To reinforce this point the body is not seen as ritually polluting until that final part of the cremation process; until then it is more sacred than impure. One important reason for this status lies in another interpretation of death and cremation in Hinduism focused on the entire process as a kind of sacrifice.

## Cremation as sacrifice

In Chapter 5 we looked at the way in which human cultures often seemed to want to take control of death and make it appear to serve positive ends rather than be a negative terminal point of life. This same theme is also evident in the traditional view of life and death in India where it is quite possible to interpret the cremation as a kind of sacrifice, one which is connected with the distinction between a good and bad death.

Parry's description of good and bad deaths provides very fruitful information for illustrating the human control of death (1994: 158ff.). The good death is one in which a person is prepared through fasting and drinking Ganges water, the body is weakened so that the spirit may leave more easily and so that faecal material will not spoil the final moments. In other words death is a kind of voluntary offering of the body to the deities; one should not cling to life. A bad death is one which snatches life away as in an accident, or when vomit or faeces stain the body. Those dying good deaths are said to burn easily, and in popular perception their body is viewed as almost self-igniting and glowing with a divine radiance. Bad deaths, by contrast, yield bodies which turn black and are hard to burn.

The preparation for death is like the preparation of sacrificial offerings. The burning area is prepared as are sacrifical sites, the wood for cremation is like the wood used for offerings to the deities. The way the pyre is lit and materials added to it all reflect the rites of a sacrificial offering. In fact the cremation is called the sacrament of fire, *dah sanskar*, or the last sacrifice, *antyeshti* (Parry, 1994: 178).

## Conquering death

This ritual of Hindu cremation provides yet another example of the human desire to transcend the negative aspect of death. This drive to conquer death underlies most chapters in this book, expressing as it does a fundamental dimension of cultural life in so very many societies.

It comes to another focal point in Parry's study of death in Benares in the group of ascetic males called Aghoris, who frequent the burning *ghats* along the Ganges at Benares (1994: 251ff.); a *ghat* is a holy place which may take several forms: here it is a riverside platform for cremation. The Aghoris belong to a type of monastic order of ascetic individuals who go about naked or wearing shrouds taken from dead bodies. They have matted hair, sleep on biers used to carry the dead, eat ashes from the cremation pyres and carry a bowl made from a human skull. They appear to be very aggressive, are foul-mouthed to ordinary individuals and are not only reputed to eat dead bodies but also to engage in human sacrifice. Their religious devotions involve sex with prostitutes, preferably at the time of menstruation, when they are also said to practise *coitus reservatus* which means that they have orgasm without the ejaculation of semen. The symbolic significance of this pattern of apparently odd behaviour becomes clearer in the light of the death rites of these individuals, for Aghoris are said not to die. Instead they are believed to enter into a form of final meditation. Their dead bodies are not cremated but are buried in a meditative posture within the grounds of their monastery. Their skulls are not cracked and, in popular belief, their bodies are said not to decay. A shrine is set up over their grave and is marked with the phallic shaped emblem of Shiva who is also the deity of the cremation ground.

Taken together these features represent an individual who transcends death through this form of asceticism which is focused upon phenomena of death. These are people who break all the boundaries of normal life, they ignore the distinctions between ritually pure and ritually impure things. They do not subject themselves to the same rules as other people. The Aghori is like Lord Shiva and embraces death in a kind of eternal meditation. In other words, these few individuals represent in their own life and behaviour that goal of transcending death which, in quite different ways, runs through the cremation and post-cremation rites of ordinary Indians. Accordingly, while still alive, they are regarded as possessing spiritual power from which their devotees hope to benefit. In some respects they resemble the Leopard Skin Chief of the Dinka peoples of the Sudan described later in Chapter 9. In both cases there are individuals whose pattern of death represents a conquest of death and furnishes a channel of power for the living.

## Buddhism

Buddhism favours cremation as the preferred means of disposing of human remains, not least because the body of the Buddha was, itself, cremated after his death in the sixth century BC. Tradition tells that his cremated remains were divided into eight parts and distributed to different regions within India.

The pots containing these remains were placed inside mounds called 'stupas'. When, later, the Indian Emperor Ashoka, who instituted a form of Buddhist revival in India, subdivided these remains very many more stupas were constructed as a means of fostering piety among the faithful (P. Harvey, 1991: 82). While the religious significance of the stupa is grounded in the mortal remains of the Buddha or, as in subsequent stupas, in the remains of some famed spiritual leader, its architectural form has been increasingly elaborated so that each part of the architectural structure has been invested with significance.

The stupa is both a simple and an extremely complex structure. In simplicity it is a square within a circle. It represents in three-dimensional architecture what a mandala represents in two-dimensional paintings. In one sense a stupa is a mandala, a condensed set of symbols reflecting on the nature of the cosmos and of the life and nature of the Buddha. A hemispherical mound rising from the ground with a square structure near its top which terminates in a spire. In terms of symbolic interpretation and its capacity to stimulate meditative reflection the stupa is, as Snodgrass explains in his magisterial study of stupa symbolism, 'ineffable: in the last analysis the meaning of the stupa cannot be expressed' (1992: 5). In a direct sense the stupa represents the physical remains of the Buddha and symbolically expresses his entry into nirvana at his death and his achieving real Buddha nature. One tradition of interpretation within the history of religions sees the stupa, centred around a vertical axis, as representing the *axis mundi*, the centre of the world. The abstract idea of the world tree, which is often taken to symbolize this centrality, may well be associated with the Buddhist devotion to the Bodhi tree associated with the Buddha's enlightenment and which is symbolically represented at the top of the stupa (P. Harvey, 1991: 87; Irwin, 1991: 46ff.). Stupas serve as a focus of devotion and piety for many Buddhists whether in their architectural form or within art (Rhie and Thurman, 1992: 99).

This Buddhist approach to the structures containing cremated remains, or even other sorts of belongings of holy people, can be interpreted as an expression of conquest of death. These are not negative symbols of the triumph of death over humanity but of the fact that in particular individuals the bitterness of life has been overcome. The power in the symbolism is interesting precisely because it is the symbols of physical death, in the form of cremated remains, which become the focal points for devotion and for religious practice which sets itself to triumph over the material problems of existence. In this sense we might, perhaps, speak of the stupa as containing the ashes of and for enlightenment.

## Tibetan Buddhism

The funeral rites of Buddhist Tibet were various. Traditionally they included cremation, placing corpses in water, burying them or cutting them up for wild animals to eat (Anuruddha, 1959: 167). The purchase of wood for cremation was costly for the poor and burial was disliked lest the soul desire to remain with the body and produce a kind of vampire. This expense helps explain why so called sky- or air-burial or the exposing of the chopped up body to birds and animals was employed; even remaining bones might be hammered into powder and mixed with dough for the birds to eat. Finally, the bodies of celebrated religious leaders might be mummified and retained in temples where devotions could be made to them (Evans-Wentz, 1960: 26). Behind Tibetan Buddhism there lies the pre-Buddhist Bon tradition of Tibet which is said to have had its own extensive commitment to death rites but not to have engaged in dismemberment (Hoffmann, 1961: 23).

The reason why Tibetan practice has gained a degree of celebrity in Western societies lies less in these varied funerary rites of corpse disposal than in the verbal rituals used before, during and after physical death. Evans-Wentz was much influenced by early twentieth-century anthropology at Oxford, especially in the person of his supportive teacher R. R. Marett (1941: 307). In 1927 he published a version of what he called *The Tibetan Book of the Dead*, in which he introduced to an increasingly appreciative audience a text which described a set of relationships between the soul and the body of the deceased and between that soul and an assisting priest.

Called in Tibetan the *Bardo Thodol*, this text provides a kind of psychological and religious picture of the 'Bardo', or state of being between the former life and the next incarnation. The priest or monk who is called to the dying person engages his own spiritual power to employ verbal ritual to explain and describe to the dying person the experiences he or she is now undergoing. The goal is to help the consciousness to separate itself from the body in order to allow the body itself to die and to understand its transitory state. So it is that the person undergoes a form of liberation through hearing the verbal ritual and is enabled to pass through a threefold series of Bardo states within a 49-day period before it reincarnates in another body. The use of words is important because of the emphasis placed upon the dying person's consciousness and on the need of being mindful and attentive to the very process of dying just as the goal of life is to develop one's attention to the way things are and appear to be (David-Neel, 1970: 164). In other words dying is not simply something that befalls a person or happens to someone but is an active process in which the dying person is intimately involved and can positively assist in what happens next. This reflects the Tibetan Buddhist understanding of death and life as 'modifications of consciousness' (Evans-Wentz, 1954: 45).

So it is that the priest should speak clearly into the dying person's ear and, through the instruction given, the dying person is told not to hold and cling to this life but to set out on the journey into the next phase of existence. Here the general idea of death as a journey sets the scene where 'cosmological regions are more aptly described as being different states of mind' (Colvin, 1988: 74). After the disposal of the corpse and for up to 49 days after death, the rituals continue, using an image of the dead or even with the priest mentally imagining the deceased person and the soul and engaging in the verbal ritual with them. There are accounts of the feelings and emotions the soul will undergo as it encounters various deities and even, for example, the mood encountered on coming to be conceived in the womb as male or as female. It suggests that those about to be conceived as a male will feel a deep attraction to the mother and a hatred of the father while the girl embryo will feel a strong attachment to the father and a repulsion towards the mother (Evans-Wentz, 1960: 180).

This Tibetan Buddhist tradition, furnishing as it does one of the best known examples of a highly schematized approach to death, dying and the afterlife, has recently been reasserted in more contemporary terms in *The Tibetan Book of Living and Dying* (1992) by the Tibetan-born teacher Sogyal Rinpoche. His book extends and applies the traditional Tibetan approach to death in Western contexts and has much to do with using the imagination to come to terms with various human attitudes to mortality. The novelty of his book lies in the completely explicit engagement with death, not only our own death but also the death of others. He gives advice on how to use the imagination within meditative practices to gain a balanced approach to death and to overcome fear of it. He also describes ways of helping other people as they prepare to die. In doing this his approach is highly eclectic as he quotes the work of medical professionals such as Cecily Saunders and encourages people of all religions and none to use the symbolism of their own perspective within the meditative practices he outlines. The attraction of this approach is that it, apparently, gives access to secret knowledge and allows the modern desire to conquer death to be met through a combination of traditional wisdom and contemporary psychology.

## Competing and complementary rites

The way human cultures develop sometimes means that a society may possess more than one outlook on life. This may involve direct competition as well as collaboration between ideologies and ritual schemes and may also be the outcome of the merging of traditions over time. Four brief examples must suffice as far as death is concerned, the first in Japan, the second in Sikkim, the third in Romania and the fourth in England. The first two show cases of mutual coexistence, while the third demonstrates a mixing of traditions and the fourth a more voluntary addition of a rite to traditional practice.

In contemporary Japan the traditional religion of Shinto coexists with a form of Buddhism and it is this Japanese Buddhism which provides people with death rites and underlies the common Japanese expression that people are 'born Shinto and die Buddhist' (Reader, 1994: 169). One anthropologist has described this situation as one in which 'for ordinary people Buddhism is, by and large, a system for the removal of the dead' (M. Bloch, 1992: 53). The Shinto pattern of ritual life studiously avoids anything to do with death and stresses the strengthening of life, its fertility and flourishing.

In Sikkim in the southern Himalayas, Buddhists, representing the form of Lamaism which initially flourished in Tibet, engage in one set of funerary rites for a deceased person inside the dwelling while another set of death rites is conducted outside the house by Mun priests who represent an ancient tradition of Sikkim. Geoffrey Gorer (1984) furnished a very full description of these complementary rites which he studied in the 1930s before Sikkim became largely closed to outside visitors. He described how bodies were disposed of by burial, cremation or by being thrown into a river, depending upon the circumstances of death and the horoscopes cast by the lamas, and studied the apparent contradiction between the Buddhist belief in transmigration and the Mun belief in a more permanent version of heaven or hell. He also wrote about the Mun engaging in animal sacrifice as well as spirit possession as a means of guiding the spirit on its way to the afterlife.

One important issue raised by Gorer's account is that of attitude towards the dead. In this Sikkim case he speaks of both sets of elaborate ceremonies as 'performed to get rid of the dead; the dead are terrifying and should be feared, not loved. Death has no consolations' (1984: 362). It may be possible to generalize from Gorer's observations to say that where the dead are feared, for whatever reason, their mortuary ritual will be extensive whereas where they are not feared mortuary rites will be considerably more brief. This will depend upon the extent of ideology concerning the state and capacity of the dead held by a society.

In the recent custom of rural Romania it was also the case that the dead must be appropriately mourned and honoured lest they engage in some form of retribution upon the living (Kligman, 1988: 159). This example reflects the dynamics of a close-knit community where the many obligations which living kin have of each other is extended into the post-mortem world. The Romanian context also reflects a situation in which elements of pre-Christian culture have become part and parcel of Christian rites in village death rites so that, for example, coins may be placed in the coffin 'to appease the gatekeepers' of hell so that the soul may be allowed to proceed on its journey to judgement day (1988: 162). While this example will be read by many as quite alien to formal Christian teaching on the afterlife, there are many other ideas which are widely accepted and yet which are almost equally foreign to theological thought. One example concerns the composition of the afterlife in terms of the family. In Transylvania, for example, a widow is said to join her husband's family after death while an unmarried girl stays with her family of birth (1988: 163). There is nothing in formal Christian theology which justifies such opinions yet many Christian cultures express beliefs in the human family continuing as a unit after death, despite the fact that, for example, a well known element of the wedding rite in many Christian traditions says that marriage is 'till death us do part'. Another important feature of the Romanian study shows how, for historical reasons, villagers not only go on to combine elements of belief and practice drawn from the Greek Catholic and Greek Orthodox traditions but also adhere to what Kligman calls contradictory conceptions of death and the afterlife (1988: 160, 162). The conflict lies in the formal contradiction between a tripartite theological definition of the afterlife in terms of heaven, hell and purgatory, and a more secular binary distinction between this world and that world which frames the laments and popular discourses on death. There is, perhaps, no need for Kligman to describe these features as religious and secular since both express elements of practical faith, albeit in different contexts. The widow and the priest, for example, have different concerns and draw upon the varied sources to express them.

The fourth and final example concerns a small number of people in England, and probably in numerous other traditionally Christian societies too, who also draw from different sources for short periods after the death of their kin. This is especially done by attending Spiritualist meetings some time after the formal funerary rites have been conducted by established denominations; these, in particular in the Protestant tradition, possess relatively few means of focusing on the immediate state of the dead. Through funeral rites the dead are consigned to God's domain in a most general sense and are uncontactable. For some mourners this is insufficient: they want proof or some sort of evidence that the deceased is 'well'. Very little research exists to enable us to say whether these mourners fear these dead people or why they wish to contact them, but certainly it is likely to be the case that while a priest of a regular denomination will perform the initial funeral rites, it is a quite separate and unorthodox practitioner who will attempt to establish contact with the dead.

## Zoroastrian-Parsee death rites

Zoroastrians not only constituted an ancient religion in Persia, now Iran, but also migrated to India and beyond, where they are known as Parsees. The Zoroastrian religion is one of the oldest continuing religious traditions in the world originating in Persia perhaps even before 1500 BC. Its two basic ritual elements were fire and water with daily plant and animal offerings made to the fire which was, itself, perpetually maintained.

Zoroastrian belief in life after death focused on the idea of a spirit which was, in the ancient tradition, believed to travel to an underground kingdom, aided by mortuary blood sacrifices. Rituals took place daily for 30 days and then less often until after some 30 years, when the soul was reckoned to be part of the ancestral fellowship of the dead and was commemorated on the last night of each year when souls were said to return to their old homes (Boyce, 1979: 12ff.).

With time the Zoroastrians developed a belief in a more joyous form of afterlife focused on the idea of the resurrection of the body; in fact it is likely that this was the first religious tradition to arrive at this route to a realm of Paradise. The ancient sacred texts of Zoroastrianism are very clear on the destiny of the dead and tell the living not to 'put your trust in life, for at the last death must overtake you and dog and bird will rend your corpse and your bones will be tumbled on the earth. For three days and nights the soul sits beside the pillow of the body' (Zaehner, 1956: 133ff.). The texts describe the journey to the bridge of judgement and beyond where a man is met by a beautiful girl who, though unrecognized, is the embodiment of his good deeds. Finally he, or indeed she, for the texts give full weight to the salvation of women, experiences fragrant breezes from heaven until finally achieving the Endless Light where he is fed on the 'butter of the early spring'. Similarly the wicked person passes into an underworld of pain and torment, meeting an ugly woman and eating the vilest food until the final day of resurrection. What is interesting about this sacred text is that, in the most general sense, it resembles *The Tibetan Book of the Dead* in providing a description of the ways followed by the journeying soul.

It may be that the abandonment of burial and the emergence of the ritual of exposing bodies for vultures to devour the flesh before any remaining bones were buried was associated with this belief in the soul now departing to some heavenly realm prior to its being united with the body at a future date.

The ancient form of burial was thus replaced by exposure of the body and Zoroastrians became well known for this enclosed space or *dahkma*, a word which originally meant grave, or Towers of Silence as they became popularly called. The body was left on a platform and did not touch the earth; vultures ate the flesh and then the remaining bones were placed in a central pit. Cremation was never traditional because the dead body was regarded as an extremely ritually polluting object owing to the fact that much evil must have become focused on it to bring it to death. Indeed, Zoroastrianism possessed as a key belief the fundamental opposition of forces of good and evil between which people needed to choose. Accordingly, the sacred fire could not be contaminated by the polluted corpse.

In the twentieth century the migration of Parsees to urban centres in Persia, India and elsewhere inaugurated some major changes in death rites as it became increasingly difficult to sustain Towers of Silence within or close to cities. Accordingly a cemetery was established in Tehran in 1937 and in Bombay some Parsees have even used cremation, though not without protest from more traditionalist devotees (Boyce, 1979: 222). While priests had a role in the mortuary ritual, the actual conquest of death belonged more to the moral life lived by the individual which would become apparent in the post-mortem judgement of the dead.

Adaptation to new circumstances has continued, for example, in the USA and in Great Britain. British Zoroastrians have come to use both burial and cremation as funeral rites, given that exposure of the dead was culturally inappropriate. Neither practice is ideal, given what we have already said about the ritual purity of the natural elements. Still, adaptation is vital and even though many say they would like to be taken to India for their bodies to be exposed, this is difficult to achieve and expensive to execute. John Hinnells has explored the thoughts of contemporary British Zoroastrians on these issues and has found that the great majority, some 90 per cent, ultimately preferred cremation to burial. The problem of corpses polluting the flame, so sacred to Zoroastrians, was approached by some who argued that this was acceptable because British cremation involved intense heat and not actual flame, especially in electric cremators (1996: 270). Extensive prayers cover the period of preparation of the body, its burial or cremation and subsequent memorial days, and there is some suggestion that these human acts of a person may benefit the *fravashi*, or the heavenly self of the deceased ancestor, enabling them to progress from lower to higher orders in the post-mortem world (Nigosian, 1993: 84).

## The journey and the prayer

Although we have not dealt explicitly with the texts of the prayers associated with these rites of Indian and Persian origin, they all occur within a rhetoric of the journeying soul, a motif which is also well known in other religious traditions (Collins and Fishbane, 1995). Whether in terms of furnishing guidance through supernatural realms, with their perils, judgement and blessings, or providing sustenance through food rites, the living support the dead in their transition. The fact that death, most especially in the Zoroastrian case, is deemed ritually polluting emphasizes all the more the need for verbal ritual in ensuring that this phase is safely completed to the advantage of the dead and the living. What is important is that death continues the journey experienced in life so that the motif of travel is perfectly appropriate for what now takes place. The degree of fit between the rhetoric of spirituality in life and in death is an important issue which has particular consequences during periods of social change, whether for the Zoroastrians in England or for non-religious Britons engaging with traditional Christian ritual. The degree of consonance or dissonance between the inner language of an individual and the public language of the rite remains of importance for the ultimate success or failure of mortuary rites.

# 7 Ancestors, Cemeteries and Identity

One of the most distinctive features of life is the fact that for the greatest part of humanity's history, as it is known to us, men, women and children have belonged to families within identifiable communities. This fact of kinship and ethnicity underlies all known human societies and provides a foundation not just for individual and group identity but also for coping with death. It is against this background of kinship duties, obligations and cultural expectations that death brings significant changes to bear. Close kin of the dead see that funeral ceremonies are properly carried out so that the desired post-mortem status may be attained. Concurrently, the identity of surviving kin also undergoes a change as the eldest child now becomes the head of the family and may inherit the goods of the deceased, or as the surviving partner becomes a widow or widower. Through the funerary rites not only are ancestors made but they reciprocate by benefiting their descendants.

This chapter considers a variety of such ancestral influence on descendants, whether in conferring a cultural identity or in standing witness to that opposition to death which often marks the human response to mortality. This offsets the overemphasis on grief in relation to death in Western societies, as though bereavement only involved emotional states of grief, whereas in fact most deaths involve changes in life circumstances touching matters of money, inheritance and shifting social status.

## India

In India the eldest surviving son owed a debt of obligation to his parents, especially his father, in conducting that part of the cremation ceremony when the skull was cracked. This act acknowledges the relationship between immediate generations but does not constitute any extensive sense of ancestors. While the power of older people over their younger offspring was considerable in traditional India it tended not to be exerted after death. This was because of the deep influence of the idea of individual merit in the system of karma which underpinned belief in salvation. Merit was to be gained from individual actions and not from the ancestors through some sort of blessing. This is an important point needing some emphasis for it highlights the fact that the relationship between the living individual and the dead often reflects the total scheme of salvation in a culture. Societies with strong ancestor cults emphasize the blessing, curse or benefit coming from the ancestors to corporate groups of descendants rather than the private salvation which an individual may be granted.

In traditional India, life was often described as ideally passing through four stages: student; householder; semi-recluse; total recluse. These last two phases indicate that a man who has been a powerful head of a household now begins to withdraw from his social responsibilities and obligations. If he did go as far as entering the final stage it involved performing a ceremony which symbolized his own funeral and marked a separation from ordinary social life in preparation for actual death and the subsequent journey on the path of transmigration of the self. Here the individual withdraws from those aspects of life involvement which would support and reinforce the status of being an ancestor. The whole realm of karma, the system of moral reciprocity in which the future state of the self was determined by acts performed in the former life, replaces the realm of social obligations. Karma is sometimes described as a rather impersonal scheme of cause and effect and, accepting that description, it is possible to see how it is an alternative to the highly personal pattern of obligations inherent in ancestor cults.

As already discussed for India in Chapter 6, funerary rites constitute the prime arena within which the status of ancestor is conferred upon the dead, just as descendants have to use this period as a time when they begin to pay their dues to the dead who are now becoming ancestors. It is in the religions of East Asia and in some African tribal societies that such ancestral relationships became most highly developed.

## Chinese religion

In traditional Chinese societies the place of the ancestors was privileged. Their funerary rites were attended to with care and first involved burial; then, after a period of years, the bones were exhumed, placed in containers which might be partially reburied before finally being placed in more permanent and elaborate tombs. Records of the names of these deceased people were inscribed on ancestral tablets located in ancestral halls belonging to particular clan groups. These funeral rites have been described as 'converting the volatile spirit into a tamed domesticated ancestor' (R. S. Watson, 1988: 204). This is not a simple task nor is it done for everybody. This is an important observation demonstrating the fact that death can involve many social consequences and political dimensions.

R. S. Watson's account of contemporary funerary rites argues that in south-east China, at least, the dead possess not a single soul but three souls, or aspects of soul. One is believed to reside in the grave, one in the ancestral tablet and one in the underworld (1988: 208). Very soon after death, perhaps the next day, the dead is rapidly buried in an unmarked spot in the neighbouring hills. Little care is taken over this spot since it is temporary. Between seven and ten years later, the skeleton is disinterred and the bones cleaned by an expert before being placed in a pottery urn which is, in turn, partially buried in the soil. For many people this may be the last resting place, for descendants may stop visiting this urn and its location be simply forgotten. For important persons, however, the bones may ultimately be buried in a brick tomb. This last rite may occur decades after the death and only if descendants deem it worthwhile. Very few seem to achieve this last stage of the threefold process.

The names of the dead are added to ancestral lists in homes while those who are politically important for particular kinship groups may also be included on ancestral tablets in ancestor halls. As time goes on those on domestic lists are removed as newer generations die and are added to the list. For many, the names are lost from lists and the location of bones is forgotten; they disappear from the social world as from the realm of the ancestors. This shows how the remembrance or survival of the dead depends upon the interest shown by the living; the living, in turn, express interest depending upon the kind of benefit they derive from the ancestors. One distinctive aspect of this benefit lies in the political alliances and power-links created by groups associated with particular graves. Indeed groups of people may decide to focus their concern on a particular person and to merge their several economic interests in so doing precisely because the focal ancestor becomes the pivotal point for their new-found united action.

The rich are more likely than the poor to survive the course of time since their descendants or such uniting groups of kin will probably place them in graves in auspicious locations. These locations are established by money derived either from the wealth of the dead or from the estates of one or more living individuals who now wish to be associated with the deceased. Examples exist of groups of relatively loosely linked kinsfolk deciding to choose a long dead ancestor as one they will now corporately honour. By so doing they reinforce their bonds one with another through this common ancestor and use their new found unity for economic and for local political purposes (R. S. Watson, 1988: 212).

The siting of ancestral graves is itself of great importance for Chinese descendants because of the ideology of *feng shui* (literally 'wind and water'). The principles of *feng shui* involve a kind of divination concerning the direction and location of favoured sites. It is a practice still used extensively in funerals but may also be used for commercial ventures in deciding how best to locate business or commercial premises. Ritual experts decide upon the optimum location of burial sites.

In traditional times the Chinese emperors occupied an extremely significant place in society and in the relationship between the people and heaven itself. Death was marked with much ritual and included the burning of possessions the emperor might need in the afterlife. Mourning rites were adopted throughout the empire. The emperors were buried in tombs with a sacrificial hall housing their spirit tablet. Ritual, a form of worship, was performed twice a month in these halls and at other prescribed times throughout the year. One interesting aspect of death rites involved the choosing of a new name for the deceased, one that would be inscribed upon the ancestor tablet and by which he would be known to his descendants.

In modern China and some other East Asian societies, including North Korea and Taiwan, high political leaders have been accorded elaborate state funeral rites, as was the case when Chairman Mao Tse-tung died in September 1976. Public weeping and attendance at the rites, at which Communist Party officials played the central role, took precedence over the immediate family and their involvement. One theme that has been identified both in the events following Mao's death and also the death in April 1975 of his great political rival, General Chiang Kai-shek, leader of the Chinese in Taiwan, is that of transforming 'grief into strength' (Wakeman, 1988: 267).

### Grief into strength as rebounding violence

This may be interpreted not only in terms of the 'rebounding violence' themes explored in earlier chapters but also as a form of 'words against death'. For its own survival society does not allow its members to linger in states of depressed grief but overcomes it with a sense of victory and triumph. The very building of the large memorial hall to house Chairman Mao's body was completed in six months, involving 'more than 700,000 people from all over China' and was interpreted by the Chinese Communist leadership and many others as an act of devotion to Mao and of the continuing triumph of his ideals (Wakeman, 1988: 278).

When Chinese left China, they often retained these practices. For example, Chinese immigrants to Hawaii established a cemetery in 1851 using the traditional method of *feng shui* to decide on its auspicious location (Purnell, 1993: 194). This was a place on a hill bounded by water on three sides, regarded as particularly suitable for it restricts the free movement of souls. A symbolic spirit-gate at the entrance to the cemetery also serves to prevent spirits from 'wandering'.

After some seven years the bones are exhumed and placed in ceramic pots which are located in a special bone house. Initially this was done until a convenient time arose when they could be taken back to the ancestral town in China. But as time went on and it became clear that many Chinese would live permanently in Hawaii, the bone house became the final destination of many of these remains. In April and May each year, these Chinese families hold the Ching Ming Festival of the dead in which they seek the blessing of these ancestral personages for themselves and for the fertility of nature. Food items and tea are offered and rites are performed at the tombs of the unknown Chinese soldier and the Earth Mother and also at the bone house.

Cremation was avoided by the Chinese, except for those who had transgressed particular religious rules. For the Japanese, by contrast, cremation was preferred but the cremated remains were carefully retained and placed in urns in vaults. The Hawaiian Japanese retained many of these customs and often set up pagoda-like memorial stones over sites of cremated remains. These layered structures symbolized earth, water, fire, wind and air. In all their rites, respect for the ancestors is deemed important for the continued welfare of contemporary Japanese.

In all these cases of Indian, Chinese and Japanese cultures the fact of descent and inheritance is of great cultural significance and mirrors the deep respect in which the ancestors are held. This has remained true in many cases where members of the cultural group also exist far from their original territory, as we shall see when considering identity in the context of emigration. It is precisely in the rites used for the ancestors that 'words against death' find their ongoing power and give to society its durability of significance.

## Maori ancestors and death

This can be seen clearly in New Zealand where traditional Maori rites also phased funerary ritual in a way which mirrored a belief in death more as a process than as an event of one rapidly passing moment. Death was not viewed as complete until the actual body had become fully decomposed. This could involve a temporary burial until the flesh had largely gone from the bones. At that stage the second ceremony, *hahunga*, took place amidst renewed vocal expressions of grief; any remaining flesh was scraped from the bones before they were finally buried. Reflecting the process of death the spirit of the deceased was believed to remain amongst the living until the decomposition process had been completed; mourners would address the dead, encouraging them to go to their ancestors to *Hawaiki*, the place of the ancestral abode (Schwimmer, 1966: 60). This approach to the fate of the dead also helped explain any experiences the living might have of that widespread human sensation of experiencing the dead as still present some time after their death. Still, this Maori example offers a clear example of the fate of the body being matched by a transition in status of the dead from being one amongst many living in a family to being one of the ancestors whose domain was elsewhere.

Before the nineteenth century, the dying Maori was traditionally placed in a separate shelter, covered with ancestral objects and surrounded by close kin, until death came. Joan Metge (1976: 28, 261–4) describes this historic period. The corpse, surrounded by the kin who now maintained constant formal wailing for the first few days after death, was left unburied for up to three weeks so that all visiting kin could pay their respects. The corpse was finally hidden in a cave, a tree or in the earth and wrapped in mats.

Exhumation took place a year or two after death and the bones were scraped, painted in red ochre and exposed at the traditional meeting place before being buried in a secret burial ground. The spirits of the dead were believed to undertake a northwards journey before finally entering the underworld realm of the goddess of death and childbirth, where they finally met and became one of the ancestors.

The contemporary tradition retains elements of this pre-nineteenth-century practice. Women raise a high pitched wailing, the wider family organize the funeral leaving the closer kin to grieve and to receive visitors coming to pay their respects. The formal wailing is resumed as each new visiting party approaches. This is a good example of the performance of grief which unites both social and psychological factors. Visitors address speeches to the dead who are also directed towards and commanded to go and join the ancestors. Burial takes place three days after death and usually follows a Christian rite. After the burial the mourners perform a rite of washing to remove the *tapu* ('taboo') from themselves. When the burial party return to the *marae*, or community meeting place, and the *tapu* is raised from it they set about the funeral feast and, with it, trigger a shift in emotion with 'more cheerful themes' (Metge, 1976: 263). Alcohol and music take their effect as the gathered community helps the grieving family before leading them back to their home and to the place of death from which the *tapu* is also lifted. Over the next year occasional events occur culminating in a final community meeting or *hui* which involves unveiling a memorial to the dead.

Metge describes the Maori as people who believe in sharing rather than hiding their grief and she speaks of the way in which the formal wailing seems to give a natural outlet for the grief of many Maori women. Children are party to all these events so becoming familiar with death in a community context from a young age. The occasion of the funeral is also that at which many people in their twenties or thirties make their first formal speech at the *marae* and do so under the influence of the emotion of bereavement as they thank those who support them in their bereavement. In this Maori case we see very clearly in the extensive practice of speech-making the power of words, whether spoken to the dead or to other members of the community, in asserting the significance of the ongoing life of society. Verbal ritual enhances support and gives firm profile to the community's past and future.

## Identity, emigration and ancestors

Emigrant groups are very instructive as to the significance of death rites as a means of asserting the identity of a community through its own dialogue with death. A case in point is that of Italians in America who brought with them the custom of placing photographs of the dead on tombs, a practice which became possible from 1851 when a monumental form of daguerreotype was introduced (Meyer, 1993: 10). Though some American Catholic authorities went through a phase objecting to this practice which was alien to most North American cultures, it asserted itself and now, with improved technological processes, the images of the dead become increasingly sophisticated.

It has been argued that for nearly a thousand years leading up to the twentieth century the Catholic tradition, with its doctrine of purgatory, kept the living and the dead in a kind of reciprocal relationship which has been called a 'mutual economy of salvation' (Davis, 1977: 93). Through the prayers and good deeds of the living, dead family members might reap the benefit of such merit. In the late nineteenth and early twentieth centuries, Italian Americans employed women to sing eulogies for the dead, and at the annual All Souls' Day the family set out a plate of spaghetti for the dead relatives (Matturri, 1993: 17).

This kind of strong connection between the living and the dead found support in the Roman Catholic theology of purgatory as an intermediate state, when the soul might be purged of sin and assisted through the prayers and merit of the living. A quite opposite picture emerged in the Reformed Protestant tradition of Scotland. Initially the Scottish Reformers, as they turned their backs on Catholic theology and ritual, ignored all religious ritual at funerals. In the *First Book of Discipline* of 1560 the funeral was a silent and bare act not requiring the assistance of any minister of religion. However, in John Knox's *Book of Common Order* of 1562, wider scope was left for local choice (Gordon, 1984: 46). Here the doctrinal position of Reformed theology with its belief in God's grace in Christ and predestination meant that as far as salvation was concerned there could be no fruitful relationship between the living and the dead.

This is a crucial point, for it is in societies which believe that a beneficial relationship may exist between the living and the dead that kinship facts of descent are used to establish the ancestors as significant individuals. Often the relationship is believed to be reciprocal as the ancestors benefit in the afterlife from rites performed by the living while they, in turn, bless and foster the living. In the case of Christianity this led to distinctive patterns of church building and cemetery construction which we explore for the early Christian period after, first, considering the case of Roman emperors. This case of silence at funerals is also instructive because, at first glance, it permitted no words to be spoken against death. On reflection, however, this can be seen to be due to the belief that it was God who, through the divine decrees of predestination, had already spoken the definitive word against death. The silence of the funeral symbolized belief in the finality of the divine word.

## Cemeteries and ethnic identity

However, normal life usually rejects such silence and asserts itself at the time of death. The links with forebears have many meanings, whether directly existential in doubting death's finality or in rehearsing an identity gained through inheritance, succession and ethnic identity. For many cultural and subcultural groups cultural identities are closely associated with public funeral rites and patterns of memorialization. This becomes particularly important in the USA where so many ethnic groups from widely differing parts of the world immigrated and laid the foundation for distinctive communities throughout the nineteenth and early twentieth centuries. Those identities were marked through cemetery construction (Sloane, 1991).

In many respects two rather different processes were at work in those cemeteries. On the one hand cemeteries or, more usually, parts of cemeteries have reflected a definite ethnic identity as immigrant families from particular nations have been buried together and furnished memorials reflecting their national origin. On the other hand, one of the major goals of cemeteries in America has been described as 'linking members of its culturally diverse population into a symbolic unity' (Matturri, 1993: 31).

An example of the first process, of marked cultural distinction, can be found in a cemetery devoted to Ukrainian Americans at New Brunswick in New Jersey where the 'spirit of being Ukrainian' is said to shine through the memorial stones (Graves, 1993: 55). This particular cemetery follows the custom of burying people according to their profession or walk of life so that, to cite a few cases, doctors, artists and priests are buried with those of their own vocation. Their headstones also reflect their professions with, for example, priests having a chalice and holy communion wafer on their headstones. The main focus is upon the male occupations, wives being buried with their husbands. Even so, the second process of uniting diverse cultural groups is also achieved in many cemeteries with the boundary wall embracing various sub-groups as a symbolic expression of the USA itself embracing diverse communities. Sometimes a particular cultural tradition comes to be shared by other groups. This was the case, for example, in New Orleans where the descendants of French Catholics buried their dead in above-ground vaults, partly because the water table was very high and people did not like the idea of waterlogged graves. The Episcopalians also came to adopt this practice over time.

In such cemeteries, architecture itself stands as a human creative response to death as well as a marker of historical identity. The inscribed messages on memorials express not only a human past but also a hope for the future, showing that particular ethnic groups, just as humanity in general, are committed to life. In such cases not only do 'words against death' appear as part of the total religious tradition of the group but they also bear a more local accent, whether Japanese, Ukrainian or any other group.

What is interesting is that burial has remained the prime form of North American funeral; cremation has been of minor significance for many reasons. Traditional religious opposition played some part (Welfle, 1935) and its pagan background also influenced others (Irion, 1968: 11; Phipps, 1989: 23). Some argue that funeral directors and trade journals associated with death professionals have, for their own economic reasons, emphasized the preference for burial (Jackson, 1993: 161). But the significance of group identity and of a sense of history focused on particular cemeteries ought not to be ignored for many parts of the USA. One distinctive example comes from Mormon cultural life in which a sense of history is coupled with a unique doctrine of family, death and the afterlife.

## Ancestral Mormonism

For Mormons, family and kinship are of fundamental importance and the dead being treated, in some respects, as ancestors. The Church of Jesus Christ of Latter-day Saints was established in the USA in 1830 by its first prophet Joseph Smith. After his death in 1844, the Mormons migrated west into what would become the state of Utah. In addition to ordinary chapels or places of worship, they went on to build special temples which now exist all around the world and which may be attended only by Mormons in good standing in the Church. Along with the temples there emerged new doctrines concerning special rituals which took place in temples and which guaranteed to faithful Mormons a special place after death in the future realms of eternity (Shipps, 1985).

Central to these rites are baptism on behalf of the dead followed by ordination to the Mormon Priesthoods and other rites which seal husband, wife and children together not just for this lifetime but for all eternity. All of these rites can be performed vicariously, done by the living on behalf of the dead. Mormon belief sees the human family as progressing on the path to an ever greater degree of divine status with these deceased people being able to enter into new benefits in the afterlife precisely because rituals have been performed on their behalf in earthly temples. The larger that family becomes, the greater its sense of achievement and, in a sense, of salvation.

The idea of the extended family lies behind all this ritual and deeply motivates an intense family loyalty and concern over family history. Mormonism is the only contemporary religion which has developed the idea of genealogy as a special kind of religious duty. Thus many Mormons, especially older ones, spend a significant amount of time tracing their family tree to establish exactly who their ancestors were. As part of this search the Church has actively recorded and computerized hundreds of thousands of records of birth, marriage, death and baptism throughout many countries of the world, especially in the UK and northern Europe, areas from which thousands of new converts migrated to the USA in the mid and late nineteenth century to lay the foundation for the new state of Utah and its Mormon society.

As a family trace their ancestors they set about undergoing a wide set of rituals on their behalf. So, for example, if the grandparents' names and facts of life are discovered their living descendants will undergo baptism on their behalf before being ordained, married and so on in their stead, in the temple. Mormon belief sees these rites as giving the ancestors a choice of entering into the fullness of Mormon religion in the eternal worlds beyond this life. This is a very interesting case where the living descendants clearly and distinctly alter, or at least provide the basis for altering, the status of the ancestors. But the living also benefit from this vicarious work for the ancestors in the sense that their whole family, earthly and in the heavenly afterlife, flourishes more fully as ever larger numbers of ancestors come into the group of those experiencing salvation, or an increase in glory as the Mormons describe it (D. J. Davies, 1987: 115).

The close link between temple and eternity is seen in the fact that after death the body is prepared by being washed and dressed in the special temple clothing otherwise only used in the temple. For men this includes a special apron-like garment which carries extensive symbolic meaning for Mormons and which some believe reflects the very garments made for Adam when God first drove Adam and Eve out of the Garden of Eden. In centres of Mormon culture the funeral directors are likely to be Mormon and will carry out these preparations. In other parts of the world there are members of the Church who will assist the bereaved by caring for the dead person themselves. There is a funeral service at the local Mormon church, not at the temple, and the body is buried. The Mormon Church does not forbid cremation but possesses a very strong preference for burial. In the USA this reflects a wider popular preference for burial than is the case in Britain where cremation is now the dominant mode of funeral. But the Mormons also prefer burial because they have a strong belief in the resurrection from the dead and see burial as a natural prelude to the future resurrection. The grave is blessed as a resting place until that future date arrives (Cunningham, 1993: 183).

In this example we can see how an individual Mormon's sense of his or her own identity is very much caught up in the identity of their ancestors. Not simply in a historical sense of knowing who their forebears were, or where they came from, but in a more dynamic sense of becoming bonded together in an actual family network extending increasingly further back in time as more genealogical work brings new family members to light.

In fact the temple ritual of Mormons is the first major example in relatively modern Western societies of a preoccupation with ancestors and their salvation. We may even speak of the Mormon Church as consisting in 'soteriological lineages', a phenomenon that is quite novel in modern societies. Here the death rites of the funeral are set within the much wider framework both of working on behalf of the dead and working for the family. Unlike many modern religions Mormons have much to say and much to do when confronted by death, which may be one major reason why their message possesses a relatively wide appeal in a world where family values are easily shattered and where ignorance over death is intense. Mormons see death as a process through which the dead person passes to another world just as they believe that birth is a process through which a pre-existing spirit is given an opportunity to come and experience life in a body of flesh. Not only is the individual self given a past and a future eternal framework of existence but it is also not left in isolated loneliness but set amidst an extensive ancestral network of relations. The 'words against death' spoken by Mormons are uttered long before the funeral – the devotee undergoes temple rituals during life, rituals which give assurance that death can and will be conquered through the keeping of vows and the living of an ethical life. The funeral is simply the time when those powerful words begin to take effect.

This Mormon example draws heavily from the Christian tradition whilst also adding quite distinctive features of its own. Indeed, so many cultural developments are grounded in Christianity and its tremendous success as a religion of salvation from death, and the causes of death, that it is important to return to the early stages of that religion to see how it addressed death in ways that became appealing to entire civilizations.

## Early Christianity and graves

In early Christianity we witness the birth of a movement in which family and kinship came to be set within a much wider framework of a new community, that of the Church, serving as a form of what might be called spiritual kinship involving beliefs which starkly confronted death. Early Christians died despite the hope, held by many, that Christ's second coming would be so soon that not all of their first generation would 'sleep' in death. St Paul too, it would seem, thought that he would be amongst those who at the last trumpet 'would be changed' at the same time as those who had already died would be 'raised imperishable'. This suggestion in 1 Corinthians (15:52) is even more clearly spelled out in 1 Thessalonians: 'we who are alive, who are left until the coming of the Lord, shall not precede those who have fallen asleep' (4:15). Indeed precedence is to be given to the dead, to those of the early generations who have 'fallen asleep'. Only after they have experienced resurrection will living believers be 'caught up in the clouds' to meet the Lord.

This deeply held belief in the resurrection of the dead, a hallmark of early Christianity, probably helped burial become established as the preferred form of Christian funerary rite, though there is some debate over this (Nock, 1932). For early Christians who were Jews, this followed the long established Jewish practice of burial (often double burial involving ossuary jars for the dry bones), which had come to be associated with beliefs in a resurrection even before the time of Jesus, as attested in the opposing views of Pharisees and Sadducees. For those Christians of the early centuries who had, for example, been Roman, burial ultimately replaced their traditional pattern of cremation. 'At one Roman cemetery, for example, in the early second century only cremation is found, in the mid century a mixture of cremation and inhumation, while by the end of the century inhumation was predominant' (Price, 1987: 96). For Christians, resurrection would be the mode of entry into a heavenly domain where salvation would be fully known. Though the belief that Jesus had been resurrected, leaving behind only an empty tomb, was determinative of the choice of burial rather than cremation for subsequent generations of Christians for centuries, mixed practices occurred throughout Europe as some Christians continued former death rites, including cremation. As we have already said, one should not draw too simplistically on the idea that the resurrection of Christ was a doctrinal issue which immediately caused cremation to give way to burial under some sort of doctrinal imperative, not least because of the influence of belief in the soul (Nock, 1932). By the time Augustine wrote his *City of God* in the fifth century, it was easy for him to portray a Christian tradition firmly committed both to a belief in the immortal soul and also to the resurrection of the body (XX: x, xx; XXII: v). For him the resurrection-body was certainly important with, for example, dead babies being included in his argument in the belief that a 'sudden and strange power of God shall give them a stature of full growth' (XXII: iv). He was not so sure about abortions but was open to the possibility that they too would be provided with bodies (XXII: xiii). What Augustine did assume was that burial was the norm for Christians. But, of course, the practice of burial had not been the universal mode of dealing with the dead in the ancient world. Cremation had been a widespread, though not exclusive, funerary rite in the ancient classical world. With Christianity establishing itself as the religion of the Roman Empire, however, pagan cremation gave way to Christian burial. This was certainly the case by the sixth to seventh centuries AD.

## Imperial deities

One prime context in which the Christian view of death and funeral rites came to establish itself as a powerful means of addressing mortality concerned the emperor himself. In the world of Imperial Rome and in the funerary rites of the later emperors, following Julius Caesar and his official deification, the human identity of the deceased emperor was believed to be transformed and given a divine status (Price, 1987: 72). While the ancestors were also much in evidence, with their busts or representations being carried in the funeral procession, the verbal dimension was of particular significance through formal funeral orations.

The idea of apotheosis, or the process by which a human became divine, had a Roman history extending to the second century BC and was associated with ideas of the deceased person ascending to the realm of the gods or of his soul doing so. With time the funeral emphasis on emperors focused increasingly on the funeral pyre and the cremation of the dead with coins of the second century even depicting six-storeyed pyres (Price, 1987: 93). Along with the lighting of the multi-structured pyre there went an associated rite of releasing an eagle from the pyre. This magnificent bird was said to conduct the soul of the emperor to its new divine realm.The importance of the cremation of the emperor as part of the process of apotheosis was further enhanced as, in the second century, inhumation became increasingly common for the general population. Scholars debate this point because it is not completely certain whether perhaps the actual body of the emperor was buried while a wax effigy was cremated. Part of the problem lies in the fact that the Greek verb *kathaptein* could mean cremation or inhumation while the Greek *soma*, or Latin *corpus*, could refer to either the dead body or the cremated remains (Price, 1987: 96). However, it appears that when the emperor Constantine, who had converted to Christianity, died in 337 he was buried rather than cremated. Instead of the ritual of the pyre and of apotheosis there were Christian burial rites conducted by the clergy. This is a particularly good example of how a funeral rite which once served to assert one kind of change in identity shifted its significance quite dramatically as the overall framework of meaning changed. It is also important because it shows how the Christian view of death was now successfully penetrating a world culture on what would prove to be a path that would influence a great part of world civilization within a thousand years.

## Martyrs and style

Returning to the early Christian period it is important to record that not all pagans had engaged in cremation. Indeed, the practices of those who used burial were followed, in some significant ways, by Christians. We have already implied that it is wise not to assume too readily that it was a deep commitment to Christian beliefs in resurrection that led to burial replacing cremation in the ancient world; funeral rites as such were not made to carry the heaviest symbolic load in emergent early Christianity though they would increasingly do so as time went on.

As Howard Colvin has shown in his important study *Architecture and the After-Life* (1991), Christians initially buried their dead alongside pagan neighbours before adopting separate cemeteries. Memorial banquets of Christians matched the preceding pagan form of commemoration, and the same craftsmen produced similar sarcophagi albeit with Christian motifs on them. The growth of Christian mausolea as architectural markers of the dead also followed contemporary pagan patterns. When a mausoleum was built on the site of a martyr's grave it often came to serve as a place of religious pilgrimage and spiritual benefit. Colvin presses the interesting argument that while the bodies of the dead were polluting to pagans, they served as sources of spiritual power in the case of Christian martyrs (1991: 105). He also sees the rise of many local martyrs' graves as serving the end formerly achieved by local pagan deities. From about the fifth century it seems that baptisteries, built to cope with the large numbers being initiated into the increasingly official Christian religion, and mausolea were built in very similar styles. St Ambrose, who died in 397, built a baptistery near his cathedral in Milan on a plan copied directly from a mausoleum recently built just outside the city. The octagonal nature of both of these fed the architectural symbolism that it was on the 'eighth day' that Christ was risen. Death was a motif both in baptism, where the faithful died with Christ and were born again into new life, and in the funeral rite of burial where the dead were laid to sleep in the hope of the resurrection.

The practice of burying the dead outside the city was continued by Christians, who often developed two major church centres in a town. One was inside the walls for the regular worship of the congregation and the other outside the walls as a funerary church often including the *martyrium,* or place of a martyr's relics, which served as a sacred focus around which the Christian dead could beneficially be buried. If Christians enjoyed the fellowship of worship during their life they also wanted to be in physical proximity to the fellowship of the dead when in their grave. It did not matter that the sites of the living church and of the dead church differed because the martyr's relics were a dynamic presence on their own account as 'the magnetic body of the holy man' (Colvin, 1991: 123). As time went on the desire of Christian people to be buried in churches presented increasingly difficult problems of space. Two general patterns emerged. The first dropped the older tradition of burial outside the town and instead developed cemeteries within town boundaries and also buried people, especially eminent clergy and laity, within the main church. The second followed the increasing conversion of Europe with a corresponding increase of parish churches built either in association with pre-existing cemeteries or on sites that soon came to house cemeteries. Either way the dead were housed in or near the church reflecting the early Christian location of the dead.

## Christian doctrine and buildings

Harold W. Turner has rehearsed this pattern of development of Christian churches in relation to the dead in his important phenomenological and theological study of places of worship, *From Temple to Meeting House* (1979). He established a firm distinction between two types of space used in places of Christian worship, one being a house of God (*domus dei*) and the other a house for the people of God (*domus ecclesiae*). He thinks the meeting-house style presents the authentic norm for the Christian tradition in that the people gathered for worship are more important than some building in which a divine presence may be housed. Though early Christians met for worship in houses of particular believers it was still the case that 'the construction of funerary buildings ... was the first architectural activity of the early

Church'; so, for example, St Peter's in Rome began life as a covered cemetery (1979: 166). Harold Turner sees the growth of Christian churches in close connection to the graves and remains of the dead as an unfortunate development, involving a regression to that theme of world religions where sacred places too readily exert an influence over the living. In fact he thinks that the growth of martyr-churches as places of special spiritual power involved 'an explicit denial of the New Testament revolution' (1979: 168).

This sort of pattern of burial near to sacred spots has been strictly perpetuated to the present day in some Christian countries where the physical location of the dead after burial is itself an important symbolic assertion of their social identity in relation to the traditionally prevailing religious ideology. In their important and instructive study of death in Portugal, for example, Feijo, Martins and Pinal-Cabral make this point very clearly in arguing that those buried inside churches or in churchyards remain close to the social life of their village, unlike those buried in large city graveyards who are abandoned and left to their own devices (1983: 24). They also document the fact that church authorities have long objected to burial inside churches despite the fact that such practices have actually occurred.

In the UK, this tradition was maintained throughout the medieval period, when its society, along with that of the rest of Europe, was extensively and predominantly rural. During the seventeenth century problems over space began to arise in larger towns and cities, especially London, which necessitated the opening of new cemeteries, sometimes outside the town. But it was in the nineteenth century that the major shift to new cemeteries emerged because of the astonishing rise in population associated with Britain's entirely new phase of social history born through industrialization and its concomitant urbanization. Chris Brooks in his *Mortal Remains* (1989) has traced the impact of social change on cemeteries in Britain in the rise of the new economically powerful groups such as merchants, but more importantly he draws attention to that shift from 1801 when less than 20 per cent of the inhabitants of England and Wales lived in towns to 1901 when 75 per cent lived and worked in urban settings (1989: 1). This population change also involved an employment shift from agriculture to industry, a change which sociologists have often associated with the process of secularization. The period from the later eighteenth through the nineteenth and into the early twentieth century has often been regarded as the age of secularization involving major changes in attitudes towards religion which might be glossed by saying that as mankind gained mastery over nature, in terms of the means of production of wealth, so nature lost its mystery in the human mind and imagination.

The arguments for this view of secularization are well known, embracing as they do the rise of free thought and popular education in association with working-class culture and various political ideologies, and especially in connection with the new outlook on life engendered by the discovery of evolutionary theory. These are important issues for cremation and for the framework within which the identity of the dead makes sense. Amongst the most important of changes inaugurated by the Industrial Revolution was the visible alteration of the environment. New kinds of buildings and structures transformed the face both of rural and of small-town England in the obvious form of terraced housing and the parent factories, some of which even became the subject of socially aware artists of the Industrial Revolution (Dixon and Muthesius, 1978: 59ff.). But there were also bridges, aqueducts, railways, hundreds of new urban churches and new civic cemeteries. Then, beginning at the end of the nineteenth and increasing throughout the twentieth century, the new institution of the crematorium became increasingly visible. Through such crematoria the identity of the dead could be manipulated very rapidly to yield ancestral remains which could either be buried under permanent monuments or else allowed to be rapidly blown away by the wind. There are numerous symbolic aspects of this cremation process which merit some analysis.

## Sweden and France

Despite the increased modernization of the world, distinctive cultural practices remain and it is worth considering the examples of Sweden and France as Western European societies at the close of the twentieth century. As a background to the Swedish context, recent surveys show that funerals conducted by the Lutheran clergy stand at a high 92 per cent for a population where 5 per cent attend church on Sundays, 45 per cent reckon to believe in God, and 38 per cent say they believe in life after death (Bäckström, 1992). Swedish crematoria are, most frequently, owned by the Lutheran Church as the state church. Because ordinary taxpayers usually also pay a church tax, the cost of their own funeral service at the crematorium is covered in advance.

Swedish crematoria differ from those in England in the very significant fact that they usually contain a cold room for the storage of bodies. It is not unusual for the period from death to the final interment of ashes to last between two to three weeks, more than double the time likely in Britain. This is partly due to the fact that there are proportionately fewer crematoria than in England, but also because many Swedish families wish to gather together from various parts of the country, which is better done on Fridays with its following weekend than on other weekdays when work and wages may be lost. This, necessarily, means that Fridays become crowded at crematoria. It is also increasingly common for families to hold the funeral service at the local parish church rather than at the crematorium. Therefore the coffin, which may well have been kept in the crematorium cold room, is brought to the parish church for the funeral rites and afterwards is taken back to the cold room to await cremation at some future date. Thus the act of cremation is distanced from the funeral service itself, not only in terms of time but also of place.

In terms of church ritual both the form and content of the cremation service is identical to that of the burial service as far as what takes place within the church is concerned. Though there is a variety of options in words of committal there is no indication that one body is to be buried while another is to be cremated. Even the idea that a funeral – by burial or cremation – finally results in a body returning to the earth and to dust is retained, both verbally and ritually. It is customary during the Swedish Lutheran rite for priests to make the pattern of a cross three times on the top of the coffin in fine earth while saying: 'You gave *him* life. Receive *him* into your peace. For the sake of Jesus Christ give *him* a joyful resurrection.' Though these words offer clear affirmations of standard Christian 'words against death', the rite of using earth in a rite designed as a cremation service might appear contradictory to those whose liturgy, however minimally, includes some direct reference to cremation. But in practical terms, once it is understood that many of these cremation ceremonies are conducted in churches at a considerable distance from the crematorium, and that the cremation may not even take place that day, the symbolism becomes more obviously appropriate. In Sweden the cremated remains have traditionally been interred in recognized locations so that there has been very little opportunity for the growing British practice of private placing of remains in places of personal choice. In this Swedish context cremation and burial have become very closely aligned in symbolic terms. This is particularly apparent within the cremation service where a rite that formally took place in the graveyard has now been brought within the church. Towards the close of the service the family of the deceased, followed by other relatives, friends and members of the community, leave their seats and come to the front of the church where the coffin stands on its bier. They walk around the coffin, stop for a moment at its head and stand in honour and memory of the dead. Many will place a flower on it before making a slight bow or, in the case of women in traditional villages and towns, a curtsy and then return to their seats. In a burial service this practice takes place in the cemetery, where family and friends walk around the grave and throw in their flower. In other words a custom originating, and still used, in burial has been transferred to cremation.

In terms of ritual time the speed of Swedish cremation is slow, as already mentioned. Quite the opposite is the case in some French crematoria as, for example, the Bordeaux Crematorium which is typical of a crematorium in a large town which also serves an extensive rural community. Here it is very likely that a funeral service will have taken place at a local parish church, which will be Catholic. The formal rite in the chapel of the crematorium is brief and simply commits the body for cremation, but it is the next phase of the process which presents a complete inversion of the Swedish situation. The coffin is immediately removed from the chapel and is cremated there and then. The family and mourners retire to a waiting room where they may listen to music or otherwise occupy themselves for the period of one and a half to two hours while the body is cremated, the ashes reduced to the customary granular state, placed in a container and given back to the family. The family then return to their home area with the cremated remains which may well be buried in the family grave at the local cemetery. However, such speedy practice will not be possible as cremation grows in popularity in France and as pressure increases on each crematorium's capacity.

In these cremation rites, we see a variety of ways in which the dead are made to symbolize the past and allowed to influence the present, just as in the cemeteries of ethnic groups and the martyr-graves of early Christianity. Social change is reflected through these rites and, in particular, we see how the dead may be increasingly used or abandoned as sources of benefit to the present. In the Mormon case ancestors are actively made and are expected to be a source of blessing for the present and future. In many cases of modern cremation the dead may be dramatically marginalized. In historical terms it may be that the decrease of kinship as a driving force in social life is accompanied by a dependence on other forms of life-conquest than that of death rites provided by traditional religions. The Yanomamo of Venezuela and Brazil (Chagnon, 1968: 50) demonstrate an intimacy with their dead by crushing their cremated bones and eating them in a plantain soup – a ritual far removed from some contemporary Britons who even seem to forget the remains of their dead, simply leaving them at the crematorium. The difference may have much to do with the way certain kin may or may not be marginalized during life and also have a part to play in the ongoing symbolic life of the community after death. This raises a major issue of the degree to which death remains a confronting phenomenon for different societies. It may be that for increasing numbers of contemporary Britons, for example, there is a growing forgetfulness associated with death. Rather like retirement, it is an issue for another day and not part of the consciousness of everyday life. This may well be true in the sense that contemporary mainstream religions pay relatively little attention to death in their teaching. But the situation is constantly dynamic and the current rise of interest in death and bereavement may signal a return to the horizon of death as a significant feature in life, one that evokes the challenge of conquest.

# 8  Jewish, Christian and Islamic Destinies

Judaism, Christianity and Islam represent the three great contemporary religions which emerged in the Near East. All are grounded in the power of divine words addressed against evil and death, and exist to pronounce those words for all to hear. Behind and alongside these were others, represented for example by ancient Babylonia, Persia, Greece and Egypt. All had their distinctive beliefs about life, death and the afterworld and probably had some knowledge of the religious and philosophical ideas of India. Behind these perspectives lay the problem of reconciling bodily decay with some inner sense of life as consisting in more than simple bodily existence. The most widespread solution to this problem lay in the distinction between the body and the soul as, for example, in Plato's philosophy of the relationship between an immortal soul and a human body, which imprisoned it during life. Though this view touched Judaism as well as deeply helping fashion early Christianity, and the Western intellectual tradition in general, in this chapter our focus falls primarily upon Christianity not only because it is a salvation religion primarily concerned with 'words against death', promising salvation from death through the death and resurrection of Jesus of Nazareth, but because many have accepted it as such.

Jesus' death stands central to Christian salvation. This differs fundamentally from the death of the key religious figures in any other living world religion and, in terms of this book, this factor is reckoned to lie at the heart of Christianity's success as an international and cross-cultural religion. Christianity has afforded the world the most successful community-focused adaptation to death known to humanity in terms of the number and variety of cultures in which it has come to operate. In a derived way Islam shares in this capability which may yet increase its power in many local contexts. Judaism's belief in resurrection was transformed by early Christianity and made international, leaving little for Judaism to achieve beyond its own, relatively narrow, cultural boundaries. The much earlier Zoroastrian notions of resurrection never became linked with a large and expanding world community, while Hinduism's transmigration doctrines were so linked to the Indian caste system that world expansion was impossible. It is this very success which makes it important to explore something of the variety of Christian forms of words against death.

## Christianity

No death in the history of the world has been interpreted so extensively, and in so many different ways, as the death of Jesus of Nazareth. It has influenced the thinking of millions and motivated their ethical life. It has underpinned traditional Christian cultures. It is the clearest example of a 'model' death, being, paradoxically, not only a model *of* death and a model *for* death but also a model of *life* and for *life*.

Though this is not the place for a theological discussion of doctrines concerning the death of Christ, it is important to focus on two issues which Christians have, traditionally, set at the heart of their religion. The first concerns the death of Jesus as a sacrifice for sin and the second, the joint belief in his death and resurrection as representative of the death and future hope of all people; both express the idea of transcendence underlying this book. We have seen how Bowker sets such sacrifice at the centre of his interpretation of death (1991). In many parts of the New Testament, especially in the Epistle to the Hebrews, Jesus is viewed in the light of the Old Testament Jewish belief in sacrifices for sin. One strand of the tradition speaks of Jesus as a perfect form of sacrifice which was prefigured in the animal sacrifices of the Jewish Temple. Though not usually spoken of as such, his death is a kind of sacrificial slaughter. Just as animals were killed in the temple as an offering to God, including offerings for sin, so the death of Jesus and the shedding of his blood through crucifixion is interpreted as a sacrifice for sin.

Theologians still argue about the way in which Jesus himself perceived his own death but many lay great stress on the shedding of blood, even though crucifixion itself normally involved tying and not nailing people to crosses and death was more likely to be through asphyxiation rather than loss of blood. The Gospel of St John gives one good example of such a theological interpretation built into the form of the gospel story where, after his death, a soldier is said to pierce Jesus' side from which flowed blood and water (John 19:34). This image of Jesus as a sacrifice lies beneath the idea of him being the sacrificial 'lamb of God' (John 1:29; Rev 19:7, 9). These sacrificial ideas came, in the course of time, to generate the idea of the Mass or Eucharist as a kind of sacrifice. Indeed the doctrine of the Sacrifice of the Mass has been established at the very heart of Roman Catholicism for the last thousand years in particular. The doctrine of transubstantiation was formulated in the thirteenth century and taught that the true substance, the inner nature, of the bread and wine of the Mass was transformed into the true body and blood of Jesus even though no visible change took place in the outward and visible aspects of these elements. This doctrine triggered the development of many rituals of piety and devotion to the symbols of the sacrament themselves. The point, as far as death is concerned, is that the death of Jesus was symbolically rehearsed or repeated at each Mass. And it is in this way that Christianity increasingly became a religion with a strong concern with death. In the Requiem Mass in particular, the death of Christ comes to be closely associated with the death of a particular human being making the symbolic structure focused on death and its transcendence even stronger. In these rites the act of eating was also closely related to the deep fact of death and the high hope of resurrection, the consummation of hope was integrally related to the consumption of the sacramental food (cf. D. J. Davies, 1990b; M. Bloch, 1992: 37).

Similarly prayers for the dead, whether said privately or as part of a Mass, have been of tremendous importance in Christian attitudes to death (Ariès, 1991: 146). They afford a prime example of 'words against death', albeit under the constraints of a theology which processes souls through some intermediate state to their final heavenly glory. Protestant traditions usually completely rejected this sort of doctrine but, in its place, stressed the belief that in his death Jesus was a substitute for sinners. His blood would cleanse sinners from their evil and bring them salvation and the preaching of the word of the Gospel constituted, in the terms of this book, the prime 'words against death'. They come to sharpest focus in St Paul's exalted discourse on the resurrection of Christ and of Christian believers, including his rhetorical question 'O death where is thy sting? O grave where is thy victory?' (1 Corinthians 15:55). These lines form part of a reading closely associated with funeral services and comprise one of the most direct Christian liturgical moments of 'words against death'.

Within the Christian tradition the idea of death is very closely linked with that of sin, especially in St Paul, whose doctrine of the Fall speaks of sin entering into God's perfect world through human disobedience, and of death emerging as a consequence of sin (Romans 5:12–17). Jesus is then interpreted as being the second Adam, the one whose life is obedient and whose death brings a restoration of a spiritual life to men and women as the sting of death is drawn through Christ's resurrection. In terms of practical symbolism, death and decay are viewed as the outcome of disobedience and sin. This is the origin of the phrase 'earth to earth, dust to dust', for in the Book of Genesis God is described as speaking to Adam about his disobedience, telling him that he will have to work hard to earn his bread from the very soil, for 'out of it you were taken; you are dust, and to dust you shall return' (Genesis 3:19).

The significance of the traditional account of the death of Jesus lies precisely in the belief that his body did not return to dust, through decay, but was transformed into a resurrection body. In other words the link between sin and death was broken. The new link was to be between the resurrection of Jesus and the future resurrection of believers. So it is that Christianity took to burial in a very committed way as a kind of symbolic replay of the death of Jesus and in the hope of a replay of the resurrection at some future date.

For the greater length of its history Christianity has employed burial as its key mode of human disposal. In an obvious way this reflects the death of Jesus, especially in an echo of the credal words that he was crucified, dead and buried. As far as we have access to the facts, Jesus was buried in a tomb, probably a tomb cut in the rocks and resembling a cave. It was the Jewish practice at that time to place the dead in such tombs until the process of decay was over. The bones were then collected and placed in an ossuary, a kind of small stone box. This is a typical form of the process of double burial outlined in Chapter 1.

## Historical cameos

Just as with any feature of a culture's life, death rites are seldom static and death possesses a history within each society with archaeological evidence providing more extensive collections of material on this single feature of society than on any other human institution, not least as far as Christianity is concerned. With the passage of time it is not always easy to interpret the precise significance of remains from former eras and a great degree of caution is needed lest too much is read into ancient burials and cremations.

One of the most informative historical studies of death rites, already mentioned in earlier chapters, was that of A. D. Nock of 1932 which illustrates this need for caution in showing how vague cultural fashions, rather than specific ideological drives, could influence changing practices. Nock focused on the Roman Empire and on the fact that its extensive use of cremation gave way to burial over a period of some three hundred years. He shows that while the rise of Christianity, and even the influence of the mystery religions, had been used to explain the change of practice, neither seemed to fit the facts.

By sketching some of Nock's observations we can see just how important it is not to fall into easy generalizations or guesses over why certain practices rise or fall in popularity. He shows how both burial and cremation coexisted in Greece and the Near East during the Roman Empire. Even in Egypt cremation is adopted as a passing phase. Sometimes burial and cremation occur together as 'buried and burned remains were placed in the same grave' (1932: 328). Yet by the first century BC burial was the more common in Egypt. Even in the second century after Christ, cremation and burial coexisted. The rite of cremation remained of important significance for the Roman emperors, probably up until the time of the newly Christian emperor, Constantine. The rite seemed to express part of the transformation by which the human emperor became deified. Even so Nock shows that whether through burial or through the burial of cremated remains, the tomb could continue to be a place of some significance for the living.

Nock's conclusion, as already intimated, was that the change from cremation to burial in Rome in the second century of the Christian era cannot be explained as anything other than 'a change of fashion' (1932: 338). By this he means the habits of the rich which steadily became adopted as the habits of the poor. Burial, he says, 'seems to have made its appeal ... because it presented itself in the form of the use of the sarcophagus. This was expensive and gratified the instinct for ostentation' (1932: 338). Doubtless, as time went on, the slowly Christianized societies of Europe saw in burial real theological opportunities to reflect the death and resurrection of Christ, but it must not be assumed that these theological ideas were the prime factors in effecting the change of custom. This is an important point to be held in mind when considering the change from burial to cremation, effected in close collaboration with the Christian churches, in Britain throughout the twentieth century.

## Folk beliefs in Christian cultures

While many books on Christian belief focus on the ideas of established theologians, presented as systematic and rationally interlocking sets of beliefs, very little attention is usually paid to the often unsystematic beliefs of ordinary devotees. While Chapter 9 considers several examples of such popular practice it is worth emphasizing here that folk beliefs are profoundly influential in people's lives. As far as death is concerned there is a great deal of popular belief associated with the idea of the soul and its departure from the body on its way to God or in purgatory (Vulliamy, 1926; Christian, 1989: 84; D. Clark, 1982: 130). As many examples could be provided as there are Christian communities, but a few will give a sense of their diversity, as in Finland where traditionally the soul was believed to stay in the room with the dead for several days after death. A hole might be made in the wall for it to leave. As late as 1965, accounts speak of a family taking it for granted that a butterfly that flew into the house and landed on the face of a young girl was the soul of her younger brother who had recently died and who had loved his sister very much (Achté, 1980: 3). Though the dead might be encouraged to return home on All Saints' Day, such return visits were normally discouraged by lopping off branches and writing the name of the dead on the exposed trunk of a tree on the way to the cemetery or, in an account from Lincolnshire, by tying the feet of the corpse in the coffin (Obelkevich, 1976: 297). In Eastern Europe we find Catholic villagers in Romania maintaining extensive funerary rites which are not obviously derived from Christian ideology, as in not accepting cremation because of the idea that it burns the soul as well as the body, or that if tears of grief should fall upon the dead they would disturb the resting soul (Kligman, 1988: 165, 197). In more directly mythical form, that region of Transylvania also contributed much to the literary genre of Dracula, the one who existed between life and death and drew sustenance from the life-blood of others. Similar myths of the living dead not only exist in many societies but have also been extensively developed in

European literature, furnishing ways of reflecting on the nature of death and life (Twitchell, 1981).

## Double burial in contemporary Greece

In more traditional Christian terms the Eastern Orthodox Church stands out through its strong focus on the resurrection of Jesus and of the life of the Christian in relation to that resurrection. With this in mind it is worth exploring an example of Greek Orthodoxy as it operates at the local and domestic level of life. This will also serve as a concrete example of the process of double burial mentioned in Chapter 1.

In a study of a village near Mount Olympus in modern Greece the anthropologist L. M. Danforth gives a profoundly humane account of the place of the cemetery and of double burial in the life of the villagers, most especially of the women (1982). His book is not only well illustrated with photographs by Alexander Tsiaras depicting what people do at times of death and exhumation of bones, but the sensitive text also cites the songs people sing at the funeral rites, texts which express human reaction to death.

When a person is very ill and thought to be near death, the Orthodox priest is called to administer Unction; this is the Anointing of the Sick. Prayers are involved for the body's healing and for the purification of the soul through forgiveness of sins. Here the distinction of the body and the soul is marked liturgically in a distinction which plays an important part in subsequent funerary rites. Popular belief describes the soul as leaving the body at death. As Danforth describes it, 'many people believe that at the moment of death a person's soul, which is described as a breath of air located in the area of the heart, leaves the body through the mouth' (1982: 38). An easy death indicates a relatively healthy soul while a slow death reflects bad relationships between the dying and the survivors, who are not permitted displays of grief lest they hinder the passing of the dying person.

Once dead, the body is washed and dressed in new clothes and laid out in the house by neighbours or kin who are not very close. This leaves the close kin free to express their grief. The church bell is tolled slowly and the priest comes to the house. After he has recited some of the funeral prayers the body is removed outside and placed in a coffin. Within twenty-four hours a procession takes the body to the church for the funeral service which includes a rite where relatives kiss the body for the last time. This is followed by burial. The stress of the prayers lies on the separation of the soul and its journey into rest and on the entombed body. The body is placed in the grave and its hands, feet and lower jaw, which were earlier tied up, are now untied and the priest pours a bottle of wine over the body in the form of a cross. The liturgy concludes with words from the Psalms and the Book of Genesis:

You shall sprinkle me with hyssop
and I shall be clean,
You shall wash me
and I shall be whiter than snow.
The earth is the Lord's and the fullness thereof,
the world and all that dwell therein,
You are dust and to dust you will return. (1982: 42)

The coffin is closed and the grave is filled in. As people leave they throw in a handful of soil saying 'May God forgive him'. Food is eaten by many at the cemetery, though not by the closest family. All return to the house, wash their hands and touch a tray of burning charcoal before entering the house. So it is that an element of the pollution of death is removed. The priest blesses some bread and wine and gives this food which is described as *makario*, or blessed, to the close relatives. The clothes of the dead are now given away or burnt to aid the departure of the dead. All these rites mark the social change of identity of the dead as a person belonging to the household. It is as though the home of the dead is now in the cemetery, for the grave is likely to be visited practically every day by some of the women. This is kept up for a long period of time, but usually less than five years, before the rite of exhumation finally takes place.

Again following Danforth's account of a particular case, when the time came for exhumation family and neighbours went to the cemetery. The brothers of the deceased first started to dig and when their emotion increased the task was taken over by young women. When they came close to the corpse an older widow took over the task of uncovering the skeleton. On finding it she made the sign of the cross on herself, wiped the skull and placed it in a white cloth. It was passed to the bereaved mother who kissed and cradled the skull as though it were the body of her dead daughter. Later it passed around those present who all greeted it. After all the bones were recovered they were placed in a metal box. Throughout these proceedings cries of anguish were made by close relatives and laments sung by others. Soon the village priest arrived with candles and incense. He recited part of the funeral liturgy already mentioned at the first burial of the body while pouring wine over the bones three times in the form of the cross. Later everyone returned to the family house for food, drink and general conversation. Here the popular laments, which include personal references and the formal liturgy of the Church which is more universal, combine to form 'words against death' which bind together the individual and the wider community of faith in a transcending of death.

One important aspect of death for these local Greeks concerned the state of the exhumed bones. In terms of popular thought the state of decay was seen to reflect moral judgements on the life of the deceased. Good clean white bones indicate a sure separation of soul and body and a good moral life, while partial decomposition or dark bones may well indicate sin of some sort, whether in the deceased or in a former relation. Danforth argues that this is only one view present in traditional rural communities of Greece; others are more pragmatic and talk about the site of the grave or an earlier illness that affected decomposition. Even so, he mentions part of the official theology of the liturgy which seems to reflect this popular attitude. The priest refers to the possibility of great sin in the deceased: 'let his body indeed dissolve into its elements, but his soul do You appoint to dwell in the tentings of the Saints' (1982: 51). Throughout Greece there is a wide variation in these rites. After the exhumation the bones are often placed in ossuaries but they may also be reburied, for the final time. In urban areas these traditional processes tend to be organized by professional agencies and not carried out by neighbours and kin, while graves and places in ossuaries may be rented for limited periods only.

This total process of burial, exhumation and final placing of the bones reflects a period of change in the identity of the dead as they pass from the active world of the living to the middle phase of what we might call passive waiting in the grave before finally being viewed as belonging to the world beyond this one. This period also reflects one in which the bereaved undergo a process of change as they come to accept and live with their bereavement. The five-year period between burial and exhumation is a period in which the survivors, especially the women, carry on a kind of 'conversation with the dead' which marks a relationship which draws to a close with exhumation.

This brief account ignores many important features of death which in themselves are important in grasping the social, psychological and economic aspects of Greek life. It is important, for example, to know that it is the youngest son, and probably his wife, who is responsible for the funerary rites and not the eldest, as amongst Jews or as in India, for it is the youngest son who looks after the aged parents and finally inherits the family home. So, too, with the songs which provide a popular grasp of life, death and grief. The fact that these are sung together by women who have all, in their turn, experienced grief is likely to be important in helping them to live with the fact of death, as discussed in Chapter 3, which exemplifies the motif of 'words against death'. Perhaps they even maintain a culture of death rather than a culture of the forgetting of death which has often been criticized in late twentieth-century England.

## Soul in systematic theologies

Having discussed the non-systematic nature of beliefs in everyday faith, it is perhaps useful to look briefly at some examples of systematic theological discussions of the soul, if only to show how the idea assumes a place of practical orthodoxy. This practical orthodoxy in Christianity may well be matched in the faith of some contemporary Jews if Rabbi Dan Cohn-Sherbok is correct in saying that 'the doctrine of the resurrection of the dead has in modern times been largely replaced in both Orthodox and non-Orthodox Judaism by belief in the immortality of the soul'. He sees the demise of the Jewish belief in a future resurrection as going hand in hand with an increase of belief in a 'scientific understanding of the nature of the world' (1987: 270).

In terms of the history of Christian doctrine I have written in detail elsewhere about the way in which by the time of the Reformation in the sixteenth-century Protestants largely agreed with Catholics on the nature of the soul despite so many other bitter oppositions (D. J. Davies, 1997). Indeed, it was only in 1513 at the Fifth Lateran Council that the Catholic Church pronounced the immortality of the soul to be an official dogma of the Church (Pine, 1968: 170). The Protestant John Calvin in his *Institutes of the Christian Religion* uses the phrase 'cottage of clay' when referring to the body as 'the residence of an immortal spirit'; here spirit and soul are synonymous (1.xv.1). He presses the point 'that man consists of soul and body ought not to be controverted' (1.xv.11). He is dogmatically sure that 'when the soul is liberated from the prison of the flesh, God is its perpetual keeper'. For Calvin, then, the soul is 'an incorporeal substance' (1.xv.vi). Still, he remains sure of the resurrection of the body even though 'It is a thing difficult to be believed that bodies after having been consumed by corruption shall at length ... be raised again'.

From the Reformation to the present day, the identity of the dead has followed complex pathways (McManners, 1981), while twentieth-century academic theology has witnessed an intellectual divide between some Protestant theologians and the ongoing Catholic doctrine of the soul. Paul Tillich argued that 'eternal life' and 'immortality' have been confused by many and that the Greek idea of the immortality of the soul had largely supplanted what he calls 'the symbol of the resurrection' (1964, Vol. 3: 436). He would prefer to see that idea of immortality of the soul soundly rejected by Christianity, to emphasize the resurrection of the body with its acknowledgement not only of the positive significance of the material creation but also of each individual's uniqueness. The Anglican theologian William Temple also placed great weight upon the resurrection: 'Man is not immortal by nature or of right; but he is capable of immortality and there is offered to him resurrection from the dead and life eternal if he will receive it from God and on God's terms' (1935: 472). An even more recent Anglican voice expressed the opinion that 'we ought to reject quite frankly the literalistic belief in a future resurrection of the actual physical frame which is laid in the tomb' (Richardson, 1987: 274). Many others have discussed this issue showing the importance of ideas of the afterlife to the way life is lived before death (Cullmann, 1951, 1958; Moltmann, 1985).

119

## Cremation, soul and identity

Despite these academic theologians, most contemporary popular Christian belief does focus on the soul and involves a relative underemphasis upon the body, for the identity of the dead is increasingly associated with the departed soul and not, in any specific way, with a future resurrection of the body. This is particularly true in England for members of more Protestant religious traditions but, interestingly, Roman Catholics tend to stress in their ritual both the idea of a departing soul and also that of a future resurrection body.

This has one very significant consequence as far as the acceptance of cremation is concerned in that in most countries with a Protestant Christian heritage cremation has been quite widely accepted as a standard funeral pattern while Catholics have been relatively slow in their acceptance of cremation. One reason for this may well be that the cremation ritual symbolizes and expresses the pre-existing belief that it is the soul that really counts and not the body. Accordingly the rapid destruction of the body in the cremator symbolizes the discarding of the shell so that the soul may freely fly to God (Voelker, 1987: 12–14). Only very occasionally do some Christians raise the idea that cremation may actually burn and destroy the soul (Kligman, 1988: 165). We will argue in Chapter 13 that modern cremation appeals to secular individuals precisely because it expresses the total end of the deceased.

## Soul in popular images

Folk Christianity has many beliefs concerning the soul; one of the most common speaks of the soul leaving the body after death. Lindsay Prior has, for example, compared the way in which the soul is dispatched rapidly in Irish Presbyterian and Anglican culture compared with a longer involvement with the soul in Irish Catholicism. 'The disposal of the soul is a process which occurs quite abruptly in Irish Protestant culture. It occurs on the day of the funeral alone. After disposal there will be no prayers for the dead and no further ritualistic concern with repose of the soul. Even in Irish Anglicanism this is the case' (1989: 165).

One of the most sensitive analyses of death and illness in a sociological context, including the relationship between the soul and the body in relation to cremation, is that of Rory Williams in his study of attitudes to death amongst elderly people in Aberdeen. His findings reflect many of those in this book especially on the fact that some people accept cremation precisely because of a belief in the soul, seeing cremation as not hindering a re-uniting of friends or partners in some future state (1990).

David Clark tells of the practice in his study of a Yorkshire fishing village where, 'as members of the family left the house (for the funeral procession) care was taken to leave the door open in the belief that this facilitated the departure of the dead person's soul' (1982: 130). In the course of research for this present book, including information from a major teaching hospital, one has encountered the practice, taught by some as part of nursing's oral tradition, that a dead body is left for a period of time in its death-bed so that the soul may have time to depart. This practice is even represented in contemporary literature where one of Michael Arditti's characters is at the death-bed of a friend and recalls one of his memories of his mother, 'describing how she'd been trained to wait an hour before laying out a body to allow time for the soul to escape' (1993: 245).

## Soul in hymns and poetry

The significance of hymns is very great as far as popular Christian religion is concerned, not least in connection with death. It is here that we find a clear articulation of 'words against death'. Following the Reformation, hymns came to lie at the heart of Protestant spirituality complementing formal liturgies to produce a complexity of great power. In some Protestant churches the hymn-book served as a kind of alternative lectionary or guide to the liturgical year as in the widely used collection of *Sacred Songs and Solos* originally published in 1873. One of its hymns, written by Sabine Baring-Gould (1834–1924), gives a classic expression of the relationship between soul and body which is likely to have been amongst the clearest teaching on the subject many ordinary Christians are likely to have derived from their church membership. The first verse describes that future day when, 'On the resurrection morning, Soul and Body meet again; / No more sorrow, no more weeping, No more pain.' Then the second and third verses describe the fact that 'Here awhile they must be parted; / And the flesh its Sabbath keep', the tired body is depicted as waiting its final animation which comes with the resurrection day when, 'Soul and body reunited', the believer wakes up in a resurrection-likeness of Christ.

From a much earlier generation and a tradition deeply influenced by Catholic thought, the metaphysical poet John Donne (1573–1631) could also speak of the soul and body in a relatively similar way. His poem 'Of the Progress of the Soule' depicts the flight of the soul to heaven after death, leaving behind the body until the day of resurrection when, once more, they reunite to form an even greater – because immortal – unity. Replacing the Platonic image of the body as the prison of the soul he sees it as an eggshell ruptured to release the bird-like soul that takes its flight to heaven:

This to thy Soule allow,
Thinke thy shell broke, thinke thy Soule hatch'd but now.
And think this slow-pac'd soule which late did cleave
To a body, and went but by the bodies leave,

> Twenty perchance or thirty mile a day,
> Dispatches in a minute all the way
> Twixt heaven, and earth ...

The body belonged very much to this earth and should be meditated upon as such:

> Think that thy body rots ...
> Think thee a Prince, who of themselves create
> Wormes which insensibly devour their State.

Still, that earthly body still possesses a heavenly goal when it is transformed and reunited with its soul to enjoy an eternal bliss whose pleasures never end:

> Joy of a soule arrivall ne'er decayes;
> For that soule ever joyes and ever stayes.
> Joy that their last great Consummation
> Approaches in the resurrection;
> When earthly bodies more celestiall
> Shall be, than angels were, for they could fall ...

Donne clearly reflects the long established idea, which functions as practical orthodoxy within Christianity, that the soul departs at death to be reunited with its body at the resurrection to form a whole that is more than the sum of its parts.

As Donne came from a Catholic family so, by contrast, a century later Isaac Watts (1674–1748), from Dissenting stock, could also write of death and the Christian's attitude to dying in realistic and descriptive terms but again with an almost Platonic view of the soul and its prison-house of a body:

The pains, the groans, the dying strife, fright our approaching souls away; we still shrink back again to life, fond of our prison and our clay. Oh, if my Lord would come and meet, my soul should stretch her wings in haste, fly fearless through death's iron gate, nor feel the terrors as she passed.

So, too, Charles Wesley (1707–88) expresses his view on the soul in the first verse of his hymn 'A charge to keep I have / a God to glorify / a never-dying soul to save / and fit it for the sky'. A similar echo comes in E. Caswall's (1814–78) hymn 'Days and Moments Quickly Flying', where worshippers are told that 'soon our souls to God who gave them / will have sped their rapid flight'. This hymn goes a little further than most in also speaking almost in terms of a pre-existing soul: 'teach, oh teach us to remember / what we are and whence we came'.

One religious tradition, that of The Church of Jesus Christ of Latter-day Saints, or the Mormon Church, not only reflected but also developed this nineteenth-century expression of the classical approach to the soul. One popular Mormon hymn by the early Mormon hymnist and poet Eliza R. Snow speaks of the soul's pre-existence, its forgetfulness of that pre-existence during earthly life and its final return to heaven where the heavenly parents await it. It includes the words:

O My Father thou that dwellest
In the high and glorious place,
When shall I regain thy presence,
And again behold thy face?
In thy holy habitation,
Did my spirit once reside?
In my first primeval childhood,
Was I nurtured near thy side?

The hymn describes the hiddenness of this knowledge of pre-existence as far as human memory is concerned and that it is only through the new revelation of truth within Mormon religion that humanity comes to a knowledge of its real identity.

For a wise and glorious purpose
Thou hast placed me here on earth,
And with-held the recollection
Of my former friends and birth.
Yet oft-times a secret something
Whispered 'You're a stranger here',
And I felt that I had wandered
From a more exalted sphere.

This hymn reminds Mormons of the duty that lies upon them in their earthly life: to fulfil the potential they have already shown in their pre-existence and to persevere in the work done in Mormon temples to enhance the salvation of themselves and their kinsfolk. It is particularly interesting that Mormons hold both a strong doctrine of a soul, including its pre-existence, and such an emphasis on the future resurrection of the body that they strongly adhere to burial rather than encourage cremation (*Ensign*, August 1991).

Though this emphasis on the soul is tremendously powerful in many streams of the Christian tradition, there are other currents which prefer to speak of the resurrection without dwelling too much on the soul. Very often the image of sleep helps describe the state of the dead prior to the future resurrection. In the hymn 'The Glorious Morning' by William Hunter, contained in Sankey and Moody's section of almost 21 hymns on death, amidst a wider band of some 140 hymns on aspiration after heaven and the heavenly existence, he speaks of 'the saints who sleep, with joy awaken, / all arise, all arise, / their clay-cold beds are quick forsaken, / all arise, all arise'.

Another facet of nineteenth-century hymnody of death is the notion that each dying person passes directly to heaven as an individual. In *Hymns Ancient and Modern Revised* (1922), the twentieth century begins to make its presence felt with only some four hymns for the departed. All of these support the soul idea in some way. Even in 'Now the Labourer's Task is O'er', which ends with the verse 'Earth to earth and dust to dust, / calmly now the words we say, / leaving him to sleep in trust, / till the resurrection day', death is described earlier by saying 'now upon the farther shore / lands the voyager at last'.

Similarly, by contrast with the extensive coverage of death and heaven in the eighteenth and nineteenth centuries, twentieth-century hymn-books begin to stress ever more strongly the present nature of Christian life and faith. In the Methodist Church's new hymn-book of 1983 there is no single entry on death. There is a section of 17 hymns devoted to 'The Human Condition', but none deals with death as such. There is a section of some 15 hymns dealing with 'The Church Triumphant' and that includes several actually referring to death. Charles Wesley seems to have a clear sense of the Church Triumphant both in his 'Leader of faithful souls', and 'Guide of all that travel to the sky', where he speaks of Jesus as the guide on the soul's journey to heaven, and in 'Come let us join our friends above ... though now divided by the narrow stream of death'. This picture of the stream, or of the sea, regularly indicates the nature of the journey from earth to heaven. Swimming and flying seem to be the two major modes of transit for the pilgrim soul.

The significance of all these hymns lies in the fact that they express a rhetoric of death in ways which offer a variety of interpretations to the singer or hearer. In fact the genius of Christian religion, as in other religions, lies, as we have already mentioned, in this pool of potential orientations to death; a resource for grief and adaptation to death.

## Secular words and music

Much more could be said about hymnody as an expression of life-concerns showing that death has, increasingly, been granted a lower profile in British church life throughout the twentieth century. Even so it remains rare for a funeral to take place without some hymns being sung or sacred music played. Increasingly common is the use of secular music and songs which may be played in the form of recorded songs as detailed in Chapter 4. Whereas only a decade ago it would have seemed impious to play pop music at a formal funeral service it would now seem appropriate to the life that is passed. The words might bear no reference to life after death but, through being a favourite song or pop group of the deceased, it gains a significance as an item that expresses something of the depth of the dead person's personality. In this much more secular perspective, words are still used against death and may serve a very powerful goal of fostering comfort in grief. This is a significant point indicating the power of ritual, whether religious or not, to achieve positive ends for those engaged in it.

## Soul in liturgy

Whether in soul or resurrection body language, it is in the funeral ritual of the main churches that Christian 'words against death' have found their most formal expression. The very first words of the 1662 *Book of Common Prayer* of the Church of England are 'I am the resurrection and the life, says the Lord; he who believes in me, though he die, yet shall he live'. Taken from the Gospel of John (11:25), these have become part of the culture of death in many Christian societies. Similarly, in the committal statement made by the minister as earth is cast onto the coffin which has just been lowered into the grave, the words resound: 'For as much as it hath pleased almighty God of his great mercy to take unto himself the soul of our dear brother here departed, we therefore commit his body to the ground; earth to earth, ashes to ashes, dust to dust; in sure and certain hope of the resurrection to eternal life.'

This particular prayer replaced the 1549 entry which was more directly Catholic in form containing the words: 'We commend into thy hands of mercy ... the soul of this our brother departed', a significant shift of emphasis in which God is said to have taken the soul while the survivors deal with the body. Even so, the ultimate hope lies in the resurrection. After the Lord's Prayer there follows a further prayer which reinforces the idea of the soul whilst also going on to give the body a future purpose: 'Almighty God, with whom do live the spirits of them that depart hence in the Lord, and with whom the souls of the faithful, after they are delivered from the burden of the flesh, are in joy and felicity.' The prayer ends by referring to our perfect consummation and bliss, both in body and soul.

No liturgy exists in isolation but, for both regular and even occasional attenders, forms part of a total grammar of liturgy used by a church, an entire set of words which not only address death but also the principles of life itself. Only a brief consideration can be given of this here, and that only in the one case of the Church of England. In the *Book of Common Prayer* of 1662, references to the soul, for example, are relatively few, but where they occur they are powerful. In the prayer of humble access at the Holy Communion service the priest, speaking for all the people, asks that 'our sinful bodies may be made clean by his body, and our souls washed through his most precious blood', referring to the sacrificial death of Christ. Then in the words of administration of the sacred elements the priest says: 'The body of our Lord Jesus Christ which was given for thee, preserve thy body and soul unto everlasting life.' Similarly in a final prayer after Communion the people say: 'And here we offer and present unto thee, O Lord, our souls and bodies.'

In terms of funeral services, the Church of England's *Alternative Service Book* (1980) is noteworthy in almost entirely avoiding the use of the word soul at all. In the funeral rite the phrase handling the idea of an eternal personal identity comes through the expressions 'We entrust *N* to your merciful keeping' and 'We have entrusted our brother to God's merciful keeping, and we now commit his body to the ground (or to be cremated) earth to earth, ashes to ashes, dust to dust in sure and certain hope of the resurrection to eternal life'.

The use of the verb 'entrust', along with the person's name, seems to indicate an entity which, distinct from the body or from cremated remains which are committed to the ground, is now in God's care. But only one of the optional prayers refers directly to souls when God is addressed as 'Eternal Lord God, you hold all souls in life: shed forth we pray, upon your whole church in paradise and on earth the bright beams of your light'. This prayer expresses, or at least strongly implies, the idea that souls exist and have their being in paradise.

One of the clearest examples of this double emphasis on body and soul comes in the *Funeral Services of the Christian Churches in England* published by the ecumenical Churches' Group on Funeral Services in 1986. The Anglican service contained in that book follows the use of 'entrust' as just described. The ecumenical service in the book goes much further than the *Alternative Service Book* by actually having a section entitled 'Declaration of Committal and Entrustment' (1986: 14). The clause, putting our whole trust and confidence in the mercy of our heavenly Father, is used both in the committal prayer for use at the grave side in burial and at the crematorium in cremation. The key issue is that the distinction between committal and entrustment seems to parallel the idea of body and soul. It is the body which is committed for either burial or cremation while it is, for want of a better description, the non-corporeal identity or soul which is entrusted to God. There is also a subsequent service entitled 'The Disposal of Ashes' where the text runs 'we now commit his ashes to this place, earth to earth, dust to dust'. Ironically the phrase 'ashes to ashes' is omitted in a context where it would appear to be both literally and ritually appropriate, perhaps involving a loss of verbal power in this context.

Historically speaking it is worth recalling that the Church of England made an early response to cremation, albeit in a very small way, in the *Prayer Book* as proposed in 1928. Although this book was accepted by Church authorities, it was not accepted by Parliament and never attained legal status. Even so, it was published and provides one insight into a view of cremation relatively early in the twentieth century. After the burial service it contains two very brief additional rubrics. The first assumes that the burial service would also be used for cremation but suggested that the words 'commit his body to be consumed by fire' replace the words 'commit his body to the ground, earth to earth, ashes to ashes, dust to dust'. The second rubric implies that the burial service might also be used as the basic rite for burying cremated remains. In that case the words to be used should be either 'commit his ashes to the ground, earth to earth, dust to dust' or 'commit his ashes to their resting place'.

The Roman Catholic Rite printed for use in the *Funeral Services Book* (1986) makes a direct reference to the soul in the 'Commendation' section where it says 'We commend to you, O Lord, the soul of your servant'. The set reading following this commendation is drawn from Psalm 129 and includes the verse 'My soul is waiting for the Lord', which is then reiterated by the people. The idea of the soul now setting out on its journey to God is clearly echoed in the antiphon: 'May the Angels lead you into paradise, and Martyrs welcome you as you draw near and lead you into Jerusalem, the heavenly city.' A subsequent prayer asks that Mary commend to her Son the soul of his servant who has departed this life, 'that through her maternal intercession, he may quickly reach his longed-for home in the heavenly fatherland, and live for ever and ever'.

The clearest distinctions are maintained in subsequent prayers between the soul and body, the sharpest coming in the prayer which requests that, when his body has been put to rest, his soul may rejoice in paradise. At the level of popular Catholic thought some believe that the souls of dead marriage partners are reunited after death and that the phrase 'till death us do part', used in the marriage service, applies only to the period of parting when one spouse has died and the other is still alive. Once both are dead, then parted by death no longer they are at one in the realm of paradise.

Returning from folk belief to the formal liturgy, the final prayer, one that is also reflected in innumerable Anglican churches each week though not written into any regularly used formal liturgy, runs: 'May his soul and the souls of all the faithful departed through the mercy of God rest in peace.'

What is quite evident from these funeral services is that Roman Catholic usage is perfectly happy with an explicit distinction between body and soul while the Anglicans retain this distinction implicitly through the dual language of trust for the soul and commitment for the body. Either way, the overall ritual sense is one of transcendence and the overcoming of death in words that are full of certainty and assurance.

## Judaism

Judaism is one of the most ancient religions of the world with a history extending to a thousand years before the beginning of the Christian Era. Some of its key ideas have deeply influenced both Christianity and Islam. As might be expected from such a period of time, the beliefs of this faith have emerged and developed with time. So when approaching the issue of death rites and beliefs we can expect a picture of variety and change rather than any single and specific belief.

Though there are indications of some belief in a shadowy post-mortem existence in the earlier Hebrew biblical texts, a firmer belief in an afterlife does not take shape until the time of the Maccabees in the second century BC. That period, of strife and self-sacrifice in war, was one which placed a premium on a future life which followed after martyrdom in this world. By the time of Jesus there was a distinction between the Pharisees, who did believe in a life in a world to come, and the Sadducees, who did not. The means of the future life was one of dispute. The Jewish text the Wisdom of Solomon, probably written in the first century of the Christian Era, places the 'souls of the righteous in the hands of God' where no torment can touch them (Wisdom 3:1). Similarly in the work of the Jewish scholar Philo of Alexandria, who lived at approximately the same time as Jesus, a great emphasis is placed upon the immortality of the soul.

In the Talmud, a Jewish theological resource produced from approximately the fifth century of the Christian Era, the major emphasis lies on the resurrection of the body and not upon an immortal soul. In his study of these doctrinal developments, Louis Jacobs argues that Jews did not, in any systematic way, develop beliefs about life after death until the Middle Ages. Then, he argues, 'among medieval Jewish philosophers the doctrine of the resurrection was never abandoned but the emphasis was undoubtedly on the immortality of the soul' (1992: 97).

Jacobs goes on to discuss various modern Jewish attitudes to life after death. He shows, for example, how the Reform Movement in the nineteenth century 'did give up the belief in the resurrection of the dead', even removing references to the resurrection from their prayer books, stressing instead the idea of the immortality of the soul (1992: 102). Still, other more conservative Jews do believe in the resurrection of the body. This variation is reflected, to some extent, in the fact that in urban Britain the great majority of traditional Jews continue to practise burial while only relatively few adopt cremation. The varied nature of the Jewish approach to death, and especially in terms of the mixed belief in resurrection and immortality of the soul, should alert Christian authors to the often mistaken assertion that the Hebrew view of death focuses on the resurrection of a unified body while the Greek conception lies squarely on the immortality of the soul. It is quite clear that no such clear-cut distinction is possible.

In terms of burial practice Jews, especially those in Israel, prefer to bury the body on the same day as the death. The general emphasis is upon simplicity and speed, with the body washed, dressed in white and buried directly in the soil without a coffin. The earth is believed to have a purifying effect upon the corpse which, otherwise, is potentially polluting in a ritual sense of pollution. The actual funeral customs can vary to a marked extent not just between more traditional and more modern Jews but also between those who adhere to religious beliefs and those who are secular.

The Jewish anthropologist Henry Abramovitch has given an interesting account of some of these variations along with his study of a *hevra kadisha*, the Jewish name for a burial society or group of individuals who perform the funerary rites for the dead (1986). He tells how the body is ritually washed by immersion in a ritual bath, how the eldest son places soil over the eyes before the corpse is wrapped in a white sheet. The eldest son recites the *kadish* prayer of praise to God and people make a tear in their clothes. In some traditions male lineal descendants of the dead were not allowed to attend the interment because of a belief, originating in the medieval mystical tradition of the cabbalah, that if they followed the corpse they would encourage the presence of strange, demonic-like half-souls, which had been created from any wasted semen of their dead father (1986: 128).

One way around this belief is for the bereaved to precede rather than follow the corpse. Some other cabbalistic traditions encourage circular dances to be performed around the corpse, but these are not common elsewhere. After the corpse is placed in the ground the mourners pass between rows of friends who encourage and support them. Small stones are placed on the grave after burial and on subsequent visits. To some orthodox Jews such stones are preferable to flowers since stones are symbols of permanence while flowers are so, obviously, ephemeral. After the funeral at the grave people return home to begin the period of *shiva*, or seven days of mourning. They sit on low seats and wear torn clothing and the men do not shave. Memorial candles are kept burning, prayers are said and neighbours come to comfort the bereaved. A 30-day period of lesser mourning follows while some prayers are said by the son for eleven months after the death of the parent (Unterman, 1994: 134).

Secular Jews may also be much more involved as active rather than passive agents in the funeral process and may speak eulogistic words and not merely recite *kadish*. What is clear from several accounts of death in Judaism is that the religion's main focus is on life rather than death and on doctrines of death. Where the belief in an afterlife exists the death rites are believed to aid the progress of the soul to its rest and peace in God, while for secular Jews the emphasis falls upon the memory of the dead and the comfort of the survivors. What is instructive in this case is that, whether or not belief in an afterlife is important, the use of powerful words about the deceased remains important as part of the treatment of death by the survivors.

## Islam

Islamic belief in the resurrection of the body is very firmly established to the point that the practice of cremation is firmly opposed. Allah it is who creates people from clay, who sustains them, causes them to die and finally calls them from their graves. Before death it is good for the dying Muslim to be in the company of those who can recite the *shahada*, the utterance of faith that there is no God but God and that Muhammad is His Prophet. In this way Muslims leave the world as they entered it, accompanied by texts proclaiming the reality of God and His revelation (Bennett, 1994: 107). At death the body is washed by people of the same sex, is dressed in white and carried for prayer at the mosque prior to interment. The prayers are focused on the holiness and greatness of God with requests that God have mercy on the deceased as upon Abraham and his descendants.

One prayer shows very clearly how the Islamic rhetoric of death sets the single individual firmly into the total community of Islam, past and present. 'O God, forgive our living ones and our deceased ones, and those of us who are present and those who are absent, and our young ones and our old ones, and our males and our females. O God, those of us whom Thou grantest life keep them firm on Islam, and those of us whom Thou causest to die, cause them to die in the faith. Deprive us not, O God, of the benefits relating to the deceased and subject us not to trial after him' (Chaudhri, 1983: 60).

Other more private prayers are made for the individual who has died. At the burial various texts may be used including the Quranic verse 'from the earth we did create you and into it you shall return, and from it we shall bring you out again' (20:55). What is so obvious in this pattern of ritual is the deep influence of the scriptural texts of Islam over the prayers and actions with the emphasis lying on God and the divine action rather than upon the accomplishments of the individual. As far as humanity is concerned the focus falls on a people under God rather than upon the individual who now passes into an interim state, usually interpreted as sleep, prior to the afterlife of paradise or hell (Bennett, 1994: 110).

Local variation in practice is great in a religion such as Islam which has penetrated so many cultural worlds, especially in the Middle East and Southeast Asia. In Java, for example, the dead person is washed while being held on the laps of relatives; all get wet. It is as though the corpse is a baby again and is receiving loving attention. It is an act of strong will described as requiring the relatives to be *tegel*, 'resolved to do something odious, abominable and horrible without flinching ... despite inward fear and revulsion' (Geertz, 1960: 69). Geertz describes how the Islamic religious leader jumps into the grave to address the corpse on how it should respond to the two visiting angels who, by Islamic tradition, visit the deceased shortly after the burial and interrogate them as to their faith and witness to the Prophet. These informative words demonstrate that death is not the end but that much is to follow. Similarly, Geertz describes the Javanese Islamic response to death as one not grounded in hysteria, sobbing or expressions of grief but a 'calm, languid letting go, a brief ritualized relinquishment of a relationship no longer possible' (1960: 72). This he describes in terms of the indigenous concept of *Iklas*, or 'willed affectlessness'. Here the overall rhetoric of death is set within the goal of an attitude of life which is sought as a general outlook, one in which an afterlife is given an important place.

One important contribution Geertz makes to the discussion of afterlife beliefs lies in his description of the fact that 'three separate notions of life after death' are 'often held concurrently by the same individual'. One is Islamic, the idea of death, resurrection and reward or punishment in heaven, another involves simple extinction at death and the third embraces the notion of reincarnation (1960: 75). The popular ideas of reincarnation are often held to involve rebirth into the same family. This complexity of mixed beliefs is, perhaps, more widespread in many religions than systematic and official religion realizes or acknowledges. Certainly it presents a picture in which the individual may choose a perspective which answers to particular needs; in this sense local religion furnishes an extensive pool of potential orientations to overcome the idea of death in a variety of ways.

## The books and words

Judaism, Christianity and Islam all represent religions of the book. This foundational source derives its power, very largely, from the belief that the sacred text was God-given and comprises divine revelation. The growth of traditions of biblical study, exegesis and preaching along with formal liturgies all gave to such words a power which enhanced humanity's commitment to language as its very partner in self-consciousness (Goody, 1977: 112ff.; 1986: 1ff.). Here the great traditions of official theologies often influence rituals which may become extremely durable and permeate the cultures of many societies. That very durability provides local communities with religious formulae which they may make their own through local practice and, as it were, the accent of their own world view. The words which ensue become all the more powerful as a rhetoric of death, and against death, for they are very words of an ongoing and living community. In the case of Christianity and Islam, in particular, they are also words of communities which see themselves as expansionist and capable of transforming human nature and commitment into a higher order of service and submission to God. As such they well express Maurice Bloch's idea of a rebounding conquest. It is the very human nature which has, symbolically, died to itself in order to be submitted to God which now dies, physically, so that it may be resurrected to a new reality with God.

# 9 Ancient and Local Traditions

Since every human society possesses some form of death ritual there is, obviously, no end to the examples which could be documented when thinking of the indigenous and ethnic groups of the world at large. The cases described below have been selected primarily to demonstrate the way ritual influences the changing status of the dead while also indicating the variety of human action taken against death. Some reflect local variants drawn from contemporary world religions while others express indigenous beliefs of a locally more ethnic kind. Most focus on contemporary practices but the inclusion of the ancient traditions of the Egyptians and of the Chinchorro of Chile provide a more historical perspective to funerary rites, and it is with these that we begin. These examples were chosen to contrast cases where the dead are cherished and others where they are hated. Each could be explored in much greater depth to show how the language associated with bereavement and the funerary rites expressed these attitudes. 'Words against death' are often expressed as words for and against the dead and, in an evaluative sense, it is important to see that each society varies in the way it has come to terms with mortality. Local circumstances and style of life obviously influence this to a great degree so that, for example, the geographically static Egyptians cannot be expected to deal with death as did the nomadic Gypsies.

## Mummies east and west

One of the most dramatic forms of dealing with death and, in one sense conquering it, lies in mummification when the body is preserved from its ultimate decay. Although this practice is usually associated with the ancient Egyptians, one of the earliest cases known comes from the Chinchorro people of ancient Chile who were preserving their dead from as early as 5000 BC.

### The Chinchorro of Chile

The Chinchorro lived in settlements on a fertile coastal strip between the Pacific Ocean and the Atacama Desert from about 7000 BC. Their material needs were easily satisfied by this area and it seems that they invested a considerable amount of time and effort in preserving their dead, most especially their children and even foetuses. This is an interesting fact since children are often found to receive minimal funerary attention in a majority of cultures. The Chinchorro may have derived the idea of artificial mummification from the natural mummification which occurs in the Atacama Desert conditions, but other more social factors, which lie beyond our access, would have been present. Of the 282 mummies known, 47 per cent were naturally and 53 per cent artificially mummified (Arriaza, 1995: 97). The mummies which Bernado Arriaza has classified as 'black mummies' were subjected to complex processes in which the body was skinned, practically taken apart, the flesh removed, the bones dried and then the whole put together again having been reinforced by sticks, twine, reeds and paste. Even facial skin seems to have been replaced on the filled-out skull after the brain had been removed. A scalp of hair was also placed on the mummy along with some sealion skin before the whole body was painted with a black manganese paint. Arriaza describes some of these mummies as complex works of art, more like an image or statue of death than as a simple body (1995: 106). Other, red, mummies were less complexly treated before being painted with an iron oxide paint. The mud-coated mummies were not eviscerated but, unlike the other mummies, they seem to have been cemented to the floor of their graves.

The Chinchorro had no written language so that, unlike the Egyptians who started mummifying some 2000 years later, we have no means of interpreting the significance of their mummification. The fact that food and some fishing materials were buried with mummies might indicate a sense of a future world where such things would be of use. Much later practices of mummification in the Andes led to the mummies being honoured, as amongst the Incas who dressed and fed their mummified rulers and carried them in processions, suggesting they still played a part in ongoing social life. In the absence of texts much belongs to speculation but Arriaza, whose work is very significant in this field, is happy to suggest that speaking 'symbolically, without artificial mummification their society would die ... Metaphorically, preserved ancestors can be equated with a dry fish in a maritime society' having the power to nourish others, albeit in a spiritual sense (1995: 140). This speculation reinforces the fact that without information we can say nothing about 'words against death' in this case but it is extremely unlikely that all this ritual of mummification and burial took place in silence or that it did not address itself to the fact of death. The fact that the Chinchorro lived in small groups and that the facial individuality of the dead seems to have been retained after mummification suggest that death was a personal issue as well as one which triggered a social response.

## Egyptian mummies

To travel from pre-literate Chile to literate Egypt involves a significant step in time and space but a smaller step as far as the treatment of the dead was concerned. Both practised mummification even though the ancient Egyptians did not begin the practice of seeking to preserve bodies by chemical means until approximately 2500 BC. The process reached its peak about 1000 BC yet continued in a lesser form until about the seventh century AD in the early Coptic, or Egyptian Christian, period.

This chemical base is reflected both in the word 'embalming', referring to the Latin phrase *in balsamum* or being placed in various aromatic oils, and in the word 'mummification' which is probably derived from the Arabic word for bitumen, *mumiya*, the black liquid in which corpses were sometimes soaked (Hamilton-Paterson and Andrews, 1978: 36). Another substance called natron, a mixture of sodium salts, was packed around the corpse and helped draw off its moisture. For the more extensive form of mummification the brain was removed, through the nose, while the internal organs were taken from the abdomen and chest, though the heart and kidneys were often left in place. These organs were themselves chemically treated and placed in special jars called canopic jars. They formed sets with specific organs being placed in separate jars within a distinctive chest, and with the four sons of the falcon god Horus sometimes represented on the lids of these jars. These baboon-, human-, hawk- and jackal-headed individuals guarded the lungs, liver, intestines and stomach respectively (Hamilton-Paterson and Andrews, 1978: 91).

The corpse was finally carefully wrapped in bandages and placed in a case. All of these stages were associated with religious rituals which had the overall purpose of securing the body and the departed soul or life forces of the deceased for a future existence after death. Special groups of embalmers and priests collaborated in preventing the physical body and the more intangible spirit from being lost forever. Though the actual process of mummification probably took around 40 days, the total ritual period lasted some 70 days. This closely reflects the Old Testament account of the mummification of Jacob in the Book of Genesis (50:2, 3) which is explicitly said to have taken 40 days within an overall funerary period of 70 days. Joseph, like his father Jacob, was also embalmed and mummified 'and placed in a coffin in Egypt' (Gen 50:26). It is interesting that the first book of the Bible should end with an account of two great figures in the history of Israel being embalmed and mummified.

The Egyptian practice was, as we have already mentioned, related to a system of religious beliefs concerning life after death. The life of a person was reckoned to be made up not just of the physical body but of three additional features. Firstly the *Ka*, which was the life force which left the body and came to have an existence of its own at death, when it was thought to exist both in connection with the mummy and in a special chapel, often at ground level, where it could be sustained with food offerings. Secondly, the *Ba* was a kind of manifestation of the dead as a combination of the *Ka* plus the dead body. It could take the form of a bird with a human face but needed to return to the tomb at night. The third dimension of the spirit was that of the *Akh* which introduces a rather complicated idea into the Egyptian answer to death. The *Akh* was part of the individual which had its existence amongst the stars, far removed from earthly involvement; in this sense it reflected a distant part of eternity. Between the three elements of *Ka*, *Ba* and *Akh*, the dead Egyptian possessed a set of different spheres of post-mortem existence. The first two related to the former way of life while the latter was far more transcendent, with all three together providing a broad working set of beliefs which could help explain the dead as nearer and as more distant post-mortem beings.

The most famous popular aspect of Egyptian funerary rites, apart from mummification, concerns the pyramid structures built over burial chambers of the embalmed dead, notably of the rich and of royal houses in Egypt. These pyramids were a form of architectural protection of the rich dead, including the special grave presents and gifts for the dead to assist them in the next life. Many features were built into these elaborate tombs to prevent access by robbers (Spencer, 1982: 74ff.). There were, obviously, other kinds of tombs in Egypt which were not capped in a pyramid, but the pyramid form stands out in symbolic assertion of the human will to express the hope and belief that life continues after death. The tomb art depicted the religious beliefs of the Egyptians and constitutes a ritually impressive set of what we might describe as 'art against death'. In pictorial form it displayed the powerful myths and invocations used by the priests in the various stages of embalming and constitute a fine example of 'words against death'.

In Egypt these beliefs about life after death went hand in hand with a myth about the gods, especially Osiris, which helped integrate the destiny of the pharaoh with the destinies of ordinary Egyptians and showed how human beings wrestle with the fact of life and death and the hope of transcending the despair of mortality. Less well known than mummies or pyramids are the extensive funerary texts which described the relationships between the dead and the deities and probably were recited during the process of embalming and entombing the deceased. These funerary texts are represented, for example, in what has come to be called *The Egyptian Book of the Dead*. They have been described as 'of great importance ... in the belief that their recital would secure for the dead an unhindered passage to God in the next world, would enable him to overcome the opposition of ghostly foes, would endow his body in the tomb with power to resist corruption and would ensure him a new life in a glorified body in heaven' (Wallis Budge, 1967: xi). This Egyptian case brings together a series of oppositions to death, not only the hieroglyphic texts but also the process of embalming and the architectural realism of the pyramids and other tombs. Here 'words against death' are set very firmly in writing, in stone, and upon the physical bodies of the dead. In fact a great deal of cultural energy was devoted to this endeavour.

From ancient worlds we turn to the practices of two contemporary groups which, in some respects, are the symbolical opposites of each other. In both cases we rely on anthropological accounts of the societies concerned, first the Merina of Madagascar where the dead continue in a state between the living and the ancestors, and second, the Gypsies who seek a firm divide between the living and the dead.

## Madagascan death rites

The example of the Merina from Madagascar shows how the dead are transformed into ancestors with whom the living are bound in an ongoing community of periodic contact. Maurice Bloch provides an extremely full account of these death rites, which are very briefly sketched here (1971). After death the body may be buried in a temporary earth grave and, at some later date, be transferred to the tomb of the group to which the dead person belonged and which he had helped to maintain during life through financial payments. These ancestral tombs were very elaborate structures, part of which lay under and part above ground. At particular times these tombs had the soil dug out from a descending staircase and the locked door was opened to allow the living relatives to gain access to a chamber with shelves on which were laid the wrapped-up bodily remains of the family's dead. These would be taken out of the tomb, rewrapped in new bindings and used in a kind of dance. In this dance the bodies, which by now might be no more than skeletons, might be thrown in the air and even fall on the floor. They were, as it were, 'crushed by the process of reburial in order to become an impersonal descent amalgam' (Bloch, 1989: 170). Afterwards they were returned to the tomb along with any bodies of the relatively recently dead who had been brought to the ancestral land and its tomb from other parts of the island. This ancestral territory is very important to the Merina, symbolizing their own focus of identity which is all the more important when they live and work away from that location. In the most direct of ways, these people return to their ancestral grave when they die, for as their body decays and is moved from the top shelves to the bottom shelves of the tomb, they return again to the dust and earth of that territory.

## Gypsy death rites

In a stark contrast with Gypsies' traditionally nomadic way of life, the dead Gypsy comes to a fixed halt in the grave. This marks a strange change, for the grave is the opposite of the moving caravan; it is much more like the fixed house of the non-Gypsy. Okely (1983) interprets Gypsy death rites by arguing that, in death, the Gypsy comes to be like a non-Gypsy, involving a kind of symbolic turn-around reflected in the way the corpse is dressed in clothes turned inside out. At death, Gypsy identity is, similarly, turned inside out. And this is quite the opposite of the Madagascan case where the dead body becomes more intimately connected with the home ground in death than ever it was in life. In death the migrant Madagascan comes home to the ancestral territory and to their true identity in which the dead come to be one with the very soil of the land of their kinsfolk; death integrates the kinship group.

By sharp contrast the British Gypsy attitudes to death and burial are very negative and there is a major division between the living and the dead. Gypsies often classify the world into things that are ritually positive and things that are, in a symbolic sense, unclean. Death and funerals belong to this category of unclean, or of ritually impure things. They prefer death to take place in hospitals belonging to non-Gypsies, whom they call Gorgios, in the belief that the ritual impurity of death may be carried by the Gorgios. This mirrors the Gypsy attitude to birth, which they also regard as a ritually impure process and prefer to take place in hospital. The dead body is dressed in clothes that are turned inside out and taken on its last journey to a church where, after a Christian funeral service, it is buried. Family members engage in dramatic public expressions of grief depending on their degree of kinship relationship to the deceased person. The closer the relationship to the dead the more dramatic is the performance. Ultimately a headstone is placed above the grave.

In the USA Gypsies, who largely immigrated after 1865, hold funerals involving considerable expense of a conspicuous kind. Even so the English Rom Gypsies still only utilize 'relatively modest' gravestones which 'blend inconspicuously with' those of middle-class Americans (Erwin, 1993). This would reflect Okely's interpretation of British Gypsy death rites which, she thinks, reflect a process in which a group distances itself from the dead who have lost their Gypsy identity and become more like Gorgio outsiders. This belief offers a stark example of the living defining the dead as belonging to quite a different domain from the living in terms of kinship relation and the ethos of communal life. The living do not wish to have contact with the dead and seek to make the grave a place the dead remain in, hence the traditional custom of burning and destroying the belongings of the dead. This is matched by the Gypsy dislike of ghosts and of the continuing identity of the dead as entities which may wish to continue relationships with the living.

What is interesting in terms of the formal funerary rite is the fact that a mainstream church is chosen for the service: in England the Church of England and in the USA usually Roman Catholic churches or even Greek Orthodox (Trigg, 1975: 198ff.). This suggests that the official 'words against death' are, therefore, drawn from beyond the Gypsy community and reinforce the wish of the living to have the dead firmly kept in their place and at a distance.

## The Americas

In the history of religions much attention has been paid to literary traditions describing death and processes of consciousness believed to be associated with the soul after death. We have already considered this above for *The Egyptian Book of the Dead* and in Chapter 6 for *The Tibetan Book of the Dead*, but it is also the case that many oral traditions have addressed themselves to similar issues through the myth and belief systems fostered in the local cultures of the world.

### Native North Americans

Often ultimate destiny is seen to depend upon human endeavour and ethical striving. One example, from the Winnebago, traditional Native North Americans, describes a path through various hazards which the individual must traverse after death. The dead encounter a steep ravine which the individual feels he could not possibly pass. It is then that they remember the advice of the ancestors to 'plunge right through'. Similarly when meeting an apparently impassable barrier of sticks, when being covered with evil and foul smelling phlegm, and when seeing the earth all afire they know they must 'plunge right through'. Finally they are given sacred and sustaining food and reach the realm of ancestors who meet and welcome them (Beck and Walters, 1977: 206ff.).

The idea of the soul plays a major part in many Native American traditions and is often associated with belief in two souls, one being closely associated with bodily movement and the other with dreams. This latter dream or free soul ultimately becomes caught up in the world of the dead which leads to the bodily soul leaving soon after, causing physical death (Hultkrantz, 1979: 131). The extensive tradition of Navajo mythology set the dynamic power of life and its absence in death within the overall theory of 'holy winds'. Such winds come to the growing foetus to give it life and to cause it to flourish, while at the end of earthly existence, these vivifying winds are withdrawn from the human body leaving it to die (McNeley, 1981: 56). Similarly, Cheyenne tradition saw death as resulting from the soul, *tasoom*, leaving the body and travelling on to its destiny, either with the Great Wise One or, for those few who had committed suicide, to extinction as they took the negative path from a fork in the Milky Way (Hoebel, 1978: 92). At death the Cheyenne rapidly set about their funeral rites, which included binding the full-length body in cloth and placing it either in a tree or else on a platform above the earth, though it could also be covered with rocks. A dead man's horse was shot and left at his grave site, and a dead woman's cooking utensils at hers. The speed of the procedure was said to be because the deceased could not set out on the all-important journey to the next world until the funeral rites were completed. The practice of placing the dead on platforms or in trees, sometimes prior to interment, or above ground in cairns was a widespread practice in North America, though some tribes did bury and a few did cremate, especially on the west coast (Hultkrantz, 1979: 138).

The idea of the dead taking a journey until they come to a division of the ways, whether to bliss or terror, is extremely widespread in human history and is an interesting use of this-worldly human experience, that of travelling, as a model for viewing human destiny in the other world lying beyond death. Some have argued that these 'two paths' reflect human ideals to an even greater extent as when, for example, the Nordic myths of a warrior culture speak of the victorious dead passing the way of God into Valhalla while those dying of disease or old age pass along the Hel-way to the abode of the negatively viewed goddess Hel (Lincoln, 1991: 120).

Some scholars see this idea of the death journey of the soul as mirroring the very widespread practice of shamanism, of individuals who believe they have the spiritual power to undergo journeys to the realms of the gods to gain some benefit for members of their society (Hultkrantz, 1979: 133). The difference between the shaman and the ordinary person is that the shaman is able to come and go between these realms at will, as others cannot. Shamans often use a symbolic sacred tree as part of their journey to the other world; it forms the linking point as the *axis mundi* and was sometimes set up as such in the centre of ritual grounds or in the ceremonial lodge, and prayers to the spirits of the dead could be offered at this pole.

In some groups, both traditional and more recent Christian rites were combined or complemented each other, as with the Kwakiutl of British Columbia, whose Christian burial rites might be conducted before or after more traditional rites, including the famed potlatch rituals involving dances and gift-giving to guests. (Potlatch rites involved the destruction of valuable goods alongside the bestowal of costly presents upon specially invited guests of high social status. These, in turn, were expected to hold even more impressive potlatches in the future when higher-value goods would be destroyed and given as return-gifts in acts of conspicuous consumption.) On such a potlatch occasion a son might, for example, not only dance in memory of his deceased father but might also be given special names that once belonged to his father (Rohner and Rohner, 1970: 54). This shows how shifts in identity which affect both the dead and their living survivors may be marked through funerary rites.

## South America and Mexico

Not all funerals take a grand form, nor do they even require the services of religious experts. Much often depends upon circumstance and the status of the one who has died. The anthropologist Peter Rivière (1972) has described funeral rites in the cattle-ranching culture of Roraima in north Brazil. There the deceased are usually buried on the same day as they die. One interesting aspect of one funeral Rivière described shows how ordinary people sometimes have to make decisions about ritual as the very ritual is going on. This is a worthwhile counterbalance to the idea which is so easily formed in urban societies well served by professional ritual specialists that ritual is a well established set of practices. Rivière tells how, in the funeral of a young child, not only is there some discussion as to how deep the grave should be, but also a pause in the ceremony and several changes in direction before deciding which way the coffin should face (1972: 80). The rite was conducted without any priest but, at the annual Feast of All Souls on 2 November, a special Mass was said by a priest in the cemetery, special candles would be lit and prayers said for this individual as well as for others who had died over the year. This particular ceremony, known as *Dia de Finados*, or the Day of the Dead, is widespread in Catholic cultures and is sometimes associated with much festivity and joy. It is one of the rites in which life is asserted over and against death.

## Day of the Dead

One of the most extensive set of festivities focused on the Day of the Dead takes place in Mexico, mainly on the first two days of November, the days of the church feasts of All Saints' and All Souls' Days. These church feasts can extend from 18 October until 30 November, both representing the feast days of St Luke and St Andrew. Different days in this period are used to welcome particular categories of the dead, whether children or adult (Carmichael and Sayer, 1991: 16). Families clean and prepare graves, repainting and decorating them with flowers and lighting candles on them and also building elaborate offerings for the dead within each home. The dead are even said to be nourished by the food and drink offerings made for them. Many pictures, paintings, collages and statues are constructed, bought and sold and used as caricatures of death. Skeletons and corpses are depicted in a great variety of ways, many of them comic. Here death as a universal fate of people is combined with the particular loss of each individual family, the joys and sorrows of existence are brought into close proximity with each other. The general festivity parallels the Requiem Masses which are also held in a statement of the positive nature of life despite death, albeit in a much more solemn form. Here too the theme of transcendence and conquest becomes evident: life is worth living despite the fact of death and it is accomplished both at the domestic social level and at the ecclesiastical level of social life.

## Africa

African death rites obviously embrace thousands of local examples, many dealing with the shift in status of the dead into some category of ancestor. Here one major case is used to illustrate the power of words in funerary rites and to show how personal identity is deeply influenced by death. It is drawn from Evans-Pritchard's classic ethnography of the Nuer of the Sudan (1956).

The Nuer do not possess a cult of the dead – graves are unmarked and relatively quickly forgotten. As Evans-Pritchard expresses it: 'a man's memorial is not in some monument but in his sons' (1956: 162). In other words, the perpetuation of identity lies in a this-worldly dimension and not in some other-worldly sphere. But this is not simply a metaphorical statement; it also takes a formal shape through rules of kinship. Widows are not remarried, nor are they inherited by someone else, rather they continue to produce and raise children to the name of their dead husband, with their husband's brothers serving as the biological fathers. Even if she bears children to some other man they still carry the name of her dead partner. If a man dies without leaving a wife and without any surviving children it is the duty of his living kin to marry a wife in his name and raise a child to the name of the deceased relative so that the dead man may always have a name within the ongoing lineage. As Evans-Pritchard expresses it, the Nuer 'are not interested in the survival of the individual as a ghost, but in the survival of the social personality in the name' (1956: 163). Accordingly mortuary rituals do not speak of the end of a person's identity but of its continuation in the lineage. In other words it is the lineage and the presence of the deceased's name within it, not least on occasions when a list of lineage members is recited on formal occasions, which assumes significance. Here again the power of formal words is important in the face of physical death.

Another example from the Nuer will reinforce the significance of the precise social status of the deceased in relation to the death rites performed. The case concerns twins, for amongst the Nuer twins were traditionally spoken of as being 'one person', as possessing a single identity despite the fact they were two separate individuals. Twins were also said to be 'birds', a symbolic statement associated with the idea that twins were a special manifestation of supernatural power; they belonged to the realm 'of the above', of 'spirit' or of God in a special sense. Accordingly no formal funerary rites were performed for twins when they died, not even when the second and surviving twin died. When infant twins died, as they often did, the body would be placed in a reed basket in the fork of a tree in a symbolic expression of their identity as 'birds'. When an adult twin died it was not placed in a tree but nor was it buried in the same way as ordinary Nuer. Instead a grave was dug in which a platform was erected on which the body was placed and covered with a hide before the grave was filled in with earth. In this sense the adult twin maintained an identity as distinct from other Nuer right into the grave, forever remaining 'of the above' even when placed beneath the earth. Twins are ever 'children of God' and are simply not subject to the world 'of the below' as are other people.

A neighbouring tribe of the Nuer are the Dinka, and in turning to them we observe another symbolic form of conquering death, one which evokes the idea of self-sacrifice. This form of death rite expresses very clearly the idea of what we have called in this book death-transcendence. This rite focused on the death of the master of the fishing spear, an individual who occupied a deeply important place in Dinka society, as already mentioned in Chapter 5. The essence of this death is that the ritual specialist, in a sense, controlled his own death in deciding when to die. He chose death rather than have life wrenched from him; he remained in control and in that sense attained transcendence over death. When he was ill or sick and decided that the time for his death was drawing near, he asked to be buried. A grave was made for him and he was placed in it on a kind of bed with a covering platform. After speaking words of blessing and strength to his family his grave was filled in with earth. In one sense this was an example of being buried alive; in another it is a voluntary sacrifice, a giving of life and not a case of having one's life forcefully taken away.

One distinctive feature of this case lies in the verbal aspect of the whole proceeding and the way the words of blessing, which come from the one who is to die, reflect the significance accorded to words and the power of words found in the invocations made at Dinka animal sacrifices. Lienhardt (1961) argues in a most persuasive way that the verbal invocation of the one conducting the sacrifice of an ox increases in significance as the animal vitality of the beast is overwhelmed. In symbolic terms language reflects the realm of culture and of human existence while the life force of the sacrifice expresses the animal level of existence. In animal sacrifice the power of words triumphs over the cessation of the life force of the one beast that dies. In a similar sense one might argue that the words of the master of the fishing spear as he literally lay upon his death bed demonstrated the ongoing dominance of words and the realm of culture rather than the dominance of the death of individual bodies. This pattern of death reflects the death of the Aghoris of Benares described in Chapter 6. Just as they were reckoned not to die but to end their human life in a state of final meditation and were buried accordingly, so in a symbolic sense the master of the fishing spear is buried at his own command.

Among the Lugbara of Uganda there is an extensive cult of the dead in which ancestors and ghosts receive extensive ritual attention but not to prepare them for some heavenly realm. In fact they did not possess any traditional beliefs about any sort of heaven or hell, reward or punishment after life; rather the concern reflected the ongoing life of the lineage (Middleton, 1960: 28ff.). God is said to be responsible for all deaths even though the more immediate cause is thought to be a sorcerer. The dead were buried and, like the Nuer, their graves were soon forgotten, except in the case of senior men and women over whose graves trees might be planted which would carry their names. The dead are considered to possess *orindi*, a kind of soul, and may even be heard at night, but these souls are insignificant as far as the living are concerned.

In terms of the 'words against death' theme of this book is concerned, it is important to know that highly prized formal speeches are employed by the Lugbara in connection both with illness and death. These speeches are powerful not only in expressing human sincerity but also in helping to reconstitute the lineage of the sick or dead person. Middleton's very full account of the composition of Lugbara identity, composed of various life forces and supernatural elements, provides material enabling us to draw a very interesting difference between a society of this type and, for example, that of Tibetan Buddhist culture.

A dying Lugbara is likely to 'be aware of the cleavages within the lineage' and his last words are likely to seek to cause the least permanent harm to the kinship structure of his people (Middleton, 1960: 199). In fact funerals are times when arguments may break out and lineages undergo some realignment. It is a period in which the dead person's status is changed from that of a living to that of a dead kinsman. In other words, while the Tibetan arena of death focuses on the individual consciousness of the dying person, with maximum ritual effort directed to fostering full mindfulness as part of the ritual journey of the departing life-force, the Lugbara environment is this-world focused. The lineage as the prime concern of life replaces private consciousness. In general terms we might say that in the one case salvation is social order while in the other it is consciousness.

## Philippines: killing grief

In the quite different world of the tribal Ilongot of the Philippines, 'salvation' lay more in the realm of gaining a degree of psychological balance and inner calm after bereavement. At least one way of achieving this would probably surprise members of many other cultures because it involved killing another person. This case of the Ilongot people, documented by the anthropologist Michelle Rosaldo, offers an example not only of the way in which song and formal speaking serve to create certain moods (1980: 32) but also furnishes one of the most distinctive examples of coping with grief.

The Ilongot, in their pre-Christian days before the 1970s, were head-hunters. They believed that the death of a relative made one's heart 'heavy and distraught' and that through killing and the taking of a head of an enemy, the men, at least, were able to 'cast off the weight of grief and pain' (1980: 157). This aspect of the process of grief and mourning shows just how variable human death rites, in the broadest sense, can be. After the 1960s many Ilongot were converted to a more fundamentalist form of

Christianity and one of the reasons advanced for conversion lay in the fact that head-hunting was, politically, less possible and the grief of bereavement led them to this religion which was also said to be able to calm the grief-stricken heart. Ironically Renato Rosaldo (1984) has discussed his own sense of rage in grief which he interpreted through the Ilongot view of life, a scheme which Epstein has interpreted as redirected aggression (1992: 187).

## Melanesian sea burial

For peoples living on relatively small islands and for whom the sea is an integral part of life, the practice of sea burial was traditionally quite common, as in numerous of the Melanesian islands. Here the status of the deceased often influenced the pattern of disposal. The bodies of people with relatively little status might simply be cast into the sea while those with greater status are given a longer period of mourning before being placed in the water. Certain chiefs or individuals much esteemed by their family might be held back from a water burial and kept in the home encased in wooden or other containers. Many myths are associated with death and the journey the soul takes afterwards. Ghosts are often deemed dangerous and powerful and, in symbolic terms, seem to represent the status of the dead person located between the living and the ancestral planes. It is said, for example, that the ghost is weak while the body is rotting but when the smell has ceased the ghost is strong because then it is no longer a man (Codrington, 1891: 260). Even in some cases of water burial, the bones were periodically removed from established sites and piled up on the land. Parts of the body, often of the skull, were retained as memorials of the deceased and were regarded as possessing a kind of positive power of advantage to the living. This, in its own way, is an example of death not ultimately conquering humanity but of conferring a degree of benefit upon the ongoing kin group.

## Myths of death

Though relatively little attention is paid in this book to mythical explanations of death given in human societies, it is worth mentioning the fact that it is relatively common in Melanesian myths, as in those from most parts of the world, to say that mankind was originally eternal. Some human decision led to death entering the scene of human life. So, for example, one common Melanesian myth spoke of humanity as living forever. Periodically the old would enter water and cast off their wrinkled skin to emerge as young people once more. One day, however, one old woman emerged from the water in her youthful mode only to find that her child refused to recognize her. The mother had noticed that her old, sloughed-off skin had caught on a branch in the river and she went back and put it on again. Ever since then people have grown old and died (Codrington, 1891: 264ff.). Other myths speak of similar skin stories but all reflect the fact that death was not part of humanity's original or real condition. In this sense myths of the origin of death reinforce the rites which assert that life goes on after death, albeit in a transformed world. The myths express the power of words which are set against the force of nature which brings death to people.

In many cultures death is not perceived as a solely negative phenomenon. Often it is associated with some positive feature of life. In the myth just mentioned, the cast-off skin enabled the mother to continue a relationship with her child. In the myths of the Dogon of the African Sudan, the coming of death involved, for example, the emergence of art and human creativity (Griaule, 1965: 173). In many Christian interpretations of the 'Fall of Man' in the Book of Genesis, human disobedience results in sexual activity and the production of children which include positive features of pleasure.

Through the myths of death, society after society asserts its belief that human beings possess a depth which should not end in death (Dunne, 1965; Metzger, 1973). Once, they say, people did not die but then some error, fault or act of disobedience brought a radical change which meant that mortality sealed the fate of the human body. Even so the myth often goes on to trace a path of optimism or hope that some benefit in the restoration to life again will come to men and women. Such myths, in their entirety, furnish some of the clearest 'words against death'. They reach into modernity and even into post-modernity from the archaic past of the human animal and still excite optimism or evoke hope in new dialogues with death.

# 10 Souls and the presence of the dead

Some idea of soul or spirit seems to have played an important part in helping many different societies to express their conviction that life does not end with physical death. Previous chapters have explored the particular beliefs and rites of numerous societies to show how this broad belief in souls takes on different shades of meaning in each culture. This chapter focuses very largely, though not exclusively, on British attitudes towards the idea of souls, embracing the associated ideas of Spiritualism, reincarnation and various experiences associated with the presence of the dead as well as an introduction to the study of the soul in nineteenth-century anthropology.

## The nineteenth century

To provide a background to today's situation, we shall describe the beliefs of a century ago, for it was in the later nineteenth century that scholars began to think more systematically about popular beliefs in souls and the powers reckoned to animate nature. They began a scholarly discipline which has been reflected in the many anthropological studies drawn upon in most of our previous chapters. Theirs, too, was a period when Eastern and Western ideas began to penetrate each other as far as religious notions of self were concerned.

A key figure in the rise of the study of the anthropology of religion was Sir Edward Burnett Tylor (1832–1917). His interpretation of religion was grounded in a theory of how he believed primitives thought about the life force animating people. His was one rational gaze of nineteenth-century intellectualism which saw itself as penetrating what had, hitherto, been the protected territory of religious mystique (1958, Vol. 2: 535). To shed some light on what Tylor was doing it is worth setting him alongside his contemporary Sir Arthur Conan Doyle, best known for his imaginary detective Sherlock Holmes. In one sense the fictional Holmes was like Tylor's rational anthropologist, subjecting behaviour, no matter how apparently odd or weird, to a logical analysis. Yet unlike Tylor, Conan Doyle the man was personally dedicated to the idea of Spiritualism. While, figuratively speaking, it would be possible to describe Conan Doyle by saying that Sherlock Holmes marked the rational side of his life while Spiritualism defined another and more mysterious domain, it is probably more correct to see his interest in Spiritualism as a kind of logical investigation into the mystery of death and the destiny of individuals shared by many of his day.

### Tylor, animism and souls

Tylor, then, did much to clarify ideas about the soul and its role in beliefs about life after death. An Englishman born in 1832 and brought up as a Quaker, he felt unable to go to Oxford or Cambridge universities which until 1854 expected allegiance to Church of England principles. As a young man, financially well off but in poor health, he decided to travel and while in Cuba made a friend of a fellow Quaker at whose encouragement he engaged in some archaeological work in Mexico. This led to a growing and lifelong interest in anthropology resulting in some of the earliest books on anthropology including *Primitive Culture*, first published in 1871. It has even been suggested that the discipline of social anthropology was 'born ... in a Cuban omnibus' (Lienhardt, 1969: 87)! However, in several studies he explored many aspects of human life with an emphasis on the importance of evolution and on the fact that the human animal was always 'trying to get at the meaning of life' through the evidence of the senses and by reasoning out the significance of events (1958, Vol. 1: 22).

At the heart of this kind of primitive philosophy lay what Tylor called 'animism'. In fact he is now probably best known for this word, which became increasingly popular especially as a way of describing the religions of tribal peoples and those not classified as world religions. Tylor certainly pinpointed the issue of souls and life force, a topic others would explore at length, not least Lucien Lévy-Bruhl whose extensive volume on *The 'Soul' of the Primitive* aptly illustrated his view of the 'symbiosis of the living and the dead', with the individual not being 'wholly himself except by virtue of the ancestors who live once more in his personality' (1965: 341; cf. A. E. Crawley, 1909).

Animism is, primarily, a theory about souls, about those powers which lie at the centre not only of human life but also of other forms of life. As a theory about forces which make things happen it was a theory of causation. Tylor arrived at it by putting himself in the place of primitive man and trying to work out, from first principles, how people reasoned about life and death. Death was particularly important to him and he wanted some idea of why notions of immortality had emerged in relation to it. Tylor thought himself into the position which argued that man's body must be under the influence of some power. At night, for example, individuals go to sleep and appear virtually dead, yet while they sleep they dream and in their dreams wander far and wide visiting and meeting other people. If the body has been in one place all this time then, so the argument runs, something must have gone elsewhere and that something is the soul. Then, at death, when the body never wakes again, it must be because the soul has gone and not returned. This kind of reasoning led Tylor to argue that the soul lay at the basis of life and served as a foundation for religion which itself is the way of dealing with the soul after death.

Tylor believed he could show that this sort of argument did in fact occur amongst primitive people and he provided many examples drawn from a wide variety of travellers and missionaries. He is now often criticized for this speculative guesswork and for placing too great an emphasis upon logic and reasoning in the evolution of ideas of the soul (Evans-Pritchard, 1965: 24ff.). He thought that evolution applied to human understanding itself so that, for example, the early ideas of animism not only developed to become the basis for religion (he defined religion as 'belief in spiritual beings'), but also served as a kind of 'groundwork for the philosophy of religion' (1958, Vol. 2: 8, 10). Tylor also stressed his conviction that primitive man did not sit around all day engaged in primitive philosophy, indeed, he emphasized the importance of ritual as 'the gesture-language of theology', 'expressive and symbolic performances' through which men and women had sought to interact with supernatural beings and to influence them (1958, Vol. 2: 448).

Tylor's writing followed a rationalist stance and not one of personal religious belief. He assumed that all religion was naturally occurring with no such thing as revelation. He recognized that many still believed in deities and souls, even in British society of the late nineteenth century. While it is quite obvious that Tylor regarded belief as a form of survival of earlier attitudes, indeed he developed a whole theory of 'survivals', he was no campaigner against religion, as was for example the psychologist Sigmund Freud. For Tylor, religion had emerged through an original belief in powers and souls associated with death and with trying to make sense of the living and the dead. This primitive philosophy, misguided as it was, was a real attempt at self-understanding on the part of humanity. Anthropology could now help educated generations understand these early patterns of thought and ensure that they did not make the same mistake so that, for example, Spiritualism could not be a worthwhile path to self-understanding once it was realized that animism was an early stage of reflection that was now far superseded by anthropological knowledge.

## Spiritualism

It was precisely in a society in which the new knowledge, derived from biology and from anthropology, was making its impact and traditional religion was under serious criticism that several groups became increasingly fascinated both by the wisdom of the East and by Spiritualism in the West. As a definite movement, however, Spiritualism emerged in the USA in 1848 as a result of experiences gained by the Fox family (Nelson, 1969). Thereafter it was taken up in Europe and underwent periods of fluctuation, not least after the First World War when many who had lost their partners turned to Spiritualists for advice and comfort in trying to contact the dead. It is likely that most Spiritualist meetings attract a few recently bereaved people hoping to receive a message from their dead relative (Martin, 1970: 153).

In this sense Spiritualism is one way, albeit partial, of coping with bereavement as part of a total pattern of death rites complementing the formal ritual of the churches. Within Spiritualism the power of words is, once more, reflected in the way the medium gives a message believed to come from beyond this world. This applies not only to messages concerning death but also addresses the spiritual healing of the living. Vieda Skultans' study of Spiritualist seances in South Wales (1974) affords a clear example of the power of words spoken by mediums and believed to originate in spirits which guarantee that death is not the end of life. In this case the issue of death rites and the power to go on living are closely related; the power of the words comes from the fact that there is another world beyond the present one.

## Reincarnation

The broad theme of reincarnation extends far beyond the issue of contacting the dead and continues to be of interest because, while alien to Christian theology, it appears as a belief held by small groups of people across British society today. As Amy Simes, one of my own research students, has documented, practically all who belonged to the contemporary pagan groups she studied in the 1990s said they believed in reincarnation, a stance which seems to echo their wider empathy with wider forces of nature (1995: 372). Here reincarnation is not part of a karmic, merit-focused scheme of ethics but more a dynamic of nature and life-forces and it is likely that similar ideas motivate other Westerners who find reincarnation attractive. However, much more research needs to be done on exactly what people think and feel about reincarnation beliefs. It is very doubtful whether the idea of reincarnation plays the same role within the Western world as it did, and does, in Indian religion as a doctrine of the destiny of the dead holding a central place in the Indian religious tradition, especially of Hinduism, Buddhism, and Sikhism. Reincarnation ran counter to Christian belief in a divinely furnished salvation and also played little part in African and other cultures where the dead are believed to become ancestors with a realm of their own, but also contributing to the continuing communal life of society rather than pursuing their own individual existence after death.

In the East, the fundamental significance of reincarnation derived from ideas of merit, evil and salvation. It was because individuals did evil and were thereby unable to attain enlightenment, release or salvation, that they were required to live through many existences in order to improve their karma so as ultimately to attain the state of release or salvation. In this sense reincarnation is a negative necessity which offers positive hope for a long-term future. In the West reincarnation seems to provide a wide framework against which this one particular lifetime takes its significance. Its connotations seem to lie less with the negative ideas of evil and morality badly enacted than with a positive sense of depth for the inner life-force. Reincarnation becomes a framework for experience rather than an extended path leading to salvation.

In the nineteenth and early twentieth centuries, Eastern ideas and interest in esotericism led to a growth of concern with reincarnation amongst some Western elites. The commitment of Theosophy to reincarnation is one example; a much less well known influence is that of Freemasonry which does not make the idea a formal part of its world-view, for in many ways it is a non-dogmatic movement, but it has provided an arena within which some members have been able to speculate on reincarnation (Head and Cranston, 1967: 167). *The Tibetan Book of the Dead*, the *Bardo Thodol*, already discussed more fully in Chapter 6 had been translated into English in 1927 and was influential, not least on the much read psychologist Carl Jung. It had a rejuvenating influence in the 1960s as a 'guide to altered states of consciousness' (Chidester, 1990: 162) and continues to be regularly published and widely distributed in bookshops. The 1960s heralded a period of interest in Eastern religion in Western Europe and North America, increasing the profile of reincarnation and leading to psychological and other scientific attempts at analysing individuals reckoning to have previous existences. It is a concept that has also been seen to be of use in subsequent debates about feminism (Cranston and Williams, 1984: 296).

## Surveying afterlife beliefs

The rest of this chapter is largely concerned with British society in general rather than with esoteric groups. It presents the results of several empirical studies of beliefs in life after death insofar as they deal with reincarnation. The major source of information is that of the Rural Church Project (Davies *et al.*, 1990). It was assumed when interviewing people or when using questionnaires that the idea of reincarnation as such might not be the best to use. In fact there are grave problems employing that word because of the point we have already made as to its precise meaning. It may be that those who use the word do so by placing their own meaning upon it and certainly not using it in terms of its Indian significance. Accordingly, we decided that the expression 'coming back as something or someone else' would be more meaningful to people, and in that sense it was assumed that a popular notion of reincarnation existed.

It is worth stressing that reincarnation beliefs, as with beliefs on other topics, can be held speculatively or very firmly. This is why in my own surveys people were asked whether they agreed with a statement about 'coming back as someone or something else', or whether they were unsure, disagreed or did not know about the topic. It is also important to consider the pattern of belief actually held by people, to see how reincarnation beliefs fit in with other attitudes. Beliefs can be held, and probably usually are held, in cluster-form rather than in a systematic scheme. My use of the word 'cluster' aims to convey that various beliefs which may have no immediate logical or theological connection with each other are brought together to give the individual a working basis for life. Such beliefs, held in bundles together, may even appear contradictory if spelled out and analysed logically (D. J. Davies, 1996a: 23).

The fact that people sometimes seem to hold apparently contradictory beliefs without any sense of dissonance or conflict is worth emphasizing because logical contradiction need not necessarily worry individuals whose varied views are drawn on for different purposes and in different contexts. The profound significance of context for beliefs cannot be overemphasized, and here I agree with the anthropologist Ioan Lewis and his exploration of the theme that 'detachment of beliefs from their ambient circumstances produces gross distortion and misunderstanding' (1986: 21). In other words, if we listed the beliefs held by individuals we might well find that they form an odd collection when viewed critically, but within the context of that person's own life history and contemporary life-circumstance, they find their natural home and work well.

It is wise to underline this variability because one of the temptations and problems of statistical studies is that the sheer volume of figures can easily give the impression of an absolute or at least of a very fixed pattern of belief amongst people. People often accumulate their religious view of life under the influence of a wide variety of circumstances and not through formal religious education. This can easily lead to apparent contradictions in what people say since they may well never have sat down to organize their thoughts. An awareness of this somewhat arbitrary acquisition of religious dispositions is important for social researchers whose temptation is to over-simplify in establishing a small number of categories into which to fit the responses people make to questions.

One individual interviewed as part of the Nottinghamshire sample of the Cremation Research Project (D. J. Davies, 1990a) replied to the question of belief about an afterlife by saying that she had two solutions. On the one hand she thought that a 'soul essence' left the body, but on the other hand she thought that death was simply the end. She was not too sure about things. She 'would love to think your essence goes on', but either way she would be happy. In a final reflection she returned to the idea of the soul-essence going on after death, saying that she thought perhaps she did believe in reincarnation and that she thinks she could have been a Chinese in an earlier life. This, she explained, was because she was very keen on Oriental art and life, and hated the Japanese.

This example hints at the probability that while many people simply have no worked out system of belief concerning the afterlife they may find themselves putting some bits and pieces together when formally interviewed. There are several situations in life when people are pressed into formulating their ideas. Throughout this chapter we have underlined the fact that beliefs often exist as varied clusters of ideas in an individual's life. We have also emphasized the importance of context as drawing upon one aspect of this cluster rather than another. What should, finally, be drawn from these phases of response is the third possibility, namely that certain contexts help particular configurations of belief to emerge or to become established in people's minds. Being asked to talk about a belief, or feeling it necessary to express a belief, may cause beliefs to become explicit for a person for the first time. This is especially important in a society where religious beliefs are not often discussed in public or even in private, and is even more likely to be the case for people who do not normally attend church and for whom there is no easily available grammar of discourse, or pattern of words, to give voice to what is felt.

## Popular British views on reincarnation

Using the phrase 'coming back as something else' rather than the word reincarnation we have found some 12 per cent of the general public in rural areas of Britain claim some sort of belief in this mode of post-mortem existence (Davies, Watkins and Winter, 1991: 257), while an even more extensive study, in which 1603 persons were interviewed in their homes in urban areas, also found a 12 per cent agreement with this perspective on death (Davies and Shaw, 1995: 92).

These groups were drawn from random samples of people within a historical culture where there has been no formal support of such ideas and which, in fact, has positive reinforcement from quite a different model of afterlife in the traditional Christian attitude to death. Although it is only speculation, it may be that the term 'reincarnation' and the catch-all phrase 'come back as something else' cover much more than a single concept. For some it may be a perfectly indigenous notion resonating with the cyclical processes of apparent death and rebirth in nature while, for others, it is much more explicitly tinged by Eastern religious ideology.

Other research on this topic presents additional material which helps provide a historical background to these contemporary views. Geoffrey Gorer carried out two famous studies on aspects of religion in Britain involving surveys conducted in 1950 and 1963. In the 1950 survey less than 1 per cent mentioned reincarnation while in 1963 just over 2 per cent did so (1965: 167). These very low levels of explicit belief indicate no more than a variety of outlook that could be expected in a society where some members would inevitably be familiar with beliefs from other parts of the world.

Greatly increased familiarity with Indian beliefs took place during the 1960s and 1970s, especially in the USA, which probably helps account for reports of a Gallup Survey in the USA in 1981 which reflects a group of 23 per cent reckoning to believe in reincarnation. A more recent poll still, in Canada, registered 29 per cent (Harpur, 1991: 74). In the light of the research underlying this book these levels of belief in North America would not seem to be reflected in Britain. Care is always needed in this kind of survey work to distinguish between those who hold firm beliefs and those who are unsure or do not know. It is sometimes the case that large groups of 'uncertain' responses indicate a degree of change coming about in social attitudes.

One final piece of evidence reinforces this point because it is drawn from the study considered more extensively in Chapter 7 dealing with animal death. There we see a survey of an unrepresentative sample of the public drawn from readers of a specialist dog-owners' magazine who were self-motivated enough to complete a questionnaire published in *Dog World* in June 1992. When asked if they thought that 'people can come back as animals after death' some 14 per cent replied in the affirmative, 49 per cent in the negative, with 35 per cent not knowing and 2 per cent not answering. While the 14 per cent of those who thought this was possible resemble the 12 per cent who agreed with reincarnation in the general public survey of the Rural Church Project already discussed, what makes the pet owners distinctive is that 35 per cent of them were unsure about this compared with 20 per cent uncertainty in the Rural Church survey. This suggests more of an openness to this idea amongst the pet owners.

### The presence of the dead

If some ideas about immortality are derived from the media, popular literature or information from more distant cultures, others come much more directly from people's own experience, not least from those moments when the dead are recalled, remembered or more directly experienced.

In one interview a woman recounted a story told her by her brother. At their grandmother's funeral, while standing at the graveside during the service, he actually saw his son who had been torpedoed in 1942 during the war. He 'saw him as real as anybody else'. He subsequently became a medium and a Spiritualist and the woman interviewed has also come to be firmly convinced in life after death. Numerous other firsthand accounts have also been given of people who have seen relatives either before they die or after death. Quite often people do not know what to make of these moments and have very little formal framework of belief or experience through which to interpret what has happened. Sometimes they think they may be odd or abnormal until they tell of the event to another, who may echo a similar experience of their own.

The research of Hay and Heald in 1987 portrays 18 per cent of a general population sample reckoning to have had an awareness of the presence of the dead (Hay, 1990: 83). In my own research, we found that nearly 14 per cent spoke of an occasional experience of the dead while nearly 9 per cent said they often experienced such contact and 7 per cent had the experience only once (Davies and Shaw, 1995: 96). This means that approximately 35 per cent of this sample of the general public had gained some such sense of the presence of the dead.

One of the most interesting 'literary' cases of a dead person reckoned to have visited a living individual is that of the lay and professional theologians C. S. Lewis and J. B. Phillips. These two individuals are, probably, amongst the best known names of all twentieth-century religious writers as far as the general Christian public are concerned; C. S. Lewis for his extensive fiction and popular theology and J. B. Phillips for his one-man interpretation of the New Testament. In his book *The Ring of Truth*, J. B. Phillips suggests that many who believe in the Communion of Saints must have experienced the sense of nearness of those they love shortly after they have died, if only for a brief moment. This, he says, has happened to him several times. He gives a vivid description of two moments when C. S. Lewis appeared to him. He did not know Lewis well and had only met him once, though they had engaged in a fair amount of correspondence. Phillips gives his account of the appearances in this way:

A few days after his death, while I was watching television, he 'appeared' sitting in a chair within a few feet of me and spoke a few words ... particularly relevant to the difficult circumstances through which I was passing ... I had not been thinking of him at all. I was neither alarmed nor surprised ... He was just there. A week later when I was in bed he appeared again ... and repeated the same message which was very important to me at the time. (1967: 89–90)

When Phillips told these experiences to a retired bishop, the reply was 'My dear J. this sort of thing is happening all the time'.

When people reckon to see the dead it is usually within the domestic circle, normally in their own home and in contexts where they were used to seeing the deceased when alive. In my research, for example, a man whose wife had died two years previously spoke of having 'seen' her twice since her death. On the first occasion he went into his sitting room carrying a piece of toast, something his very organized wife never used to allow, and he saw her 'just sitting in the chair'. It was 'only a flash' but he was very frightened and actually telephoned a friend because 'I didn't think I was normal'. The second occasion of seeing his wife came when he was ill with an infection and had been told to stay in bed and take lots of fluid. A neighbour had been bringing him drinks and, on one occasion, he heard the sound of a cup and saucer. He turned over in bed and saw his wife standing there in the bedroom with him. Since then he reckons to hear sounds in the house every couple of months and, as he said, he does not mind being watched so he accepts it. At the time of the funeral he believed that his wife was going from being in his care to being in God's care. Since his wife's death he now believes in ghosts, which he did not before, and is a little puzzled as to what happens to people after death. This is a good example of how personal experience can lead to a reorientation of former belief.

Another individual, a woman this time, whose husband had died nearly two years ago, has not experienced him in terms of a presence but she imagines him being there and sometimes engages in a kind of argument with him 'which is almost real'. He had clear opinions about certain things and she still finds, for example, that 'his preferences in buying biscuits still win'. This individual does not believe in God and sees death as 'like going to sleep'. Her example shows the power of imagination in the post-mortem relations of the living and the dead and is probably closely related to the way in which people talk to the dead when they go to cemeteries to place flowers on graves.

A rather different perspective comes in an adult woman whose mother's body had been donated for medical research. The daughter felt that her mother was 'still around' because her body 'wasn't at rest' due to the fact that it was still with the medical profession and had not yet received a funeral.

Another woman whose husband had died several years previous to her interview said that she could still feel him sometimes touch her head. She can smell his cigarettes, can feel him near and can communicate with him. This person was of firm Roman Catholic convictions with a belief in an actual resurrection and a dislike of cremation.

These few cases illustrate how people's beliefs exist in clusters rather than in systematic forms and show how their beliefs are influenced to some degree by the experience of bereavement.

## Ghosts and near-death experience

Slightly related to the issue of sensing the dead is the question of ghosts and of near-death experiences with ghosts relating to 'other selves' while near-death experiences focus on oneself in a state apart from its body. It is worth emphasizing that most people who have some sense of the presence of their dead do not seem to interpret the experience in terms of ghosts. It may be that the very idea of a ghost enshrines a degree of impersonality and distance, whereas a sense of the presence of a dead relative is most often interpreted in a distinctly personal way. There is an immediacy and a degree of intimacy about this experience which is absent in the popular notion of ghosts; it is a field meriting considerably more research than has been done to date. Here I think researchers like Rosenblatt (1976) need to appreciate more clearly this distinction between ghosts as relatively impersonal phenomena and the sense of the presence of the familiar dead. While they may be correct in interpreting all such phenomena as 'normal psychological residues that remain after a close social relationship is terminated', they need to be more careful in describing how things appear to people because it is through that sort of clarity that explanations may be more forthcoming (1976: 65).

We already know, for example, that rural populations in England display a difference in ghost-belief between the general public at large (29 per cent) and those who are more active members of the Church of England (19 per cent). The same research found the remarkably significant fact that there appeared to be no difference between men and women when it came to belief in ghosts (Davies, Watkins and Winter, 1991: 250).

Definite shifts in cultural ideas can lead to different outcomes in belief and practice as, for example, in contemporary rural Spain where the anthropologist William Christian sees changes in attitudes to the soul and death in that 'money in the alms box that used to go for masses to the souls in purgatory ... now goes to the diocesan charity fund' (1989: 183). In contemporary Britain competing interpretations of death are likely to come both from the media and professional experts. The contemporary problem with the realm of grief, ghosts and the presence of the dead is that it occupies a domain torn between film, psychology, religion and the power of personal experience itself.

Many people probably gain their ideas of the afterlife as much from ghost films or science fiction as from the New Testament with, perhaps, the paramedical world linking the two through the two new categories of 'near-death experience' and 'out-of-the-body experience'. These descriptions of patients' experiences associated with accidents and medical operations have gained wide public attention since the late 1970s and some see them as a real basis for interpreting ideas of the soul and life after death.

While some traditional societies provided their members with categories for interpreting such strange experiences, modern life by contrast is often caught in a period of change and uncertainty. Some research suggests that where a cultural interpretation of near-death experience does exist certain individuals may still experience a degree of confusion if their experience differs in some way from the cultural pattern, as Henry Abramovitch has suggested within a contemporary Jewish context (1988). Some other research, in America, indicates that people who have undergone such experiences have a subsequent reduced sense of threat from death (Greyson, 1992).

The Christian theologian Paul Badham has placed much weight on the claim that 'if it is possible to present good grounds for believing that consciousness can function apart from the body before death, then it is intelligible to argue that consciousness might function apart from the body after death' (1984: 14). Out-of-the-body experiences provide him with just such grounds for arguing that personal identity continues apart from embodiment. Badham devotes a chapter to disagreeing with numerous modern theologians including Bultmann, Moltmann, Hartshorne and Pittinger who, as far as he is concerned, reduce the doctrine of eternal life either to some kind of transformed existence in this world or else to a place within the divine memory. For Badham there needs to be a centre of self-knowledge and awareness continuing from this life to whatever God has planned for the future. Such theological views lie beyond the scope of this book and its comparative framework.

## The dead in living memory

Our concern lies more with the distinction between physical and social death and, here most especially, with the part played by memories of the dead within the thought of the living. Physical death is a relatively obvious phenomenon: people die and are declared to be dead by the medical profession. The legal registration of death, however, marks officialdom's recognition of the change that has occurred in society. Those few painful cases where victims of accident or illness lie comatose and even 'brain-dead' raise crucial issues over death and identity which most people never have to face.

If the relationship between brain-death and the final death of the rest of the body raises both ethical and existential problems for a few unfortunate families, the undoubted physical death of someone in relation to their death in the memory of the living raises several emotional, psychological and theological issues for perhaps a majority of bereaved families in the country.

Those who are physically dead can still play a part in the conversation and history of a family as of their place of work or leisure; it may take some time for a physically dead person to 'die' in a sociological sense. While a few belong to influential groups in society and continue to live 'in history' for a very long time indeed, most ordinary citizens are unlikely to influence more than one or two generations after their death. Still, the two categories of physical and social death are slightly inadequate for dealing with the spectrum of relationships between the dead and the living. To compensate for this, a third category, that of 'death in memory', might be a useful addition to the analysis. Physical death is followed by social death which, in turn, is subsequently followed by death in the memory of the survivors. This last phase may take a considerable time and may never actually take place at all as far as certain surviving partners are concerned. This is perfectly intelligible if the identity of the living is partly composed of experiences and memories of the dead. With this in mind we return to the Nottinghamshire survey which included questions exploring the identity of the dead within the identity of the survivors (Davies *et al.*, 1990).

## Reminders of the dead

The first question concerned things reminding the bereaved of their dead. The majority, 58 per cent, felt that physical objects and situations stimulated memory while another important group, 17 per cent, found that spontaneous memories served as reminders; 13 per cent found that particular people reminded them of the dead relative; for a surprisingly small 5 per cent it was the occurrence of anniversaries which served that purpose. A final 7 per cent did not respond to this question. There is, as might be expected, and as these responses show, a great variety amongst bereaved people as to what call back memories and images of the dead. Much depends on the closeness of the prior relationship, most especially whether, as in the case of spouses, people shared the same living accommodation.

Though very little is known in detail about this complex area it is likely that two people bereaved of a third individual will have very different patterns of reminders. The spouse continuing in the family home has the constant environment of remembrance around her or him, while the party living elsewhere, say an adult child married and with their own family, may have quite a different set of memories either in the mind or, for example, in the appearance of one of the children who is a reminder of the dead grandmother.

Some cross-cultural research has shown that these links with the dead can be broken to the advantage of some people. Such 'tie-breaking', as it has been called, has been seen in North America to foster new patterns of behaviour after bereavement, especially helping someone thinking of remarriage (Rosenblatt et al., 1976: 67–85).

## Cremation and memory

Given the fact that there is a popular attitude in Britain which says that cremation makes it harder to have a concrete memorial to the dead in contrast to the fixity of a grave, we asked people if they felt that cremation had affected their memory of the dead in a way that burial would not have done. A large percentage of respondents, 86 per cent in all, thought that there was no difference between burial and cremation as far as their memory of the deceased was concerned. This is perhaps a surprising result and may hint at the part played by memory and the domestic realm of remembrance quite aside from any formal memorial to the dead. A small number, 7 per cent, thought cremation did affect the memory, while a final 8 per cent did not know.

It seems that the role of the dead in the life of the living is complex and multi-layered. When asked more specifically what part the dead play in their present lives some 66 per cent of survivors said it involved an occasional memory, while 18 per cent said they played no part and 7 per cent thought that their children somehow expressed the life of the dead relative. A final 10 per cent had nothing to say on this aspect of life.

## Dreams of the dead

Dreams constitute one significant means of survivors relating to the identity of the dead. When asked if they remembered dreaming of the dead 63 per cent said they could not, while 37 per cent said they could remember such dreams. There was no indecision on this question. People were able to answer yes or no fairly directly. The majority of dreamers had seen the dead in a positive or pleasing way and, for a few, the dreams were thought of as therapeutic. For only two individuals (3.2 per cent) were the dreams bad. By and large the dead appeared to be 'alive and well' in these dreams according to 23 per cent of the total group interviewed, but most people had no comment on this topic (Franz, 1986).

Very few were able to suggest reasons for their dream. About 8 per cent felt it might have been particular places or situations which had triggered them, and 3 per cent thought it might have been due to talking to specific people. Nobody thought that it was the occurrence of an anniversary that had triggered their dreams. One woman had not dreamed of her mother for a very long time but had started dreaming of her fairly soon before she had been contacted in this research. These recent dreams had made her think it was time for her to die herself, not least because her dead mother seemed to be calling to her. 'She is coming to fetch me', said the daughter, who was not in the least frightened by these thoughts; 'these are pleasant dreams and I look forward to them.'

Another woman, 44 years old, saw one dream in particular linking with her belief that 'death is not the end'. She is not sure whether to interpret her experience as a dream as such as her account makes clear. Her 'dream' could be reproduced for several other people:

Before my father died I had several dreams relating to his dying and after it was all over I had a pleasant one telling me not to worry any more. They are like dreams, but I can still remember it now some 15 years later, whereas ordinary dreams you can't always remember once you are awake.

## Visitations by the dead

It is for want of a better phrase that we now go on to speak of visitations of the dead in the phenomenon of sensing the presence of the dead apart from dreams. Anecdote and informal conversations with people suggested the idea of a survey question, the actual format of which may be open to criticism in that it might seem to foster the idea of such occurrences. The question posed was: 'Some people say that they have experienced the presence of a dead loved one shortly after their death. Has this ever happened to you?' Individuals did not seem to be pressed by the question into giving a positive answer, nor did they find the question odd. Just over a half of those interviewed had never experienced a sense of encounter with the dead but the rest had gained some sort of experience which they believed involved an encounter or communication with a dead person. As far as the individual is concerned these visitations, as I have called them, are quite different from dreams. This is an important point and is one reason why we deal with visitations as a different category from dreams. The major basis of the distinction lies in the fact that visitations take place during the waking state and not during sleep. By and large they involve a sense of the presence of the other person, but for a significant minority the visitation is visual and they see the person concerned; on some rare occasions a voice is heard or some sort of communication is felt to take place.

Cleiren's Leiden study showed that 14 months after a death about a third of the bereaved people studied felt a sense of the presence of the dead and also 'talked' to the dead, either vocally or in a silent inner 'conversation' (1991: 129). Finucane's interesting historical analysis of the way in which the ghostly dead appear to the living illustrates the point that up to the eighteenth century, ghosts adopted an ordinary vocal quality while by the twentieth century they tend to be mute (1982: 223). Still, since relatively little systematic work has been done on post-mortem visitations it is worth recording here what people said about their own experience in the Nottinghamshire research.

The simplest form of this sensation is expressed by the person who said of her mother: 'I feel the home is full of her presence, not in an apparition sense.' Similarly a widow said she often felt her husband's presence alongside her especially when something was on her mind. A relatively similar picture came from a person who said that every now and again she felt that someone was behind her. This she felt was a comforting presence but not of anyone in particular. It would be interesting to know how widespread an experience this is in society at large quite apart from periods of bereavement and how it might come to be associated with a particular person at the time of a death. As far as context is concerned it seems to be very largely that of the family house. These are almost exclusively domestic experiences; they are experiences of persons in a familiar place. The precise time and situation varies, as with one person whose stepmother was 'sensed' a couple of months after her death while the respondent was cleaning her teeth. One respondent contacted during the pilot stage of this research was keenly interested in Spiritualism and said he often felt the presence of dead people and, because of his Spiritualist interests, was able to give names to the states and conditions they inhabited.

*Seeing the dead*

Sometimes, sensing the presence of the dead is associated with other sensations. One person said she often felt the presence of her dead mother and often thinks that she has both 'a fleeting glimpse' of her and hears her voice. This case presents only a slight and almost indirect sense of sight. Another woman had both a clear sense of the presence of her dead grandfather and of then seeing him sitting in a chair. Yet another person 'experienced an apparition of mother years after her death. Feel she came to tell me something but don't know what. Don't feel it's finished yet, I expect to "see" her again.'

The word 'apparition' seemed to be used by people discussing this subject and without any implicit negative connotation. It is interesting that people practically never used the word ghost when they referred to sensing their own relations. There might be many reasons for this including the fact that fear only occasionally or initially enters into the experience. For example, one woman had both experienced the presence of her father and had seen him sitting in a chair. She said she was not at all frightened and actually had been comforted by it. But the interview situation may differ from ways of talking in public. There are no established formulae for talking about visitations. This was brought out very well in one particular case already cited – that of the man who walked into his sitting room carrying a piece of toast and saw his wife sitting in a chair. The second time he saw his wife was in the bedroom. He was frightened only after the first sighting but after talking about it with a friend who believed in ghosts, he found the courage not to mind the experience second time around. Another woman said she had regular apparitions of her grandfather, sometimes at times of stress. She never felt they were a threat: instead they gave strength and support.

These experiences resemble those discussed in Chapter 11 on pet death when some animal owners report an occasional sense of the presence of their dead pets. It is interesting that animals may also fall into the category of 'significant others' whose loss is much grieved but whose presence is occasionally felt by the bereaved.

*Talking to the dead*

Talking to the dead can, perhaps, be best considered by linking it with the two different contexts of the memorial site and the domestic world. The crematorium garden of remembrance and the family home are two key environments, rich in memory. Visits to graves and locations of cremated remains also permit 'conversations' with the dead associated with grave tidying and flower arranging. By contrast, many of the encounters with the dead already described in this chapter took place within the domestic sphere of home and its daily life.

In Britain crematoria gardens of remembrance and cemeteries possess obvious formal cues to memory and, though very public, they facilitate private remembering. In Britain these are recognized places where people may be alone with their thoughts. But the dead are not simply recalled on entering the garden of remembrance and forgotten on leaving it. The domestic sphere is, if anything, an even more evocative environment for the bereaved. One typical person had initially sensed the dead father's presence 'not in a supernatural way' and had often 'talked' to him. These moments had been comforting but after a period of time they ceased because 'dependence had faded'. Quite a different cameo emerged from a widow who never experienced this sense of presence but who regularly imagined that her husband was still with her. She might, for example, have an argument with him over some issue. She still felt that some of his opinions and preferences influenced her life. She still, as the example already mentioned above, bought the biscuits he preferred rather than her own favourites. Another individual was sure that she had spoken to her dead husband once and once only. She stressed that it was to him and to no one else that she had spoken, the sense of active communication was strong.

### Physical and auditory awareness

It is quite rare for people to experience being physically touched by someone who has died. One woman said she sometimes feels her deceased husband touching her head. She can smell his cigarettes and feels she can communicate with him. This individual had, in fact, practised a six-month or so period of mourning, moving from the wearing of black through grey to normal clothing. The period of social mourning did not seem to lead to a decline in her sense of her husband's presence. She stressed that she loved him now as much or even more than before his death.

A couple of individuals linked the idea of speaking to the dead with the notion of hearing the voice of a living person who was still alive but far from the hearer. One person heard her mother-in-law call out twice just before she underwent a heart attack. Another individual 'had a premonition' of her grandmother's death and then had a 'vision' of her the night she died but has seen nothing since.

In general people who have had experiences of the dead, whether by sense, sight, sound or dream, tend to find the experience comforting and supportive. A couple of cases reported an initial fear but this seemed to change into an acceptance of a more positive kind if the experience was repeated. One individual, on the contrary, did experience their dead father's presence and felt that he had wanted to 'get in touch' with the living. The survivor was distressed by this and tried not to encourage the contact in any way. By contrast, another married woman said she had never had this experience and was disappointed. Both at the time of her mother's death and subsequently on its anniversary she had 'tried to experience' her mother's presence. This indicates the positive value which many have found through visitations and which this person felt she was missing.

A rather different set of motives was found in a case of a woman who had never experienced a sense of contact but who related the fact that her dead mother had threatened to come back to haunt her. This, she added, was a very cruel thing for someone to say but, despite the promise, no visitation had occurred. Another individual who was a nurse and familiar with death said she had, in a light-hearted way, visited a clairvoyant after the death of her father but was surprised at the degree of knowledge of family relationships which seemed to emerge.

A different case emerged with a woman who said she had not felt the presence of anyone in this way but she did feel that her aunt was 'still around' in some sense because that aunt had given her body for medical research. The decision about the donation had caused some family disagreement. One man similarly reported that he felt a fellow soldier who had been killed was 'still around'.

While these varied reports of encounters with the dead in Britain touch on numerous emotions, fear seems generally not to be one of them. Though there may be a sense of surprise and astonishment, and also of concern as to the significance of an encounter, people do not seem to live in fear of reprisal or punishment of the dead. Through these many forms of contact individuals may often gain an impression of the reality of an afterlife, albeit vague. The occasions when they occur may often elicit some verbal comment or gain significance when reported to another. In these various ways experiences engender 'words against death' which may become tremendously important for the individual or family concerned. While they may not be part of public memorials or formal systems of belief they remain powerful in their effect.

# 11 Pet Death

This chapter, which presents some quite new information on the death of pets, extends our earlier discussions of human identity in relation to funeral rites to show how, in cultures such as that of Great Britain, certain animals are drawn into circles of human association to such an extent that when they die the human response is to provide a funeral rite analogous to that following a human death. This is not only because of the bonds that are severed when a pet dies but also because pets contribute towards the sense of identity of their owners. The death and funerals of pets can, indeed, attract some of the 'words against death' which human death provokes.

While we may guess that animals have been the companions of mankind for much of our racial history, we know that certain beasts have been singled out for special treatment, such as the sacred cow in India to this very day. In ancient Egypt there was a cult of sacred bulls who were mummified and given elaborate burial in underground tombs, as were certain other animals, including hawks, ibises and baboons, all reckoned to have some relationship with deities (Spencer, 1982: 195ff.).

In more recent centuries particular animals have been favoured and brought into an even closer relationship with human beings. The historian Keith Thomas gave three features to European pets in terms of the way people treat them. First they are allowed into the house and often live in very close proximity to their owners. As part of this relationship they are, secondly, very often given an individual personal name and, thirdly, they are placed in a group of animals which are usually not eaten (1983: 112). He even outlines a theological discussion of whether animals possess souls or might share in a future life, a question debated in the seventeenth and eighteenth centuries and to which we return below. He suggests that these issues 'made more headway in England than anywhere else at this period' (1983: 140).

It is the case today that in the closeness of relationship between people and animals, pets are often treated as though they were substitute persons, living in the same social space as their owners, eating specially prepared food and answering to their personal names. Given this level of contact and intimacy it is not surprising that when pets die, owners are affected in both their private lives and their more public sense of identity as daily life now lacks the pattern of feeding, walking, stroking or talking to the pet.

This makes it clear why many owners want to treat their dead pet with a degree of care and not like some wild animal whose dead body is worthless. It also suggests that the provision of a pet funeral might be added to Keith Thomas's list of the ways in which pets are treated. Indeed, it would be possible to create a scale measuring the degree of identity owners confer upon their pets by ranking the number of different attitudes held towards the animal. High on this list would be whether a funeral was provided for the pet and how its subsequent grave or remains were treated.

For many young people living in modern urban contexts the death of a pet is also likely to be the first experience of any sort of death they have encountered, apart from images in film or television (Nieburg and Fischer, 1982). This is true not only for young children and teenagers but also for many young adults and some have suggested that the experience of pet death can be used to encourage young children to think about death in general, though there are real ethical problems of disturbing children with what can be seen as premature thoughts on this topic (Leaman, 1995: 90).

Caution is proper in this area because many people aged under 40 or so in modern Western societies have not experienced personal bereavement and feel incompetent on the topic of death. In an idealistic way their wish to discuss death with children may reflect their own curiosity. Still, that is not to say that there will not be perfectly proper contexts in which some discussion of dead pets with children would be a valuable part of life experience, especially if it was not pressed into some formal and systematic account of death and dying. Many people experience and make sense of death, whether of animals or persons, in ways that are appropriate to them and not by means of some systematic psychological, religious or philosophical belief.

Certainly, some younger people do draw on their experience of pet death until their first experience of intimate human loss. One example of several I have recorded involved a young person sympathizing with an older man on the loss of his aged parent by saying that he had lost his pet dog and knew how sad the bereaved person must now feel. Though extremely well intentioned it is perfectly understandable that the bereaved individual felt the comparison slightly ill-drawn. Still, individuals can only speak in terms of their own experience and sympathy is valuable even if, at times, potentially inappropriate. Indeed, there is no guarantee that the death of a pet will not mean a great deal to some people, just as the loss of a human relative might involve relatively little emotional disturbance for others. Pet death and human loss can be interlinked, one echoing the other, as when an elderly woman's husband died leaving her to live alone except for the family dog which had been part of the close relationship between her and her husband. In some sense, her husband's identity was continued in the relationship the surviving spouse possessed with the dog. Indeed the dog was a major element in supporting her in her bereavement. When that dog then died just a couple of years later, the woman was deeply distressed and, in one sense, lost not only her pet dog but also an important link with her husband. This kind of pet death causes a form of what we might call 'echoing grief' from a previous human death. In such a case it is perfectly understandable that the owner would want some sort of funeral for her dog. This kind of significance of a pet for an elderly person living alone was briefly mentioned by the psychologist James Averill some time ago (1968: 726).

Such cases will probably be familiar to many people and underlie the growth of pet cemeteries in many town areas. It is with these emotions in mind that we turn to consider an empirical study focusing on the death of pet dogs and cats as the pets which seem to enter into closer relationships with people in Western societies.

## The death of dogs and cats

From these broad generalizations we turn to more empirical information on human responses to the death of pets by drawing on a survey of dog and cat owners carried out in 1990 by Laura and Martyn Lee and published in the book *Absent Friend: Coping with the Loss of a Treasured Pet* (1992). I was involved in analysing much of the data used in that book which were drawn from over 900 questionnaires and outlined in the final part of their volume (1992: 132ff.). Though the material is not in any true sense representative of the British public, because the responses came from readers of the specialist magazine *Dog World* of June 1990, it was the first large study of pet death carried out in the UK

With due caution we stress that those taking part possessed a deep interest in animals, particularly dogs and cats, and we expect their responses to reflect this strong commitment. The results showed that 36 per cent of the dog owners and 25 per cent of those owning cats had engaged in some sort of animal funerary rite with cremation being most common, 34 per cent of their dogs and 22 per cent of their cats being cremated. In about a third of all these pet deaths, owners sought an individual cremation with the ashes being returned to them, reflecting the trend of treating dead animals like dead humans.

What is interesting is that three quarters of the respondents felt that the death of their pet revived memories of previous bereavements not only of previous pets but also, as in the case outlined earlier, of a human loss. Indeed, a small group of 13 per cent of dog owners and 18 per cent of cat owners said they had taken time off work as a result of their pet's death and 10 per cent said they had consulted a doctor as a result of the death. Practically 75 per cent of dog and cat owners said they felt devastated when their pet died.

These results were so interesting that I constructed a further questionnaire, in collaboration with Laura and Martyn Lee, which resulted in responses from 234 pet-owning readers of *Dog World* in 1992. Pursuing the theme of funerary rites just over half, 55 per cent, of the respondents said they would use a pet cemetery if there were one near to their home, nearly 30 per cent said they would not use such a place and about 15 per cent did not know what they would do. What is interesting, in relation to the historian Keith Thomas's earlier information, was that 77 per cent of these animal lovers reckoned that animals did have souls. There was a relatively close relationship between what people thought about life after death for humans and life after death for animals.

Although this evidence is drawn from a very self-selected sample of people, it probably does reflect a growing link between humans and animals in modern urban society, and certainly in Great Britain. As people become increasingly concerned with the natural environment and, for example, oppose factory-farming methods of raising animals for human consumption, they increasingly treat animals as humans, not least in the provision of death rites.

### Human and animal remains

The fact that both humans and animals can be easily cremated results in some pet-owners requesting that their pet's cremated remains be kept and either buried or placed with their own remains at some future date. The similarity between human and animal ashes facilitates this symbolic unity of owner and pet after death. The merging of ashes reflects a kind of merging of identity between owner and pet, something made possible by cremation in a way that could never be achieved by burial.

### Symbolic animals

While animals can help form the network of relationships underlying daily existence they can, in more abstract ways, also help people reflect upon their own human life (Cusack and Smith, 1984). The anthropologist Claude Lévi-Strauss once argued that certain natural objects, places and animals were, as he put it, 'good to think' (1962: 89). So, for example, gardens are not just peaceful places but they may also help some people reflect on the ideas of peace, order, paradise and heaven. In this way physical realities help people come to grips with abstract ideas. From what we have already said it is obvious that pet death furnishes such an opportunity for reflecting on human death. But animal deaths extend beyond those of pets to include the killing and preservation of rare species, the hunting of animals as sport or killing them for meat or sacrifice. Each employs death rites of various kinds which reflect human attitudes to both life and death and now, perhaps for the first time in human history, tremendous differences are emerging between groups over these very issues. In Europe, for example, there are those who oppose bullfighting, foxhunting, bird-shooting and even the killing of animals for food while others accept all these pursuits and might even use animals in various festivals in ways others would regard as cruel. And if we extended examples across the world we would find a very great deal to say about contrasting attitudes to animal welfare as well as to human self-reflection on death and the rhetoric of death in the broader sense.

In terms of religious belief Hindus have long venerated the cow while the Parsees have an almost complete rule against harming any living thing except for a category of animals, such as frogs, regarded as an expression of evil. Christian theology, by contrast, is only just getting to grips with the issues of stewardship for the world of nature and the ethics of vegetarianism (Moltmann, 1985; Deane-Drummond, 1993). Still, pet death has remained a largely untouched topic which this chapter has attempted to remedy in a very limited way.

Pet death is a theme that increasingly appears in the media as part of a wider publicity of death and bereavement in modern society. Several pet cemeteries and crematoria in Britain have hit the headlines with their newsworthy combination of meeting a real need and sentimentalizing of animal death. The Cambridge Pet Crematorium and Cemetery has featured as a major story in the *Radio Times* (27 April 1991) along with an extensive documentary. The owner not only cremates pets but allows owners to watch the cremation and to take the cremated remains away with them in specially made boxes closely resembling small coffins. Among a growing number of examples it is worth citing the Tokyo-based Jippo pet funeral service which provides the facility of special vans 'decorated with a fairy-tale scene of green pastures and blue skies'. The entire service, from the placing of the body in its casket, its cremation within the van furnished with cremation facilities, a memorial service for the eulogized pet and the return of its ashes, takes about an hour (*Funeralis*, April 1990). Amongst the less well used services, so far at least, are those of the American Summum Company which specializes in mummification and the provision of decorated sarcophagi whether for animals or humans (*Economist*, 23 February 1991).

Because the way people think of animals, and of pet death in particular, may well reflect their deeper concerns on human death we will devote most of the rest of this chapter to presenting more detail from our 1992 survey with some additional material drawn from the earlier work as appropriate.

## Surveying pet death 1992

Returning to our 1992 survey we have a group of some 234 people, of whom the great majority, 91 per cent, were women. Just over half of all respondents, 56 per cent, were married, a small group of 6 per cent were widowed, 8 per cent were divorced, while a large 30 per cent were single. A total of 30 per cent reckoned to belong to a religious group and 60 per cent said they believed in life after death. Only 15 per cent said they did not so believe while 25 per cent remained uncertain. These responses are not surprising given that women usually believe in life after death more frequently than do men.

The distinctive feature of this survey concerned views on animals, their nature and destiny, and on owners' responses to their pets' death. As already emphasized this is no random sample of the population, not least from being very largely composed of pet-keeping women. It is also, very obviously, restricted to those who buy and read the magazine *Dog World*, and then to those who felt suitably motivated to complete and return the questionnaire. The one major advantage of these attributes is that this is as strong a group of animal lovers as one might expect to find in the general population. The disadvantage is that their responses cannot be ascribed to the general public at large or to people outside England.

## Animal souls

The idea of the soul is one of the longest standing philosophical notions still existing in modern life, as detailed in Chapters 6, 8 and 10. From Plato and the classical thought of ancient Greece and Rome, through mixed references in the New Testament and the debates of the early Church Fathers, to the high point of Thomas Aquinas, the soul has been identified as a locus of life and individuality, and as an arena of divine influence. Despite the high profile of resurrection belief in connection with a new 'body', as taught in early Christianity, the idea of the soul has not only held its place but has increased in significance over the last thousand years. Indeed, contemporary Christians give much more emphasis to the soul as the vehicle of immortality than they do to the body and the doctrine of the resurrection.

It is against this background that we consider the idea of souls in relation to animals. Despite the intrinsic vagueness of the idea of the soul and the complexity of its use in the human setting, we decided to ask pet owners if they thought that animals possessed souls. By implication this referred more to their own pets than to the realm of the animal kingdom at large. The historian Keith Thomas has shown that even in 'the later seventeenth century many otherwise orthodox clergy regarded the issue of animal immortality as entirely open' (1983: 139). He regards centuries of pet-keeping in Great Britain as an important experiential background to the popular view that animals are more than mere brutes, but even scripture – especially the Psalms – played a part in ascribing to the beasts a sense of praise towards God.

Returning to the late 1990s, it is not entirely clear just what the word 'soul' means to people as two particular questions showed rather clearly. To explore these two questions is to see the subtlety which any research needs when teasing out the emotional and philosophical dimensions embraced by this word of many meanings. So, for example, in response to this question,

'Do you think animals have souls?', 77 per cent said yes they did, 6 per cent said no, while 15 per cent said they did not know. This seems to be a very clear response with a very high level of support for the idea that animals have souls; relatively few were undecided on the issue and fewer still disagreed with it. But we should not infer from this that animal souls are assumed to confer immortality upon pets for, when asked directly if they believed in an afterlife for animals, 56 per cent said they did, 15 per cent said they did not, while 28 per cent were unsure or did not know. The following table schematizes these results and includes a final row showing what these people thought about belief in human afterlife.

|                  | Yes | No | Don't Know | Missing | Total (%) |
| ---------------- | --- | -- | ---------- | ------- | --------- |
| Souls in animals | 77  | 6  | 15         | 2       | 100       |
| Animal afterlife | 56  | 15 | 28         | 2       | 100       |
| Human afterlife  | 60  | 15 | 24         | 1       | 100       |

These results suggest that the idea of the soul serves more than one purpose in these individuals' reflection on animal life. The discrepancy between the 77 per cent who said they thought animals possessed souls and the 56 per cent who thought that life after death was open to animals suggests that possession of a soul is not always equated with belief in an immortal soul, certainly as far as animals are concerned. So it would seem that to say something has a soul is different from saying that it will have an afterlife. At one level, the idea of a soul may simply be a shorthand way of ascribing a sense of depth to life, whether it be animal or human. In this sense 'soul' resembles the use of the word 'spiritual' when used to express aesthetic, humane or profoundly artistic values. 'Soul' refers to the depth of relationship which some people have with their pets and should not be underestimated in its significance for people.

Ordinary experience teaches that some people have profound relationships with their pets and are deeply affected by their death. For many children the death of a much loved pet may lay the foundation for some small grasp of the nature of grief. Research simply reinforces and gives a sense of additional perspective to this fact of life. These relationships with pets is obvious if we sketch from the earlier 1990 survey the fact that 55 per cent of dog owners and 44 per cent of cat owners celebrated their pets' birthday, that 77 per cent reckoned their cats slept on owners' beds as did 48 per cent of dog owners. Approximately 80 per cent of these pet owners were aware of the anniversary of the death of their pet. Practically all talked to their pets and also reckoned that their pets were members of the family and it was possible to break down this sense of membership so that dogs and cats (in brackets) were said to be:

(i) equal adult members of the family: 19 per cent (23 per cent);

(ii) junior members of family: 25 per cent (25 per cent);

(iii) animal members of family: 54 per cent (51 per cent).

It is within this context of perceived relationship with pets that we can understand both the sense of grief on the pet's death and the way in which pets were reckoned to have souls. We have already seen that the word 'soul' can also carry a belief in life after death for animals, but there is another dimension to belief in life after death which emerges from the 1992 survey and the question 'do you think people can come back again as animals after death?' Some 14 per cent said yes, 49 per cent said no, 37 per cent didn't know and 2 per cent made no reply. Given that this sample is so highly biased to pet owners, to those believing in life after death, to those affirming an extensive belief in animal souls and to women, who often report higher incidence of religious belief than men, we can be fairly sure that this 14 per cent belief in the possibility of human reincarnation as animals is about as high as one might expect it to be in contemporary British society.

The following brief list of some comments made on the questionnaire returns will give a sense of the variety of beliefs about animals' afterlife and the sense of loss at their death.

'Animals go to heaven of Francis of Assisi and then return to earth later.'

'Spirits or souls rest where they were happiest in life.'

'Their spirit carries on to a further plane where they are reunited with their family.'

'I like to think life continues the same in a perfect world free from pain and evil. A duplicate perfect world so no one knows they've died.'

'The dog's spirit leaves the body as energy and links up with the universal pool of energy of other souls.'

'They become wild flowers and trees. To become the beauty that they once were.'

'Death is the end, but memories keep the love-feelings alive.'

As in the case of human bereavement, explored in Chapter 3, some individuals also talk of having sensed the presence of their dead pet as these quotations indicate:

'Their spirit is still with us.'

'They keep with their owner – have seen two of my dogs after they have died.'

'Hear and feel their presence.'

'Heard some sounds letting me know he wanted to go out – feet pattering etc. – the day after he died.'

There is little doubt that these acts of memory closely resemble reported experiences of the human dead and reflect the power of an environment to trigger imagination rendered sensitive through bereavement. The way in which the death of pets fits into the overall scheme of human bereavement should not be ignored for it affords a window into the significance of relationships for particular individuals. And, as already suggested, attitudes to the death of pets is also one way of reflecting on wider attitudes to human life and death.

## Bereavement and pet death

Three questions in the 1992 questionnaire directly addressed the subject of bereavement in a section headed 'Bereavement Support'. The first asked if people thought bereavement support necessary when someone's pet died; the second inquired whether support would be used if available; the third asked if people would be prepared to pay for professional support. The results showed that a high 74 per cent thought that support is necessary; 63 per cent felt they would use it themselves; precisely 50 per cent said they would be prepared to pay for bereavement support. There is a natural progression here from half of all the respondents who felt they would be prepared to pay for support through to practically three quarters of the whole group who felt that support was necessary. People obviously hope that their family and friends would provide the succour needed, but it is interesting that as many as 50 per cent felt that it would be worth paying for professional bereavement support.

## Echoing grief

It is very likely that the experience of bereavement shares in the nature of many other deep experiences acquired throughout life. Some anthropologists have emphasized the importance of memories and of the moods which are deposited, as it were, around those memories in our grasp of the past. This kind of mood-memory is part and parcel of the way symbols operate within our experience, influencing future encounters and, in turn, being influenced by them (Sperber, 1975).

Grief lies closer to symbolic knowledge in human beings than it does to our encyclopaedic knowledge. Each experience of grief influences earlier experiences and, in turn, is influenced by them. The death of a long-loved spouse or a mother's loss of a child expresses some of the profoundest kinds of grief. The loss of a child's goldfish, by contrast, would probably mean nothing to a friend of the family. But to the child whose goldfish has died, the loss might be considerable. This becomes all the more obvious when we consider an elderly person living alone whose dog is now her only constant companion. In terms of relationships this dog is the one whose presence is most constant and whose needs in terms of food, grooming and exercise are a significant component in the life of the woman concerned. But of even greater significance is the fact that her dog has actively shared in the life of its owner so that when it dies it is no surprise to find her with a deep sense of loss, given that her daily social world has involved, if not actually centred on, her canine companion.

The place of pets in Britain, especially urban and suburban life, is reflected in the 1990 survey which showed that some 68 per cent of dog and 61 per cent of cat owners said they had received emotional support in general on the death of their pet. At the family level 74 per cent of both dog and cat owners said they had felt supported by other members of the family when the animal had died. It is, perhaps, of sociological interest to note that on this and other questions the dog is always slightly more a 'social' animal than is the cat. A dog's death is likely to have more social consequence than the death of a cat not least because it lives a more directly social life in terms of being taken for walks and performing as a house dog. Its death may be more obviously visible than the death of a cat.

As we have already mentioned, pet death is significant in that it provides an occasion for 'echoing grief'. Grief is, doubtless, a complex phenomenon but it certainly involves memories grounded in emotion. Moods are, in one sense, the present tense of such emotion-grounded memories. Adaptation to bereavement involves movement from one set of grief-pervaded moods to moods of other more optimistic kinds which are open to the future. But people sometimes speak of the moments when the mood of grief, the memory of bereavement, is triggered, recalled and experienced anew.

The death of a pet is an event with potential for eliciting former experience of death as shown in the 1990 survey. When asked if the pet's death had revived memories of earlier deaths two sorts of response emerged. As might be expected, for a considerable minority, the death was a reminder of earlier pets who had died. Accordingly, some 34 per cent of dog and 41 per cent of cat owners were reminded of earlier pet deaths. But for some, represented in a small group of approximately 15 per cent of both dog and cat owners, the death of their pet reminded them of the death of a human being. This suggests that for a small minority the kind of relationship held with pets was strong enough to echo a human relationship. But there was another group represented by 20 per cent of both dog and cat owners who found that the death of their pet reminded them both of the death of an earlier pet and also of a human being. So in terms of pet deaths echoing human deaths we found that approximately a third of the responding pet owners felt that the death of a pet also had consequences in terms of an earlier human bereavement (cf. Isaacs, 1984).

This particular group showed that both married and divorced people actually felt that bereavement support was necessary more often than did either single people or widows. Contrary to what popular opinion might guess, people's opinion on this topic did not depend on whether they lived alone or not. In fact the trend was marginally in the unexpected direction suggesting that it was people not living on their own who perhaps felt that bereavement support was the more necessary. It may be that single people are more used to having to cope on their own while people living in families are used to gaining sympathy from others.

## Cremating pets

From what has already been said, as from many examples which could be drawn from personal experience, it is obvious that many people treat their pets as honorary persons. This involves a sense of respect towards animals which is extended to them in death. Of the 1992 sample, for example, as many as 31 per cent had had their pets individually cremated with their ashes being returned to them. Some 25 per cent had buried their dead pets at home, 21 per cent had their animals disposed of by the vet without being sure of the details of disposal, while 17 per cent had gone for mass cremation through the services of their vet. Burial at a pet cemetery was the lowest of all responses with only 4 per cent involved in it.

What is interesting is that pet cremation was reported more often than pet burial and in this the animals followed the contemporary British human path to physical extinction. When asked what they would do in the case of future pet deaths an even higher rate, some 44 per cent, said they would opt for individual cremation and 10 per cent for mass cremation. The same number of 25 per cent said they would choose burial at home, but 19 per cent said they would like their pets buried at a pet cemetery. This probably indicates that as pet cemeteries and crematoria become increasingly available they will be increasingly used. In fact 55 per cent said they would use a pet cemetery if one was conveniently available.

## Pets' and human ashes

The relatively small group of 90 or so individuals whose pets were cremated and the ashes returned to them were asked what they did with the cremated remains. Some 26 individuals simply kept the ashes but 21 individuals ticked the response box 'Kept them, to be buried with you'. This idea of keeping the ashes of a pet to be buried along with the ashes of their owner is a most striking example of a relationship between human and animal as already discussed. It also exemplifies the idea that cremation is a rite that sets people free to do what they like with the ultimate remains of a body, be it animal or human. Cremated remains by their very nature, as a simple granular substance, are easy to handle. As a substance they are open to varied use. The remains have potential in a way a dead body does not. Just as human ashes produced by modern methods of combustion permit a degree of freedom never before experienced by Western civilization so now with the ashes of pets. It would have been culturally impossible to bury a dead pet with a dead owner in any appropriate fashion, but a joint disposal is now both technically possible and, perhaps, much more socially acceptable if friends and family are prepared to undertake the task. It may be that cremated remains make this placing of owner and pet together much easier to accept for two closely similar reasons.

First because cremated remains are physically very similar irrespective of their source of origin. Light-coloured, dry, granular substances are the outcome of any cremation. It has often been said that death is the great leveller but this has never been more true than with cremation. Dead bodies are still the obvious remains of a particular individual. The fact is that a dead person is still identifiable as the body of the person known in life. This is true even though, as many mourners say, the body they see before them 'is not the person' they knew and loved. The sense that a corpse is not a person is a profound experience of life for many and is probably closely linked to the belief that the real self is somehow related to a soul that has now departed the body. To look at a corpse and to feel that it does not bear any relationship to the actual relationship once existing between the mourners and the dead is likely to reinforce either a belief in a soul or the view that death really is the end of life. When, occasionally, people speak of dead bodies in the neuter gender saying 'it was not my father lying there' etc., they are expressing their perception of a radical distinction between body and identity. It seems that some sort of liveliness in another is a fundamental trigger for perceiving personality and engaging in a relationship. The stillness of death comes as such an unfamiliar and unrecognizable posture that it leads onlookers to assume the other 'person' to be absent. Here the language of the soul comes in as one of the most convenient ways of handling this experience and trying to make sense of it. In this situation ashes are more symbolic of the person's body as it once was than of that person who now continues as a soul.

The second reason why some people might find it relatively easy to place pets' and owners' ashes together is because cremated remains are one step removed from the original body. This idea is closely related to the point just made about the body–soul distinction but differs from it in an important way. Here the ashes are seen as something different from the body that once existed. Bodies easily function as a trigger to memory, being immediate and direct. One reason why a significant minority of people prefer burial is because the buried body still functions, through the survivor's imagination, as a trigger for memory and as one basis for a continuing relationship perpetuated through visiting the grave and often engaging in conversation with the dead. Ashes, by contrast, are one step removed from the body. The physical corpse still bears some likeness to the living individual – even the buried corpse can be creatively imagined – but ashes offer no clue to the former person; they present the imagination with relatively less scope for creativity. This may be one reason why people prefer to locate them in situations which already come replete with past memories.

## Ashes and technology

It is in this sense that cremated remains take the dead a further step away from the living. This reflects Robert Hertz's anthropological argument (1960) that the first stage of funerary rites dealt with the body, which incarnates life activities, while the second stage of funerary rites dealt with the new status and identity of the dead.

Ashes are symbolically less powerful than a corpse. They present fewer triggers for grief, they represent a distancing from the dead. To say this is to generalize, because there are always some individuals for whom the cremated remains of their dead are extremely powerful points of contact in memory and contemporary experience. But, in general, ashes are symbolically different from bodies.

In this context the crematorium itself should not be forgotten as a mechanical process. We have already seen the significance of crematoria in relation to the rise of industrialized society in Britain. Here I want to propose the idea that, in one sense, ashes are symbolic of this technology which cremates bodies, be they animal or human bodies. The process itself is neutral or technological, committed to an efficient means of combustion. The cremators at a crematorium are increasingly sophisticated pieces of machinery designed to maximize the reduction of bodies to a minimum amount of remains with the barest possible emission of toxic or unsightly gases and smoke. Extensive British and European Community regulations cover these processes of combustion which make the cremation of a human body analogous to the cremation of animal remains or of any other form of 'waste'. This is quite a different picture, for example, from the Indian process of cremation which is intrinsically a religious rite governed by theological interpretation, as discussed in Chapter 6.

In this chapter, then, we have seen how those animals which contribute to the identity of their owners are responded to by a degree of grief when they die. The owners may give them a funeral and treat them as though they were, in some sense, persons, even to the point of wanting to merge their own identity with that of the pet by asking others to mix the pet and owner's cremated remains at some future date. The rhetoric of death, in terms of loss, is extended to pet animals by treating them as though they were human beings. Even more poignantly, some of the broader ideas of human afterlife may also be employed to speak of the pet as existing in some heavenly realm or as coming back as some other creature. The death of pets, then, affords a valuable entry into human ideas about post-mortality precisely because they can be 'good to think'.

# 12 Symbolic Deaths and Christian Affirmation

Physical death is such a powerful force in human experience that it has been extensively employed as a symbol for other cultural events, where one phase of existence ends and another is established in its stead. This has been especially true as far as various rites of passage are concerned, where a person is removed from one social status, and remains apart from ordinary life before being re-admitted into a new status, as was argued by Arnold Van Gennep in his classic study *Rites of Passage* (1960) and discussed here in Chapter 1. Initiation rituals, for example, may speak of the symbolic death of a boy and the birth of a man or the death of a girl and the birth of a woman (Myerhoff, 1982: 109ff.). While this comparison has often been drawn, it is important to ask whether the power of the imagery lies less in death as a negative end than in its holding out the hope of transcending death. Here the power of metaphor is very great and shows how language may be used against actual death by applying images of death to those dynamic processes in life which involve overcoming it.

Even when it comes to funeral rites the power of metaphor and symbol may operate at many levels. Clifford Geertz described a Balinese funeral as consisting 'of a host of detailed little busy work routines' which 'submerge in a bustling ritualism ... whatever concern with first and last things death may stimulate' (1960). Yet his implied criticism that some real problem of death was avoided through this bustle was, itself, questioned by Barbara Myerhoff who wondered whether, 'on another, deeper, level, less verbal, less cognitive ... we understand something about our own death in contemplating and enacting ritual involving a corpse' (1982: 118). I suspect this may be true in many contexts in which death as a dominant symbol influences attitudes through lesser and more mundane activities.

## Symbolic power of death

This universal experience of encountering death has provided a powerful image of dramatic change adopted by many cultures as a symbol of many lesser changes befalling people during their lives. In this sense death is a powerful natural symbol, so that when a culture wishes to express the belief

177

that some major change is coming about in a person's life and identity this image of death is found to lie close at hand. And here, of course, we are not talking about those afterlife beliefs holding that someone may die to earthly life and be reborn into a new heavenly existence. Such views have been common, as we have seen throughout earlier chapters. Here, by contrast, our main focus is not on life after death but on certain forms of changes of life in this world. Some of the best known examples concern the shift of identity from childhood to adulthood or from one level of awareness to a new form of spiritual knowledge. These shifts frequently take the ritual form of initiation, often interpreted through the idea of rites of passage discussed in Chapter 1.

Here we draw, once more, on Maurice Bloch's important theory of rebounding conquest, initially described in Chapter 1, to interpret certain crucial human practices which are described by participants in terms of death and rebirth. The key feature of Bloch's idea is that certain rituals add an additional level of meaning and significance to the mere biological facts of life. It is as though men and women become more than merely human through the rituals they construct, especially rites in which ordinary life is said to die before being replaced by another, higher level of existence.

## Imagination, hope and survival

It is as though human imagination utilizes both the drive for survival and a propensity for hopeful optimism to contradict the visible facts of life. To direct view, death brings people to a decaying end yet, against this cold fact, and in the very face of death, most human societies have asserted that life continues in another world, in a spiritual dimension or amongst the ancestral powers. But not only in an afterlife is death transcended. In this life, too, rites make it possible to lift the individual above the realm of death and decay. The human being may live as one who has died and, through contact with some higher power, now possesses some of that higher power to ensure that ordinary life is ordinary no longer. The words of the rites are powerful in establishing all these issues.

The highly influential sociologist Émile Durkheim provided one of the most forceful arguments for seeing religion as a set of rites which not only took individuals and bonded them together but also provided them with a sense of transcendence over the ordinariness of things. Durkheim describes this sense of power very directly: 'The man who … believes his god is with him approaches the world with confidence and with the feeling of an increased energy' (1915: 209). In fact one of the most radical distinctions this great sociologist makes in his work is between what he calls the sacred and the profane. He defines these 'two distinct and separate mental states in our consciousness' according to whether they are able to 'raise us out of ourselves' or not (1915: 212). In the same context Durkheim speaks of the 'religious imagination' and of the way it is able to 'metamorphose' certain experiences into this sacred category. Durkheim had been very much influenced by the Old Testament scholar William Robertson Smith and his famous study *The Religion of The Semites* (Carroll, Clines and Davies, 1995: 205ff.). Although his ideas were largely speculative Smith had also emphasized the significance of both fear and love in the development of human civilization and saw the emergence of a sense of unity with the deity as giving a confidence and boost to 'social progress and moral order' (1894: 154).

In Chapter 1 we mentioned A. M. Hocart (1883–1939) for his view of ritual as a way of 'securing life', of fostering and encouraging life within human societies (1973: 51). It is now time to emphasize even more that 'quest for life' which he believed lay at the heart of much ritual as an extension of the general human preoccupation to 'keep alive'. Ritual was a search for a 'full life' and not for mere existence (1933: 137). He saw that funerals were important in doing just that for those who survived. He speaks of many of his contemporaries as taking death ritual to be 'the very last occasion on which to seek life'. In this he thinks they are wrong, as he expresses it: 'that our theorists have found every kind of reason for funerals except life' (1973: 49).

With this strong emphasis on life and energy in mind we return once more, without drawing further examples from any earlier sources, to Bloch's contemporary contribution to ritual studies expressed in his theory of rebounding conquest. Bloch adds an additional dimension to these theories of fostering life and helps us understand even more clearly the way in which the image of death has been adopted as a most attractive and powerful symbol for use in other life contexts dealing with moments and events through which life is clearly fostered, confidence grows and a sense of the transcendence of ordinariness comes about. In these rites some power is believed to have conquered the individual's old and mortal self to produce a new identity and some sort of new existential awareness and, in the power of this newness, these transformed individuals go out to bring this power to others who still live at the lower level of the old existence.

## Initiation rituals

Transition from the old to the new is often accomplished through rites of initiation of various kinds. Throughout the world most traditional societies have possessed rituals which marked the sexual development of boys and girls into men and women along with rites which marked their marriage and often the birth of their children. The motif of the death of childhood and the birth of adulthood has been used in some of these rites to exemplify the changes taking place.

Also widespread are rites through which individuals come to be specialists in religious or supernatural practices. These events often make use of the image of death to symbolize the end of one phase of life. But they add to this death motif the further idea of rebirth as the commencement of the new phase of life as a religious expert. While ordination into various kinds of priesthood can carry this sense, one particularly good example is found in many traditions of shamanism.

## Shamanism

Shamans are individuals who use trance states as the context in which they take a kind of journey into some supernatural world where they engage with spirits or deities on behalf of other people who lie in some need of some help, often in the form of healing. The great Romanian historian of religion Mircea Eliade was one of the earliest scholars to describe shamanism. Referring to the use of rhythmic music, often drumming, along with the use of narcotic substances he described shamanism as a 'technique of ecstasy' (1951: 4). The word 'shaman' itself originated with the Tungu people of Siberia but the phenomenon has been encountered in very many parts of the world amongst traditional peoples, not least amongst native North and South American groups, in India (Fürer-Haimendorf, 1967: 215) and in Southeast Asia. As a term, shamanism has been regularly used by historians and phenomenologists of religion though there has been something of a trend amongst social anthropologists to speak more of spirit possession.

Whatever term is used, shamanism presents one of the foundational types of religious experience found in human societies and, apart from the ecstatic journey into a kind of supernatural geography (Collins and Fishbane, 1995), there lies at its heart the sense of a call or vocation often rooted in an experience of serious illness through which the shaman gains a sense of having died and been reborn. Eliade describes rituals associated with the vocation of the shaman in which the individual is, as it were, reduced to a mere skeleton before regaining a new power of life. The fact that some shamans are people who have been struck with illness but have recovered, and that the motif of death is also often associated with their transformation, is important in seeing the link drawn between illness and death and the power to heal. It is because they have gone through the negative state, which is basic to life, and have – in a real sense of survival – triumphed over the negativity that they now exist in a state of power ready to assist others. Here, then, we not only have one more application of Bloch's theory of rebounding conquest but can also see how the special formulae, including 'spirit languages', used by shamans serve as words opposed to negative powers. Indeed the power of positive words in the form of blessings, as of negative words in curses, could be studied at some length to reinforce the significance of verbal parts of rites in which ordinary existence, including death, was experienced as having been transcended (E. Crawley, 1934).

## Illness and near-death experiences

One dimension to shamanism lies in another phrase, that of the 'wounded healer'. This brings this phenomenon of shamanism much closer to contemporary urban society and to some Christian contexts. This image of a wounded healer was used by the Christian theologian Henri Nouwen (1972: 83) to describe Christian ministers in relation to those they serve. It is especially applicable to those who have suffered in some way and who are able to bring the experience of their personal suffering to bear upon the help they seek to bring to others. I have argued that this kind of Christian discussion of wounded healers places them within the broad classification of shamans (D. J. Davies, 1990b: 55).

In very recent times one of the clearest examples of a very similar category occurs in those people who have experienced what are called near-death experiences. Here we find people who, in perhaps the most literal sense, have been dead and because of medical technology and skill have been resuscitated. Many such survivors, as described earlier in this book, speak of having experienced a sense of going on a journey, often through a tunnel with a bright light at its end, and encountering relatives already dead or else divine-like persons who speak words of comfort and tell them to return to their ordinary earthly life. On recovery some of these who have been dead, in terms of their heart having stopped, seem to possess a new view of life, a sense of purpose and a comforting awareness of death no longer being a fearful thing. They have triumphed over ordinary life experiences, including the margins of death, and have not only survived but live to tell a positive tale of triumph which can encourage many others (Ring, 1996: 190). Here, once more, we have a set of experiences which can be interpreted in terms of the rebounding conquest motif.

This experience of having been close to death is not an especially modern phenomenon, even though modern medical techniques of resuscitation may make it more likely. Amongst the traditional Cheyenne, one of many tribes of the great plains of North America, it was believed that some people might fall into a state, rather like a coma, during which their spirit would go to visit the villages of the dead from which they were sent back to earth full of stories of their experiences (Hoebel, 1978: 92).

## Secret societies

Many secret societies have also employed the motif of death and rebirth to interpret their own initiation ritual. In Freemasonry, for example, the initiate undergoes a symbolic death within a ritual grave prior to being granted a form of new life and understanding as a Mason. Death is understood as a 'figurative death' and sets the scene for the subsequent interpretation of the new pattern of life as a Freemason (Waite, 1994: 174).

## Spiritual rebirth in Christianity

A much more traditional and long-standing example of death being used as an image of life-transformation is found in Christian beliefs and practices associated with initiation into Christian status.

The idea of death and rebirth underlies the Christian doctrine of baptism, the most important of all Christian rites by which someone is believed to become a member of the Christian Church itself. In doctrinal terms each Christian dies with Christ; the death of Christ and the baptism of the believer mirror each other. As Christ died and was buried so the believer goes down into the waters of baptism, death and water becoming symbolic equivalents. Then, just as Christ is believed to have risen from the dead so the believer rises out of the water. Accordingly believers symbolically die and rise with Christ and may be said to have been reborn.

There are two different kinds of emphasis given to this idea of death and rebirth within Christian traditions. The sacramental tradition places great stress upon the ritual traditions of the church and on the authority of the clergy. It speaks of death and rebirth as a sacramental process, one which is not dependent upon the psychology or feelings of those involved. By contrast, many within the Protestant tradition, especially in evangelical groups, see the idea of death and rebirth as something which happens in the actual experience of the believer. First there is a sense of sin and an awareness of being in a negative state, then the individual encounters a sense of newness, just as though the person had died to the old way of life and been born again into a new reality. Such believers see this as due to God's direct action in bringing a new spiritual nature into their lives.

These two perspectives have been so clear that the psychologist William James (1902) long ago defined the sacramental approach to Christianity as the religion of the once-born while the evangelical Protestant stress on conversion he called the religion of the twice-born. Similarly the sociologist B. R. Wilson used the experience of an inner rebirth as a key attribute in describing and defining the classification of the 'conversionist' type of sectarian movement (1970: 41). This 'type' of experience is not, of course, restricted to groups which might be defined as sects; it also embraces those who have come to be major leaders in mainstream churches. From the conversion experience of St Paul, St Augustine and through that of Martin Luther and many subsequent Christian figures, this awareness of the death of the old self and the birth of a new awareness has fired enthusiasm, as well as triggered revival and reformation (Rambo, 1993: 120).

What is especially important is that this personal experience is always, in the Christian context, closely allied to a belief in the resurrection of Jesus and his triumph over death (Aulén, 1970). In other words, a personal experience is combined with what is believed to be a historical moment of unique conquest, through one who is believed to be God incarnate. When this experience is shared, in what emerges as a fellowship of like-minded people, there arises a powerful community which addresses death as an enemy that has been defeated in a divine battle. The institution of the Eucharist as a repeated and frequent ritual, grounded in the memory and recall of that death and triumphant resurrection, has been one of the reasons for Christianity's historic success as a religion of world conquest. It is no accident that Christianity is a religion both preoccupied with death and with a sense of triumph over death. In the light of Bloch's theory of rebounding conquest we can understand the power felt by converts, those with the sense of having died and been reborn, that they now wish to convert others to their own state of transcendence. The 'old' nature must be replaced in everyone.

The 'words against death' which such Christians speak in funeral liturgies are symbolic expressions of their own psychological experience within their own spiritual development. This is a fundamentally important point in the history and development of Christianity, most especially amongst the evangelical groups, because it shifts the impact of death-phenomena from any realm of spirits to the inner experience of the individual. This type of person knows that death is conquered, not because of some sense of awareness of deceased kin but from a sense of awareness of the risen Christ marked in their own religious conversion. They have the proof within themselves and therefore they speak against death – and often against Spiritualism.

Though it is too stark to think only in terms of sharp classifications we may, for the sake of argument, see the other 'type' of Christian spirituality – that grounded in sacramental worship – as deriving its sense of transcendent power from the Eucharistic focus on Christ's death and resurrection along with the religious experience gained from that. This stance may also derive some real impact from the sense of experience of the faithful departed who are regularly mentioned in prayers.

From both quarters, as well as from others we have not detailed, Christianity has derived its drive to power through its belief in the overcoming of death in the historic past. For the more literal minded Christian, death and rebirth are facts of history and of psychology. For the liberal, possessing a greater metaphorical inclination, there remains a sense of the symbolic power of the Christian community founded upon the teachings and life of Christ. In practice there is probably a great interplay between both positions. Each is heir to a grammar of discourse in which death and rebirth are constantly at work through numerous levels of worship and ethics in a concerted liturgy of 'words against death'.

# 13 The Future of Death

A century ago, one Christian author pondered *The Place of Death in Evolution* (Smyth, 1897) and concluded that it was that of sorrow transmuted into joy. Many religious interpretations have done the same. If we assume that funerary rites do represent one successful human adaptation to death what is to be said about rites set more squarely within secular society?

Throughout this book I have speculated that as the human animal gained self-consciousness it found death to be a major problem. Not just in severed psychological attachments to those held dear, nor in the breaking of ties which are of sociological significance for group-based persons, but because of the more philosophical paradox of self-awareness failing to grasp its future non-existence. A point which does not, necessarily, immediately involve fear of death. I have suggested that one major feature of the success of world religions lay not only in their capacity to cope with these precise issues but also in their capacity to turn grief to advantage. In particular I have drawn attention to what I have called 'words against death', a form of positive rhetoric of death, grounded in theologies and liturgies, through which death, bereavement and afterlife beliefs are formulated and expressed. The extent to which a religion is capable of facing death and giving people, both as individuals and as a community, a sense of transcending mortality, is the extent to which that religion will flourish. Here, Bloch's idea of rebounding conquest has helped us see how funeral rites may give this sense of power to the bereaved, providing a ritual arena within which verbal rites gain their force.

We have seen how world religions formulate some of the problems and how ethnic religions have coped with death at their local level. How, for example, Indian traditions have been remarkably successful within their own cultural confines and how Christianity developed a theory and practice of death which came to transcend particular cultural boundaries. It now remains to consider other contexts, not grounded in traditional religion, where funeral customs exist to deal with death. Though relatively few groups are known which explicitly denied an afterlife, three stand out as worth consideration, namely eighteenth- and nineteenth-century rationalists, nineteenth- and twentieth-century Communists and twentieth-century Humanists.

## Secular French rites

One clear example from late eighteenth- and early nineteenth-century France is set in the context of the French Revolution and the attempt at restructuring society which accompanied it. Anti-clerical and anti-Christian groups of free-thinkers set out to replace religious acts and explanations of life with secular alternatives. For example, one leading revolutionary, Joseph Fouché, required local French cemeteries to display a notice asserting that 'Death is an eternal sleep'. Robespierre did not think such acts would be widely acceptable to the population at large, as described by Kselman in an excellent account of *Death and the Afterlife in Modern France* (1993: 125). He also shows how Henri Saint-Simon (1760–1825) seriously criticized Christianity because of its concern with, and emphasis upon, happiness in the next life rather than in this world.

Saint-Simon's associate, the social philosopher Auguste Comte, who had a great influence on later sociologists, presented a philosophical scheme of developmental stages of human thought beginning at a theological level before passing through a metaphysical stage and ending in a scientific perspective. Comte called these stages by other names which indicate the value he placed on each. The theological he called fictitious, the metaphysical he designated as abstract while the final scientific stage he called positive. This last term helps explain why Comte's sociology is sometimes called positivist sociology. But later in life and under the influence of a love affair, Comte adopted a kind of spiritual approach to life and formulated a sort of secular religion with feasts and priesthoods and with initiation rituals which even included a rite to incorporate deceased people into his expanded community grounded in love some seven years after their death.

As to the afterlife, he thought in terms of 'objective' bodily life ending at death and being replaced by a 'subjective' existence, in the 'hearts and minds of others' (Charlton, 1963: 89–91). Here, once more, we do not find silence in relation to death. Churches, if that is the correct word, were set up, for example, in London, Leicester and elsewhere, and hymns were written and sung, up until the end of the Second World War as far as the Liverpool Temple of Humanity was concerned. One hymn, dedicated to Auguste Comte, spoke of him as 'Great prophet and revealer, First of the holy Dead' (Charlton, 1963: 92). Though this social experiment in secular religion ultimately failed to evolve into a world-church, it still shows the human capacity to engage in ritual directed at death and framed by a corporate optimism.

## Soviet ceremonial

In two seminal articles, Chris Binns detailed the emergence of what he preferred to call ceremonial in the USSR of post-Revolutionary Russia

(1979: 585ff.; 1980: 170ff.; cf. Lane, 1981). Communist Party propaganda of October 1923 advocated a wide variety of secular rites including that of funerals. In the early years secular funerals were provided only for heroes of the revolution or for senior party leaders, with bands, processions and speeches at the graveside ensuring a dramatic event. Though cremation became increasingly popular as the mode of disposal for these significant social individuals (Binns, 1979: 595), perhaps the most significant opposition to mortality came after Lenin's death in January 1924. His wife asked that no memorials should be made to him, except that of following his practical example of life. Binns comments that 'no urging could have been more cruelly ignored', as towns and streets were named after him, with 21 January set aside as an annual day of mourning his death. But in particular, there followed a lying-in-state prior to the grand funeral and, unintentionally perhaps, the body was embalmed. Binns even uses the word mummification for this act, which seemed to have emerged as a result of public demand for thousands to come and see the body and pay their respects. He suggests that at a time when many religious relics were being proved fake, some a result of natural mummification, it was ideologically useful to demonstrate that science could achieve the same goal for the atheist leader. He adds that Lenin's 'miraculous preservation' might, for the masses, 'give him the aura of a saint'. The idea of the revolution and the new political reality could now be focused in the dead – yet preserved – leader, in his mausoleum at the very centre of the capitol of Communism. Here an ideological and ceremonial statement about death, as subject to the new ideology, was made in as dramatic terms as possible.

As time went on war memorials came to enshrine the names of the patriotic war-dead and were even used as the arena for youth initiation ceremonies, a clear example of the death transcendence motif. Similarly, remembrance ceremonies were held annually and, as Binns expressed it, 'death is transcended by immortal deeds'. For ordinary people a formal funeral procedure was evolved including processions, music, paying respects to the body and some statement from an official to the effect 'A citizen of the USSR has completed his life's journey. The motherland says farewell to its son, May fond memories of him remain eternally in your hearts' (1980: 180). Here death is set within the context not simply of family memory but also of the overarching purpose of the political regime. The ultimate 'words against death' set the individual within the wider corporate ideology. Certainly, both in the USSR and other European countries such as Hungary during their Communist period, large funerary areas were built where ceremonial could be conducted. Death was not relegated to some margin.

## Shared secularity

In the Communist reference to 'the motherland', in the traditional Christian affirmation of a 'sure and certain hope of the resurrection' and, for example, in the contemporary Muslim description of the death of a fellow believer as 'He responded to the call of his Lord', we find testimony to shared worlds of meaning and ultimate significance, whether this-worldly or other-worldly, as well as of a degree of authoritarianism. It is obvious from this that while 'secular' refers to an elimination of the influence of traditional religious ideas it can still embrace a collective philosophy and a collective ritual both enforced by established leaders, as in the case of Communism. A similar situation exists in Britain, for example, where the British Humanist Association is prepared to send an official to conduct funeral services for those who do not wish to have religious mortuary rites. In 1995–96, for example, approximately 3000 such ceremonies were conducted in the British Isles over a period of a year and it appears to be a trend that is on the increase.

Humanist funerals are, of course, not silent. The life of the deceased is firmly acknowledged and, in the sense appropriate to death, is celebrated. Above all else, the individuality of the dead comes to the fore as their life is detailed in its achievement. Significant relationships are described through the various circles of significance which have grown around the person while alive. These may be few, as in terms of the close and more distant family, or they may be extensive as additional circles of friends, work colleagues, guild associates, members of leisure and hobby clubs, are all included.

One Humanist memorial service provided by the American Humanist Association (Reyka, 1996) begins 'Let us be honest with death. Let us not pretend it is less than it is ... separation ... sorrow ... grief. But let us neither pretend death is more than it is. It is not annihilation. As long as memory endures ... it is not an end to love ... to joy ... and laughter.' The rite, using the symbolism of a lighted candle, involves an address including the words 'By remembering the best of this person, by recalling her finest qualities, by honouring the principle, values and dreams which guided her life, some of Jane's nobility flows into us, that we ourselves may be more noble in the days ahead'. The reading included Seneca's words 'In the presence of death, we must continue to sing the song of life', while the final 'Benediction' includes the words 'May we also on this day rekindle in our hearts an appreciation for the gifts of life and other persons ... As you return to the routine of your lives, go in love, and may an abiding peace go with you.'

This is a forceful example of the way in which a secular approach to the worth of the individual as part of a community comes to be the basis for turning death to advantage. The use of 'words against death', in the sense of benefiting from the moral principles reflected in the deceased, is very extensive. In some parts of the world this is emphasized through the use of eulogies which has increased in specific ways. Australia, for example, has witnessed the recent and rapid growth of what are often called life-centred funerals which employ a person qualified in public speaking, drama or the like to talk about the deceased and produce a ritual in which that life is rehearsed. These person-focused funerals reverse the attitude, strong in some Christian traditions, which viewed the identity and individuality of the dead as of minimal importance in funerary rites. The traditional Christian emphasis upon sin, divine mercy and an afterlife in heaven tended to devalue earthly life, probably on the basis that it had been the arena of sin rather than a sphere of pleasure. Forgiveness for the past rather than thanks for its enjoyment took ritual precedence. The telling phrase 'life-focused funerals' reflects the idea of the retrospective fulfilment of identity which was explained in Chapter 2 and which better fits the idea of post-modernity, which we discuss below, than it does the traditional world of the great religions explored in earlier chapters.

Here, then, we have an answer to the opening question of this chapter. Secular patterns of funeral ritual can achieve much in helping people gain a sense of the significance of the life that is deceased and, just as important, of life in the broader sense.

## Post-modern individuals and death

A different issue emerges when we speak of post-modernity since it need not be devoid of religious sentiment. Post-modernism is not necessarily atheistic; it is eclectic and selective of bits of beliefs. Still, this much debated word, as suggested in Chapter 2, is generally used to refer to a very individual interpretation of life, one without implied commitment to shared ideologies. Though I, personally, have serious doubts over the extent and significance of this idea of post-modernism, as far as the great majority of people are concerned, it is important to outline the attitude of mind which a small group of thinkers identify as typifying post-modernism. It depicts an individualistic world shaken free from lifestyles grounded in tradition or voluntary commitment to collective creeds and ideologies; aloof from any accepted way of thinking and acting, the individual stands alone in a world of fragmented images, sounds and smells.

More fundamentally still, it has been argued that this lone person now experiences time and space in quite new ways (D. Harvey, 1989: vii). In terms of time, rapidity of consumption or pleasure replaces a slower pace, fast food replaces long meals, a work-out in the gymnasium replaces a long country walk. Then, in terms of space, we find a growing uniformity across the world, with any one shopping mall or high street reflecting any other (Augé, 1995). Hotels across the world can be all so similar. Fashions and music rapidly pass from place to place. It is as though time is collapsing and everywhere is the same place, 'objectivity is dissipated' (Bauman, 1992b: 35).

## Negotiating individuality

While the significance of post-modernity on human identity has been widely discussed, relatively few have felt the need to extend their analysis to embrace death. Tony Walter has done so in his three-fold classification of types of death into traditional, modern and post-modern (1996: 195). Earlier chapters in this book, dealing with ethnic religions, exemplify his traditional type while the modern type is covered by both Christian and Communist rites. While Walter emphasizes the element of individual choice over planning one's own funeral, and even one's approach to death, he judiciously pinpoints the fact that even the most individualist of individuals still needs the collaboration of others in bringing about desired ends. His stress falls on the idea of 'negotiation'. 'The new authority in death and dying is not, therefore, the authority of the autonomous individual or of the post-modern consumer but the authority of persons who negotiate with each other and are influenced by what they see, hear and read' (1996: 202). In this Walter is correct: death rites necessitate collaboration. But, in one important sense, death rites also require people to collude with each other. While atheists might interpret such collusion in its full negative sense of involving fraud there is, I suspect, a more positive dimension of collusion in some ritual, especially when it involves a newly created symbolic event. One agrees to do something for someone, despite the fact it may appear unusual or odd. Be that as it may, the ritual remains social, with agreement on the fact that a symbolic event of some sort is to take place.

## Body philosophy

My own earlier analysis of post-modernism and death took a different direction from Walter's to argue that the body itself has become a prime object of concern, whether in terms of its physical health or its social image (Davies and Shaw, 1995: 104). Attention to the inner environment of the body, through health food and health clubs, or to its exterior environment of fashion dressing or fashionable holidays, serves to emphasize the fact that the body is a real and unavoidable reality worthy of attention. Here I agreed with Zygmunt Bauman's view that the human body is 'the only visible aspect of continuity' in the post-modern world. Instead of shared commitments to some abstract philosophy many do share a sense of the importance of personal well-being which is, often, set within a wider framework of ecological concern. This is one major reason why I have doubts about post-modernism with its overemphasis upon individualistic isolation of opinion. The media and various political and social movements serve to recruit many people, in their attitudes if not in actual group membership, to particular ideals about life and the world. Very many people do agree on issues of the body, they buy products reckoned to foster it and they acknowledge the importance of keeping the world free of pollution.

In many respects the contemporary upsurge of groups, often labelled as New Age groups, resembles the birth of many sectarian religious groups from the seventeenth to the nineteenth century (Armytage, 1961). The difference is that while the latter were usually based on abstract theological ideas, the New Age groups are more materialistic with various theories about gaining wholeness of body and mind through specific practices. In shorthand terms theology has been replaced by ecology, the soul by the body, heaven by earth, churches by leisure centres. And though we need to recall much from earlier chapters to qualify the comparison, we might extend these parallels to say that the churchyard has been replaced by the crematorium.

## Post-modernity and mortuary rites

The point of this comparison concerns the issue of space and time singled out by David Harvey in his analysis of post-modernity (1989: vii). The crematorium, as a post-modern structure, collapses both space and time. The body is not laid to rest 'forever' in the churchyard of a particular community surrounded by the familiar dead. Instead it is rapidly destroyed and the remains scattered, perhaps an excellent example of Bauman's 'dissipation of objectivity' mentioned above.

One very telling example of such dissipation where space certainly takes on a different meaning lies with the Celestis Corporation of Florida which offers the possibility of sending a small amount of cremated remains into outer space. Remains are to be placed in small containers, of differing quality depending on cost, which will be delivered by rocket and dispersed in such a way that each container will take its own journey in space for a very long time indeed (Phipps, 1989: 70). This example emphasizes the issue of cremation within post-modernity. While we have already seen in Chapters 2 and 6 that cremation has been widely employed as a religious vehicle for transporting the dead into the next phase of existence, here we stress the fact that cremation can also serve an important part in fostering post-modern as well as secular attitudes to death.

New mortuary techniques can trigger or foster ideological innovation. Cremation has done this and, for example, something similar may take place with cryogenics which involves freezing the body as soon as possible after death and keeping it in a deeply frozen state until some future date when medical knowledge will be able to cope with the illness from which the person died. This process has been highly developed in some parts of the USA and involves teams of specially trained persons who will attend to a dead person as soon as is practically possible after death has been medically confirmed. They take away the body to a treatment centre and prepare it for long-term deep-freezing; this involves replacing the blood system and administering special drugs to attempt to offset brain damage.

One company located in California, Alcor, has led the way in this approach to death and it is possible for individuals to take out membership prior to their decease so that the most rapid response may occur when they die (Wowk and Darwin, 1991). Many question the medical feasibility of restoring deeply frozen dead people to life again while others touch on the social problems that might face anyone who is restored to life at some future date. For critics it is easy to interpret acceptance of cryogenics as acceptance of science fiction rather than of science as such but, for the small number who give themselves to the cryogenics programme, it is a question of belief in the power of science to triumph over death as a physical process. In a slightly indirect way we may compare cryogenics with the ancient Egyptian mummification, in that both prepare the body for a future life even though the Egyptians saw the future in a heavenly realm while cryogenics firmly locate it on earth. But cryogenics also resembles the beliefs of many other religions in expressing a profound optimism that death is not the end of human life. This hope in surviving and survival stands as a distinctive feature of some human beings at all periods of history and this case simply invokes an apparently scientific procedure as the basis for that hope.

## Cremation, modernity and post-modernity

While cryogenics and the transportation of ashes into space represent extraordinarily marginal interests, the place of cremation lies much more central both to late nineteenth-century ideas, science and technology and to twentieth-century professionalization of death rites. In this, cremation marks the ideological world of modernity, where commitment to explicit ideals was matched by corporate ventures to build and manage crematoria. Against the millennium and a half of Christian burial practice the adoption of cremation in the late nineteenth century marked a major social change.

Much detailed research remains to be done on the reasons lying behind the change, especially in terms of each particular country and cultural area. What is obvious is that cremation was adopted much more readily in countries with a tradition of Protestant religion while Catholic countries were more devoted to burial. Indeed the Roman Catholic Church was opposed to cremation until the mid-1960s. One reason for this lay in the fact that in some European Catholic countries, Freemasons had favoured cremation and opposed the Catholic Church which had, in turn, set the Catholics against cremation. No such problem existed in more Protestant regions.

But there is another set of issues lying behind the adoption of cremation, especially in the industrialized cities of England. The first concerns the growth in the numbers of those dying in one restricted area and in the provision of graves for them. From the late eighteenth and throughout the nineteenth centuries, many British towns had grown considerably as large populations migrated to them to provide the workforce in the new industries. The small graveyards of old parish churches were soon over-full, often leading to bad conditions of hygiene and public health. From the 1820s to the 1850s in Britain there emerged many small companies which created their own cemeteries. New laws were passed for London in 1852 and for the rest of the country a year later enabling local authorities to prohibit further burials in existing graveyards. New burial boards came into existence and, from the 1890s, the newly established local authorities were given the right to provide new cemeteries (Dunk and Rugg, 1994: 10).

At the same time there were others who saw the future in different terms. Instead of ever increasing cemeteries, whether hygienic or not, why not cremate the dead? The year 1874 witnessed the establishment of the Cremation Society of Great Britain with Sir Henry Thompson as its President. This group worked for a change in legislation to enable cremation to be carried out lawfully. The history of the 1870s to the turn of the century is complex as far as the establishment of cremation is concerned and is not the purpose of this book (Jupp, 1990; 1993). Suffice to say that cremation was declared legal and the first official crematorium was opened at Woking in Surrey in 1885. It should not be forgotten that this was a period when industrial societies were using technology for ever broader purposes. Engineers were constantly pioneering all sorts of new machines so it is not surprising that the idea of building cremation machines sat happily with wider cultural interests. Intellectually, too, there were many free-thinkers who did not consider novelty and change from traditional customs as inappropriate.

Even so, cremation was adopted only very slowly at first. The table below shows the growth in number of crematoria in Britain over the next century or so (D. J. Davies, 1995: 4):

Crematoria in Britain

| Period | Number | Cumulative |
| --- | --- | --- |
| 1885–99 | 4 | 4 |
| 1900–09 | 9 | 13 |
| 1910–19 | 1 | 14 |
| 1920–29 | 6 | 20 |
| 1930–39 | 34 | 54 |
| 1940–49 | 4 | 58 |
| 1950–59 | 73 | 131 |
| 1960–69 | 73 | 204 |
| 1970–79 | 15 | 219 |
| 1980–89 | 4 | 223 |
| 1990–93 | 2 | 225 |

Notice how the 1930s witnessed the beginning of real growth in numbers, a process dramatically halted by the Second World War. By the mid-1960s more than 50 per cent of those dying in Britain were cremated. By then practically all the major Christian denominations, except the Greek and Russian Orthodox Churches, had accepted cremation.

Because Britain was the first Western society to reach a high level of cremation among its general population, it is of particular interest, especially in terms of the religious belief. In a very large study of people in Britain which I conducted in 1995 a kind of family funeral history was constructed to see which kind of funeral the grandparents, parents and spouses of more than 1600 people had received. It was found that nearly half (49 per cent) of those who defined themselves as atheist or agnostic (47 per cent) said that, of their more recently dead relatives, most had been cremated. This compared with 38 per cent of those calling themselves members of the Church of England and 16 per cent of the Roman Catholics (Davies and Shaw, 1995: 89). This is an important finding because it suggests that during the period of, approximately, 1950–90, those with an atheist background were much more likely to have relatives cremated than buried. There are several assumptions built into this suggestion, including the idea that those who are currently atheist probably belonged to families with a similar outlook.

I have already argued in Chapter 8 that cremation came to take on an appeal for those who were Christian in Britain. Here I stress that it was probably of even greater significance for those without religious belief. In fact, the tremendous appeal of cremation in the population at large, so that by 1996 some 70 per cent of those dying were being cremated in Britain, probably comes from this dual acceptance by both religious and non-religious individuals. For those, then, who were actively atheist or agnostic, modern cremation possessed an intrinsic appeal. Several reasons combined to make this so. Of real significance is the fact that in Great Britain the crematorium is a building owned and run by the local authority or by a private company but not by any church. This differs, for example, from Sweden where the crematoria are organized by the Church of Sweden as part of the religious provision made for the population who, until the late 1990s, paid a church tax to the state Church.

In Britain, however, the crematorium is much more a kind of neutral territory. Historically speaking the crematorium is unique in providing an arena in which people of any Christian denomination, as well as any Hindu, Sikh, Buddhist or Jew or any atheist or agnostic, can freely perform their own particular rites. Occasionally there is a problem if, for example, Christian symbols of the cross or some stained glass window are permanent fixtures. But, increasingly, the symbolism of crematoria is neutral, or at least variable, so as to serve the purpose of many different groups. This makes the modern crematorium one of the clearest expressions of contemporary society with its great mixture of beliefs and attitudes.

Secular individuals are free to use cremation quite independently of any religious practitioner or religious ritual. They may choose to have no ritual at all or else to compose or utilize a secular pattern of activity, perhaps drawing upon the British Humanist Association to provide the ritual leader. Shortly after the cremation they are, in Britain at least, free to take the cremated remains and do with them as they will. In a ritual sense there is a much greater degree of freedom from religious ritual than was possible even when someone might have been buried without religious rites but was still located in a cemetery surrounded by other people's religious symbolism.

## Two cases of ash-scattering

Against the background of these statistics two individual cases will illustrate several important points. I use these because they are not unusual and also because they show the way in which secular social contexts can leave either a family or an individual with rites to perform for themselves, apart from any wider religious interpretation.

The first case is drawn from a conversation with a recently bereaved younger man and illustrates the need for creative activity in an area of grief and private action. On the death of his father, the family opted for cremation and decided to scatter the ashes in an area of outstanding natural beauty in one of the British National Parks, in a valley that the father had loved as an amateur ornithologist.

On the day in question, the wife and son walked for some time to try and find a location with a good view. They felt this was somehow important for the deceased as well as for themselves. They also wanted a place which they would recognize on future visits. One large rock stood out amongst other smaller rocks and attracted their attention. The suitability of this spot was then doubly confirmed for them, not only because there were bird droppings on the rock, which suggested that birds frequented the place, a fact that matched the father's ornithological interests, but also because they heard Royal Air Force jets fly overhead, coming as it were out of nowhere and rapidly passing by, and the father had worked in an industry connected with aviation.

After depositing the man's remains near to this rock the wife placed a rose on them which she had brought with her. She and her son stood in silence for some time, perhaps ten minutes or so. They then left and, as they walked on, the mother suggested putting the empty container of the ashes into a public refuse bin because 'she wanted to get rid of it'. The son was uncertain about this and felt in some ways that he wanted to retain it. But he agreed with her, so they threw it away.

The second case can be related much more briefly and involves a highly educated Catholic woman whose task it was to disperse her father's cremated remains on a lake which had been a site he had enjoyed during his later life. The experience of scattering these remains on the water had an effect upon this older, adult, daughter which was greater than she had expected. As she watched the remains of her father first floating and then disappearing she found that a sense of disbelief in life after death, which had been forming in her mind for some considerable time, came sharply to a focus. She now knew that she did not believe in life after death.

Many similar cases could be cited to illustrate the complexity of these private rites of locating ashes in appropriate places; these two have been mentioned only to show that the way cremation emerged in Britain resulted in the possibility of this private world of cremated remains, far removed from the single and public act of the burial of a body. In some respects this privatization can involve a removal of 'words against death', replaced only by a memorial silence. Whether this might involve a deleterious effect upon the will to live or accommodation to grief it is hard to say at this early stage of the practice. Even so, many people find ways of setting 'words against death' as, for example, in the relatively recent form of the written memorial published in newspapers or elsewhere. These, typically, express the sense of loss of the deceased and a continuing love for them in short poems. The great majority of local newspapers in Britain carry these messages to the dead week in and week out. They can be set within any sort of ideological framework or none, and often express direct sentiment in simple rhyme. These represent a true folk response to death in linguistic form.

## Social optimism and pessimism

A. M. Hocart speaks in his 1937 essay 'Baptism by fire' of cremation as 'life-giving by means of fire' (1952: 157). He saw cremation as part of the 'process of life-giving' which lies at the heart of his vision of religious ritual as a 'technique for securing life' (1952: 51). Here Hocart reflects the underlying assumption of Chapter 1 of this book where we stressed the adaptive significance of death rites. He also echoes the anthropologist Robert Hertz, as discussed in Chapter 2, and presages Maurice Bloch by representing this group of anthropologists who manifest a kind of optimism in the view that society does not ultimately allow negativity to overwhelm its members. This differs significantly from the sociologist Zygmunt Bauman's argument, discussed in Chapter 1, that social institutions exist to hide the fact of death from members of society lest they be numbed into inactivity by the thought of death itself (1992a).

## Euthanasia

Modern trends in euthanasia offer a clear example of the desire for death transcendence. Many people seem to share the idea that life is worth living when it possesses a certain quality of experience but feel that if a time comes when, through sickness and disease, they no longer have that degree of dignity and pleasure they feel is basic to life, then they would prefer to be killed painlessly. This idea of euthanasia or a good death depicts people wishing to be in control of their life at that future date rather than being subjected to the vagaries of illness and a drawn-out death.

One of the reasons why there seems to be such a strong moral debate over this issue lies in the fact that many Christians, especially Roman Catholics, consider that it is God alone who has the ultimate control of life and of death and that it is improper for human beings to assume responsibility for the moment of death. In a very similar way this is also a reflection of the belief which opposes abortion.

## Death, life and world communities

In concluding this book we must say something about the common fact of death. As the world becomes increasingly more familiar with the thousands of societies that have composed the broad spectrum of humanity and with the rituals they have generated to help them cope with death and to turn their face to life so the potential for new rites grows. There are some contexts where an increased knowledge of human variety can lead to a rather negative or defensive attitude grounded in relativism. So, for example, some people might argue that because there are many religious beliefs, or several different sets of sacred scriptures in the world, no one of them is true. The study of comparative religion is sometimes said to make people comparatively religious and to draw them away from believing in the absolute truthfulness of any one religion and there is some truth in this observation.

But this does not seem to be the case with death ritual. The fact that practically all societies possess death rites does not mean that once people are familiarized with this variety they wish to abandon death rites as irrelevant to their own needs. Indeed, knowledge of the varied options and possibilities seems only to provide greater scope for ritual action. In Chapter 4, for example, we referred to one exhibition in which numerous artists contributed their creative reflections on how to conduct funerals and construct memorials to the dead in contemporary society. The secular nature of some present societies presents no bar to ritual. Ritual has come to be seen as something which can stand alone, apart from traditional religion, as a part of basic human and social behaviour with power to support and encourage individuals during difficult periods of life. In this sense death rites are continuing to provide both men and women as well as boys and girls with an opportunity to reflect upon themselves and upon the nature of life itself.

## Rhetoric of mortuary rites

I end this book by re-emphasizing the issue of rhetoric, that verbal arena in which one person persuades others by an eloquence appropriate to the theme in hand. No arena has challenged the human ability to frame its creativity in language more than death. The outcome has engaged the great issues of salvation, of enlightenment and of the meaning of the past and future. Most especially it has demanded that humanity consider the nature of its own sense of identity. This is as true in societies with a strong religious framework as for groups or individuals possessing a more secular outlook. This is precisely because death draws attention to the depth of existence which is focused in particular human beings.

In traditional societies the great traditions of religion give meaning and significance to life by framing death within a much broader picture of eternity and destiny through the rhetoric of salvation. In secular societies that frame changes and may take numerous forms. In Chapter 4 we briefly touched on the nature of various media as they present facts of death and ideas of life and much more could be said about the creative arts as means of dealing with death. For people whose self-identity is associated with the imagination, and its flourishing through literature or artefact, it is to be expected that novel vehicles will be drawn upon to deal with death in a non-religious world, much as described for the artistic exhibition described in Chapter 4. In societies where personal beliefs take the form of clusters of significance, drawn from many quarters, it is unlikely that any systematic belief in death and afterlife will emerge. Despite that, it is unlikely that human beings will simply see death as negating life. By engaging with death through ritual the identity of the dead will be turned to some positive effect in the ongoing memory of the living.

In the preface to his second edition of the classic treatise *The Tibetan Book of the Dead*, Evans-Wentz (1960: xv) raised a question which still carries power in the light of the diverse treatments of death we have covered in this book. He spoke of an unwillingness to die in the West which seemed to go hand in hand with a general ignorance about death. That preface was written in 1948, shortly after the Second World War, and much has happened since. Even so the issue of unwillingness to die must be set in the broad context of knowledge and schemes of understanding of death.

Willingness and knowledge may run very closely together. It may be, for example, that one reason why death is not discussed widely in Western societies is precisely because of a lack of a framework for its discussion; there is no basis for the rhetoric. This differs so tremendously from the kind of picture painted by Vitebsky's insightful and evocative study of the Sora of eastern India where 'dialogues with the dead' constitute an extensive basis for thinking about death and engaging in grief. 'Dialogues with the dead', he says, 'are not about death, but about life: it is only by having a vision of what it is to be dead, that one can have an understanding of what it is to be alive' (1993: 259). His rich ethnographic material provides one kind of model for exploring the rhetoric of 'words against death' in an exemplary fashion.

Many contemporary, urban societies may well be developing their own patterns of verbal response. To discuss death as part of a conversation on the medical condition of the deceased may, for example, be much easier than discussing it in terms of any presumed spiritual state. Medicine is clearer to most Westerners than is philosophy or theology. Perhaps one reason why the hospice movement is so positively perceived is because it locates humane questions within a broad medical frame. It is precisely when a clear philosophy emerges as, for example, with atheism or with a more New Age approach to ecology or nature, that people may talk again about their death and their preparation for it. Much contemporary talk of death focuses on personal fulfilment and upon its negative aspect, the fear of an old age lived in illness or decrepitude.

This book has engaged in broad generalizations about the power of words within the power of ritual. Yet we have not engaged in any extensive analysis of the rhetoric of particular societies; that is a complex task which needs detailed study for each culture (Oliver, 1971). That daunting necessity leads me to end this book by borrowing from one of the fathers of comparative religion, the great F. Max Müller. In concluding his famous Hibbert Lectures on the *Origin and Growth of Religion* he expresses his, and my, thought well: 'Here I should have much liked to have had some more lectures at my disposal, if only to show the influence which the first conscious contact with death exercised upon the mind of man' (1898: 382).

# Bibliography

Abramovitch, Henry (1986) 'The clash of values in the Jewish funeral', *Proceedings of the Ninth World Congress of Jewish Studies*. Jerusalem.

Abramovitch, Henry (1988) 'An Israeli account of a near-death experience: a case study of cultural dissonance', *Journal of Near-Death Studies*, 6 (3).

Achté, Kalle (1980) 'Death and ancient Finnish culture' in Kalish (1980), pp. 3ff.

Alexiou, M. (1974) *The Ritual Lament in Grief Tradition*. Cambridge, UK: Cambridge University Press.

*Alternative Service Book, The* (1980) London: Clowes/SPCK/Cambridge University Press.

Anand, Mulk Raj (ed.) (1989) *Sati*. Delhi: B. R. Publishing Corp.

Anuruddha, R. P. (1959) *An Introduction to Lamaism, the Mystical Buddhism of Tibet*. Hoshiarpur: Vishveshvaranand Vedic Research Institute.

Arditti, Michael (1993) *The Celibate*. London: Sinclair-Stevenson.

Ariès, Philippe (1976) *Western Attitudes Towards Death: From the Middle Ages to the Present*. London: Marion Boyars.

Ariès, Philippe (1991; 1st edn 1981) *The Hour of Our Death*. Oxford: Oxford University Press.

Armytage, W. H. G. (1961) *Heavens Below: Utopian Experiments in England 1560–1960*. London: Routledge and Kegan Paul.

Arriaza, B. T. (1995) *Beyond Death: The Chinchorro Mummies of Ancient Chile*. Washington: Smithsonian University Press.

Augé, Marc (1995) *Non-Places*. London: Verso.

Augustine (1945) *The City of God*, ed. R. V. G. Tasker. London: Dent.

Aulén, Gustaf (1970; 1st pub. 1931) *Christus Victor*. London: SPCK.

Austin, J. L. (1961) *Philosophical Papers*. Oxford: Clarendon Press.

Averill, J. R. (1968) 'Grief: its nature and significance', *Psychological Bulletin*, 70, pp. 721–48.

Bäckström, Anders (1992) *Den Svenska Begravningsseden*. Uppsala: Teologiska Institutionen.

Badcock, C. R. (1980) *The Culture of Psychoanalysis*. Oxford: Blackwell.

Badham, P. and Badham, L. (1984) *Immortality or Extinction*. London: SPCK.

Barinbaum, Lea (1980) 'Death of young sons and husbands following the Yom Kippur War' in Warner (1980), pp. 121–31.

Barley, Nigel (1995) *Dancing on the Grave*. London: John Murray.

Basford, T. K. (1990) *Near-Death Experiences: An Annotated Bibliography*. New York: Garland Publishing.

Bauman, Zygmunt (1992a) *Mortality, Immortality*. London: Polity Press.

Bauman, Zygmunt (1992b) *Intimations of Postmodernity*. London: Routledge.

Beck, P. V. and Walters, A. L. (1977) *The Sacred: Ways of Knowledge, Sources of Life*. Tsaile, AZ: Navajo Community College.

Bennett, Clinton (1994) 'Islam' in Holm with Bowker (eds) (1994b), pp. 90–112.

Berger, P. L. (1967) *The Social Reality of Religion*. Harmondsworth: Penguin.

Binns, Christopher (1979) 'The changing face of power: revolution and accommodation in the development of the Soviet ceremonial system 1', *Journal of the Royal Anthropological Institute*, 14 (4), pp. 585–606.

Binns, Christopher (1980) 'The changing face of power: revolution and accommodation in the development of the Soviet ceremonial system 2', *Journal of the Royal Anthropological Institute*, 15 (1), pp. 170–87.

Blacking, John (ed.) (1977) *The Anthropology of the Body*. London: Academic Press.

Blakeslee, Thomas (1980) *The Right Brain*. London: Macmillan Press.

Bloch, Ernst (1986) *The Principle of Hope*. Oxford: Blackwell.

Bloch, Maurice (1971) *Placing the Dead: Tombs, Ancestral Villages and Kinship Organisation Among the Merina of Madagascar*. Cambridge, UK: Cambridge University Press.

Bloch, Maurice (1988) 'Death and the concept of a person' in Cederroth *et al.* (1988), pp. 11–30.

Bloch, Maurice (1989) *Ritual, History and Power*. London: Athlone Press.

Bloch, Maurice (1992) *Prey into Hunter*. Cambridge, UK: Cambridge University Press.

Bloch, Maurice and Parry, Jonathan (1982) *Death and the Regeneration of Life*. Cambridge, UK: Cambridge University Press.

Boros, Ladislaus (1962) *The Moment of Truth: Mysterium Mortis*. London: Burns and Oates.

Bourdillon, M. F. C. and Fortes, Meyer (1980) *Sacrifice*. London: Academic Press.

Bowker, John (1991) *The Meanings of Death*. Cambridge, UK: Cambridge University Press.

Boyce, Mary (1979) *Zoroastrians: Their Religious Beliefs and Practices*. London: Routledge and Kegan Paul.

Breitwieser, M. R. (1990) *American Puritanism and the Defense of Mourning: Religion, Grief and Ethnology in Mary White Rowlandson's Captivity Narrative*. Madison, WI: University of Wisconsin Press.

Breuil, H. and Lantier, R. (1965) *The Men of the Old Stone Age*. London: G. Harrap and Co.

Brooks, C. *et al.* (1989) *Mortal Remains*. Exeter: Wheaton Publishers.

Burkert, Walter (1983) *Homo Necans*. London: University of California Press.

Calvin, J. (1838) *Institutes of the Christian Religion*, trans. John Allen. London: T. Tegg and Son.

Camille, M. (1996) *Master of Death*. New Haven, CT and London: Yale University Press.

Cannadine, David and Price, Simon (1987) *Rituals of Royalty, Power and Ceremonial in Traditional Societies*. Cambridge, UK: Cambridge University Press.

Carmichael, E. and Sayer, C. (1991) *The Skeleton at the Feast: The Day of the Dead in Mexico*. London: British Museum Press.

Carpay, Walter and Heyink, Harry (1996) *Midden in het Leven staan wij in de Dood*. Netherlands: Penguin Books.

Carrithers, M., Collins, S. and Lukes, S. (1985) *The Category of the Person*. Cambridge, UK: Cambridge University Press.

Carroll, M. D., Clines, D. J. A. and Davies, P. R. (1995) *The Bible in Human Society*. Sheffield: Sheffield Academic Press.

*Catechism of the Catholic Church* (1994) London: Geoffrey Chapman.

Cederroth, S. *et al.* (1988) *On The Meaning of Death*. Stockholm: Uppsala Studies in Cultural Anthropology.

Chagnon, N. A. (1968) *Yanomamo: The Fierce People*. New York: Holt, Rinehart and Winston.

Chakrabarti, S. C. (1974) 'Human sacrifice in the Vedas' in Shastri, V. *et al.* (1974) *Proceedings of the All India Oriental Conference 1974*.

Charlton, D. G. (1963) *Secular Religions in France 1815–1870*. Oxford: Oxford University Press for the University of Hull.

Chaudhri, R. A. (1983) *Muslim Festivals and Ceremonies*. London: The London Mosque.

Chidester, David (1990) *Patterns of Transcendence*. Belmont: CA: Wadsworth.

Christian, W. A. (1989) *Person and God in a Spanish Valley*. Princeton, NJ: Princeton University Press.

Church of England (1966) *The Commemoration of the Faithful Departed*. Liturgical Commission.

Clark, David (1982) *Between Pulpit and Pew*. Cambridge, UK: Cambridge University Press.

Clark, David (ed.) (1993) *The Sociology of Death*. Oxford: Blackwell.

Clarke, J. M. (1976; 1st edn 1950) *The Dance of Death in the Middle Ages and the Renaissance*. Salem, NH: Ayer Co.

Clegg, Frances (1988) *Decisions at a Time of Grief*. London: Memorial Advisory Board.

Clegg, Frances (1989) 'Cemeteries for the living', *Landscape Design*, October.

Cleiren, M. P. H. D. (1991) *Adaptation After Bereavement*. Leiden: Leiden University Press.

Codrington, R. H. (1891) *The Melanesians*. Oxford: Clarendon Press.

Cohn-Sherbok, Dan (1987) 'Death and immortality in the Jewish tradition', *Theology*, 90 (736).

Cohn-Sherbok, Dan and Lewis, Christopher (1995) *Beyond Death: Theological and Philosophical Reflections on Life After Death*. London: Macmillan.

Collins, J.C. and Fishbane, Michael (eds) (1995) *Death, Ecstasy, and Other Worldly Journeys*. Albany, NY: State University of New York Press.

Colvin, Howard (1991) *Architecture and the After-Life*. New Haven, CT: Yale University Press.

Cope, G. (ed.) (1970) *Death, Dying and Disposal*. London: SPCK.

Corr, C. A. (1993) 'Coping with dying: lessons we should and should not learn from the work of Elisabeth Kübler-Ross', *Death Studies*, 17 (1).

Cranston, S. and Williams, C. (1984) *Reincarnation*. New York: Julian Press.

Crawley, A. E. (1909) *The Idea of the Soul*. London: Adam and Charles Black.

Crawley, Ernest (1934) *Oath, Curse and Blessing*. London: Watts and Co.

Crissman, James K. (1994) *Death and Dying in Central Appalachia*. Urbana and Chicago: University of Illinois Press.

Cullmann, Oscar (1951) *Christ and Time*. London: SCM Press.

Cullmann, Oscar (1958) *Immortality of the Soul or Resurrection of the Dead*. London: Epworth.

Cumpsty, J. S. (1991) *Religion As Belonging: A General Theory of Religion*. New York: University Press of America.

Cunningham, Keith (1993) 'The people of Rimrock bury Alfred K. Lorenzo: tri-cultural funeral practise' in Meyer (1993), pp. 187ff.

Curl, J. S. (1972) *The Victorian Celebration of Death*. Newton Abbot: David and Charles.

Cusack, O. and Smith, E. (1984) *Pets and the Elderly: The Therapeutic Bond*. New York: Howarth Press.

Czech, Danuta (1990) *Auschwitz Chronicle 1939–1945*. New York: Henry Holt and Company.

Danforth, L. M. (1982) *The Death Rituals of Rural Greece*. Princeton, NJ: Princeton University Press.

d'Aquili, E. G. and Laughlin, C. D. Jr (1979) 'Neurobiology of myth and ritual' in d'Aquili, Laughlin and McManus (1979).

d'Aquili, E. G., Laughlin, C. D. and McManus, John (1979) *The Spectrum of Ritual: A Biogenetic Structural Analysis*. New York: Columbia University Press.

David-Neel, Alexandra (1970) *Initiations and Initiates in Tibet*. London: Rider and Company.

Davies, D. J. (1984) *Meaning and Salvation in Religious Studies*. Leiden: E. J. Brill.

Davies, D. J. (1987) *Mormon Spirituality: Latter Day Saints in Wales and Zion*. Nottingham: Nottingham Series in Theology.

Davies, D. J. (1990a) *Cremation Today and Tomorrow*. Nottingham: Alcuin/GROW Books.

Davies, D. J. (2nd edn 1990b) *Studies in Pastoral Theology and Social Anthropology*. Birmingham University, Department of Theology.

Davies, D. J. (1995) 'Rebounding vitality: Resurrection and Spirit in Luke-Acts' in Carroll, Clines and Davies (1995), pp. 205–24.

Davies, D. J. (1996a) 'The social facts of death' in Howarth and Jupp (1996), pp. 17–29.

Davies, D. J. (1996b) 'The sacred crematorium', *Mortality*, 1 (1), pp. 83–94.

Davies, D. J. (1997) 'Theologies of disposal' in Jupp, P. C. and Rogers, T. (eds) (1997) *Interpreting Death: Christian Theology and Pastoral Practice*. London: Cassell.

Davies, D. J., Pack, C., Seymour, S., Short, C., Watkins, C., and Winter, M. (1990) *Rural Church Project Report*, Vol. 1: *Staff and Buildings*, Vol. 2: *The Clergy Life*, Vol. 3: *Parish Life, Rural Religion*, Vol. 4: *Views of Rural Parishioners*. Cirencester: Royal Agricultural College/Nottingham Series in Theology.

Davies, D. J. and Shaw, Alastair (1995) *Reusing Old Graves*. Crayford, Kent: Shaw and Sons.

Davies, D. J., Watkins, C. and Winter, M. (1991) *Church and Religion in Rural England*. Edinburgh: T. and T. Clark.

Davies, Jon (1993) 'War Memorial' in Clark (ed.) (1993), pp. 112–28.

Davis, N. Z. (1977) 'Ghosts, kin and progeny: some features of family life', *Daedalus*, 106, Spring.

Deane-Drummond, Celia (1993) *Handbook in Theology and Ecology*. London: SCM.

*Deseret News*. Newspaper published in Utah, USA.

Desroche, Henri (1979) *The Sociology of Hope*. London: Routledge and Kegan Paul.

Dickenson, D. and Johnson, M. (1993) *Death, Dying and Bereavement*. London and New York: Open University in association with Sage Publications.

Dixon, R. and Muthesius, S. (1978) *Victorian Architecture*. London: Thames and Hudson.

Dorsett, Donald (1962) 'The Roman Catholic attitude to cremation', *Pharos*, 28 (3).

Douglas, Mary (1966) *Purity and Danger*. London: Penguin.

Douglas, Mary (1970) *Natural Symbols*. London: Penguin.

Dumont, R. and Foss, D. (1972) *The American Way of Death*. Cambridge: Schenkman.

Dunk, Julie and Rugg, Julie (1994) *The Management of Old Cemetery Land*. Crayford, Kent: Shaw and Sons.

Dunne, J. S. (1965) *The City of the Gods*. New York: Macmillan.

Durkheim, Émile (1915) *The Elementary Forms of the Religious Life*. London: George Allen & Unwin.

Durkheim, Émile (1952) *Suicide: A Study in Sociology*. London: Routledge and Kegan Paul.

Eliade, M. (1951) *Shamanism*. New York: Penguin.

Eliade, M. (1974) *Death, Afterlife and Eschatology*. San Francisco: Harper and Row.

Eliade, M. (1976) *Occultism, Witchcraft and Cultural Fashions*. Chicago: University of Chicago Press.

*Ensign*. Magazine of The Church of Jesus Christ of Latter-day Saints.

Epstein, A. L. (1992) *In the Midst of Life: Affect and Ideation in the World of the Tolai*. Berkeley, CA: University of California Press.

Erwin, P. F. (1993) 'Scottish, Irish and Rom Gypsies, funeral customs and gravestones in Cincinnati cemeteries' in Meyer (1993).

Etlin, R. A. (1993) 'The space of absence' in *Una Arquitectura para la Muerte*. Seville: Junta de Andalucia, pp. 177–89.

Evans-Pritchard, E. E. (1956) *Nuer Religion*. Oxford: Clarendon Press.

Evans-Pritchard, E. E. (1965) *Theories of Primitive Religion*. Oxford: Oxford University Press.

Evans-Wentz, W. Y. (1954) *The Tibetan Book of the Great Liberation*. Oxford: Oxford University Press.

Evans-Wentz, W. Y. (1960) *The Tibetan Book of the Dead*. Oxford: Oxford University Press.

Feijo, Rui *et al.* (1983) *Death in Portugal*. Oxford Occasional Paper 2, Anthropology Society of Oxford.

Fenn, Richard K. (1982) *Liturgies and Trials*. Oxford: Basil Blackwell.

Feuerbach, Ludwig (1957) *The Essence of Christianity*. London: Harper and Row.

Finucane, R. C. (1982) *Appearances of the Dead: A Cultural History of Ghosts*. London: Junction Books.

Flanagan, K. (1991) *Sociology of Liturgy*. London: Macmillan.

Franz, Marie-Louise von (1986) *On Dreams and Death*. Boston: Shambhala.

Freud, Sigmund (1922) *Beyond the Pleasure Principle*. London: The International Psycho-analytical Press.

Freud, Sigmund (1930) *Civilisation and Its Discontents*. London: The Hogarth Press.

Freud, Sigmund (1960) *Totem and Taboo*. London: Routledge.

Freud, Sigmund (1973) *The Future of an Illusion*. London: The Hogarth Press.

*Funeralis*. Official publication of the HT Group, Durbanville, South Africa.

Fürer-Haimendorf, Christoph von (1967) *Morals and Merit*. London: Weidenfeld and Nicolson.

Gallup, G. Jr (1982) *Adventures in Immortality*. New York: McGraw-Hill.

Garrity, T. F. and Wyss, James (1980) 'Death, funeral and bereavement practices in Appalachian and non-Appalachian Kentucky' in Kalish (1980).

Geertz, Clifford (1960) *The Religion of Java*. New York: The Free Press.

Giddens, A. (1979) *Central Problems in Social Theory*. London: Macmillan.

Girard, R. (1977) *Violence and the Sacred*. London: Johns Hopkins University Press.

Goldschmidt, Walter (1980) 'Freud, Durkheim and death among the Sebei' in Kalish (1980), pp. 34ff.

Goody, Jack (1977) *The Domestication of the Savage Mind*. Cambridge, UK: Cambridge University Press.

Goody, Jack (1986) *The Logic of Writing and the Organization of Society*. Cambridge, UK: Cambridge University Press.

Gordon, Anne (1984) *Death Is for the Living*. Edinburgh: Paul Harris Publishers.

Gorer, G. (1965) *Death, Grief and Mourning*. London: Cresset Press.

Gorer, G. (1984) *Himalayan Village*. Gloucester: Alan Sutton.

Gottlieb, C. (1959) 'Modern art and death' in Feifel, H. (ed.) (1959) *The Meaning of Death*. New York: McGraw-Hill.

Graves, T. E. (1993) 'Keeping Ukraine alive through death: Ukrainian-American gravestones as cultural markers' in Meyer (1993).

Greyson, B. (1992) 'Reduced death threat in near-death experiencers', *Death Studies*, 16 (6), pp. 523–35.

Greyson, B. and Flynn, C.P. (eds) (1984) *The Near-Death Experience: Problems, Prospects, Perspectives*. Springfield, IL: Charles C. Thomas.

Griaule, Marcel (1965) *Conversations with Ogotemmeli: An Introduction to Dogon Religious Ideas*. Oxford: International African Institute/Oxford University Press.

Grisbrooke, W. J. (1970) 'Towards a liturgy of committal' in Cope (ed.) (1970).

Hamilton-Paterson, James and Andrews, Carol (1978) *Mummies, Death and Life in Ancient Egypt*. London: Collins.

Harpur, T. (1991) *Life After Death*. Toronto: McLelland and Stewart.

Harvey, David (1989) *The Condition of Postmodernity*. Oxford: Blackwell.

Harvey, P. (1991) 'Venerated objects and symbolism of early Buddhism' in Werner (1991), pp. 68–102.

Hay, David (1990) *Religious Experience Today*. London: Mowbray.

Head, J. and Cranston, S. L. (1961) *Reincarnation: An East–West Anthology*. New York: Julian Press.

Head, J. and Cranston, S. L. (1967) *Reincarnation in World Thought*. New York: Julian Press.

Hertz, R. (1960) 'A contribution to the study of the collective representation of death' in Needham, R. and Needham, C. (eds) (1960) *Death and the Right Hand*. New York: Free Press, p. 77. (1st pub. in *L'Année sociologique*, 10, 1905–06.)

Heyink, Harry (1996) *see* Carpay, W. and Heyink, H.

Hill, E. K. (1986) 'And day brought back my night' in DeBellis, R. *et al.* (1986) *Suffering, Psychological and Social Aspects in Loss, Grief and Care*. New York: Haworth Press.

Hinnells, J. R. (1996) *Zoroastrians in Britain*. Oxford: Clarendon Press.

Hocart, A. M. (1933) *The Progress of Man*. London: Methuen.

Hocart, A. M. (1935) 'The life-giving myth' in Hocart, A. M. (1973) *The Life-Giving Myth and Other Essays*, intro. Rodney Needham. London: Tavistock.

Hoebel, E. A. (1978) *The Cheyennes: Indians of the Great Plains*. New York: Holt, Rinehart and Winston.

Hoffmann, Helmut (1961) *The Religions of Tibet*. London: George Allen and Unwin.

Holbrook, David (1971) *Human Hope and the Death Instinct*. Oxford: Pergamon Press.

Holm, Jean with Bowker, John (eds) (1994a) *Human Nature and Destiny*. London: Pinter.

Holm, Jean with Bowker, John (eds) (1994b) *Rites of Passage*. London: Pinter.

Houlbrooke, R. (1989) *Death Ritual and Bereavement*. London: Routledge.

Howarth, G. (1996) *Last Rites: The Work of the Modern Funeral Director*. Amityville, NY: Baywood Publishing.

Howarth, G. and Jupp, P. (1996) *Contemporary Issues in the Sociology of Death and Dying*. London: Macmillan.

Howes, David (ed.) (1991) *The Variety of Sensory Experience*. Toronto: University of Toronto Press.

Hultkrantz, Å. (1957) *The North American Indian Orpheus Tradition*. Stockholm: Statens Etnografiska Museum Monograph Series.

Hultkrantz, Å. (1979) *The Religions of the American Indians*, trans. Monica Setterwall. Berkeley, CA: University of California Press.

Humphreys, S. C. and King, H. (1981) *Mortality and Immortality: The Anthropology and Archaeology of Death*. London: Academic Press.

Huntington, R. and Metcalf, P. (1979) *Celebrations of Death: The Anthropology of Mortuary Rituals*. Cambridge, UK: Cambridge University Press.

Irion, P. (1968) *Cremation*. Philadelphia: Fortress Press.

Irwin, J. C. (1991) 'Origins of form and structure in monumental art' in Werner (1991), pp. 46–67.

Isaacs, Bernard (1984) book review in *Ageing and Society*, 4 (4).

Jackson, C. O. (1993) *Passing: The Vision of Death in America*. Westport, CT: Greenwood Press.

Jacobs, Louis (1992) *Religion and the Individual*. Cambridge, UK: Cambridge University Press.

James, P. D. (1989) *Devices and Desires*. London: Faber and Faber.

James, William (1902) *The Varieties of Religious Experience*. London: Longmans.

Jones, Ernest (1961) *The Life and Work of Sigmund Freud*. London: Hogarth Press.

Jones, Lindsey (1993) 'The hermeneutics of sacred architecture: a reassessment of the similitude between Tula, Hidalgo and Chichen Itza, Part 1', *History of Religions*, 32 (3).

Jupp, Peter (1990) *From Dust to Ashes: The Replacement of Burial by Cremation in England 1840–1967*. London: Congregational Memorial Hall Trust.

Jupp, Peter (1993) 'The development of cremation in England 1820–1990'. PhD thesis, London School of Economics.

Kalish, Richard (ed.) (1980) *Death and Dying: Views from Many Cultures*. Farmingdale, NY: Baywood Publishing Co.

Kearl, M. C. (1989) *Endings: A Sociology of Death and Dying*. Oxford: Oxford University Press.

Klass, D. (1993) 'Solace and immortality: bereaved parents' continuing bond with their children', *Death Studies*, 17 (4), pp. 343–68.

Kligman, Gail (1988) *The Wedding of the Dead: Ritual, Poetics, and Popular Culture in Transylvania*. Berkeley, CA: University of California Press.

Kselman, T. A. (1993) *Death and the Afterlife in Modern France*. Princeton, NJ: Princeton University Press.

Kübler-Ross, E. (1973) *On Death and Dying*. London: Tavistock-Routledge. (1st pub. 1968. New York: Macmillan.)

Lahtinen, Tuomo (1989) *Kremering I Finland*. Åbo: Åbo Akademi.

Lamont, C. (1952) *Man Answers Death: An Anthology of Poetry*. New York: Philosophical Library.

Lane, Christel (1981) *The Rites of Rulers: Ritual in Industrial Society*. Cambridge, UK: Cambridge University Press.

Laughlin, C. D. and McManus, John (1979) 'Mammalian ritual' in d'Aquili, Laughlin and McManus (1979), pp. 80–116.

Leaman, Oliver (1995) *Death and Loss: Compassionate Approaches in the Classroom*. London: Cassell.

Lee, Laura and Lee, Martyn (1992) *Absent Friend: Coping with the Loss of a Treasured Pet*. High Wycombe: Henston.

Lévi-Strauss, Claude (1962) *Totemism*. London: Merlin Press.

Lévy-Bruhl, Lucien (1965; 1st edn 1928) *The 'Soul' of the Primitive*. London: George Allen and Unwin.

Lewis, D. L. (1978) *King: A Biography*. Urbana, IL: University of Illinois Press.

Lewis, Ioan (1986) *Religion in Context*. Cambridge, UK: Cambridge University Press.

Lienhardt, G. (1961) *Divinity and Experience*. Oxford: Clarendon Press.

Lienhardt, G. (1969) 'Edward Tylor' in Raison, Timothy (ed.) (1969) *The Founding Fathers of Social Science*. London: Penguin.

Lincoln, B. (1991) *Death, War and Sacrifice*. Chicago: University of Chicago Press.

McDonald, J.F. (1966) *Cremation*. London: Catholic Truth Society.

MacKinnon, D. M. (1957) 'Death' in Flew, Anthony and MacIntyre, Alasdair (1957) *New Essays in Philosophical Theology*. London: SCM Press.

McLeod, W. H. (1968) *Guru Nanak and the Sikh Religion*. Delhi: Oxford University Press.

McManners, John (1981) *Death and the Enlightenment*. Oxford: Clarendon Press.

McNeley, J. K. (1981) *Holy Wind in Navajo Philosophy*. Tucson, AZ: University of Arizona Press.

Malinowski, B. (1974) *Magic, Science and Religion*. London: Souvenir Press. (1st pub. 1948. New York: Free Press.)

Manchester, W. (1967) *The Death of a President: November 20 – November 25, 1963*. New York: Harper & Row.

Marett, R. R. (1941) *A Jerseyman at Oxford*. London: Oxford University Press.

Maringer, Johannes (1960) *The Gods of Prehistoric Men*, trans. Mary Ilford. London: Weidenfeld and Nicolson.

Martin, Bernice (1970) 'The Spiritualist meeting' in Martin, D. and Hill, M. (eds) (1970) *A Sociological Yearbook of Religion in Britain*, 3. London: SCM Press, pp. 146–61.

Matturri, J. (1993) 'Windows in the garden: Italian-American memorialization and the American cemetery' in Meyer (1993), pp. 10ff.

Mauss, M. (1979) *Sociology and Psychology: Essays by Marcel Mauss*, trans. Ben Brewster. London: Routledge and Kegan Paul.

Max Müller, F. (1898) *Collected Works of the Right Hon. F. Max Müller*, Vol. IX: *The Hibbert Lectures*. London: Longmans, Green and Co.

Metcalf, P. and Huntington, R. (1991) *Celebrations of Death*. Cambridge, UK: Cambridge University Press.

Metge, Joan (1976) *The Maoris of New Zealand Rautahi*. London: Routledge and Kegan Paul.

Metzger, A. (1973) *Freedom and Death*, trans. R. Manheim. London: Human Context Books.

Meyer, Richard E. (1993) *Ethnicity and the American Cemetery*. Bowling Green, OH: Bowling Green University Press.

Middleton, John (1960) *Lugbara Religion*. Oxford: Oxford University Press.

Minear, P. F. (1987) *Death Set to Music*. Atlanta, GA: John Knox Press.

Mitford, J. (1963) *The American Way of Death*. New York: Simon and Schuster.

Mol, H. (1976) *Identity and the Sacred*. Oxford: Blackwell.

Moltmann, Jürgen (1969) *Theology of Hope*. London: SCM Press.

Moltmann, Jürgen (1985) *God in Creation*. London: SCM Press.

Morris, B. (1991) *Western Conceptions of the Individual*. New York: Berg.

Myerhoff, Barbara (1982) 'Rites of passage' in Turner, Victor (ed.) (1982) *Celebration*. Washington, DC: Smithsonian Institution Press, pp. 109–35.

Nandy, Ashish (1988) 'The sociology of sati' in Anand (ed.) (1989).

Needham, Rodney (1980) *Reconnaissances*. Toronto: Toronto University Press.

Nelson, G. K. (1969) *Spiritualism and Society*. London: Routledge and Kegan Paul.

Nicol, R. (1994) *At the End of the Road*. St Leonards, NSW: Allen and Unwin Australia.

Nieburg, H. A. and Fischer, A. (1982) *Pet Loss: A Thoughtful Guide for Adults and Children*. New York: Harper and Row.

Nigosian, S. A. (1993) *The Zoroastrian Faith*. Montreal: McGill-Queen's University Press.

Nock, A. D. (1932) 'Cremation and burial in the Roman Empire', *Harvard Theological Review*, XXV, pp. 321–60.

Nomberg, Sara (1985) *Auschwitz: True Tales From a Grotesque Land*. Chapel Hill, NC and London: University of North Carolina Press.

Nouwen, Henri (1972) *The Wounded Healer*. New York: Doubleday.

Obelkevich, James (1976) *Religion and Rural Society: South Lindsey 1825–1875*. Oxford: Clarendon Press.

Obeyesekere, Gananath (1981) *Medusa's Hair*. Chicago: University of Chicago Press.

Ochs, Donovan J. (1993) *Consolatory Rhetoric: Grief, Symbol and Ritual in the Graeco-Roman Era*. Columbia, SC: University of South Carolina Press.

Okely, Judith (1983) *Traveller Gypsies*. Cambridge, UK: Cambridge University Press.

Oliver, R. T. (1971) *Communication and Culture in Ancient India and China*. Syracuse, NY: Syracuse University Press.

Palgi, P. and Abramovitch, H. (1984) in *Annual Review of Anthropology*, 13, pp. 385–417.

Parkes, C. M. (1972) *Bereavement: Studies of Grief in Adult Life*. New York: International Universities Press.

Parry, J. P. (1994) *Death in Banaras*. Cambridge: Cambridge University Press.

Perham, Michael (1980) *The Communion of Saints*. London: Alcuin Club–SPCK.

*Pharos*. Journal of the British Cremation Society and the International Cremation Federation. Brecon House, Albion Place, Maidstone, Kent.

Phillips, J. B. (1967) *Ring of Truth*. London: Hodder and Stoughton.

Phipps, William E. (1989) *Cremation Concerns*. Springfield, IL: Charles C. Thomas.

Pine, Martin (1968) 'Pomponazzi and the problem of "double truth"', *Journal of the History of Ideas*, XXIX (2).

Price, S. (1987) 'From noble funerals to divine cult: the consecration of Roman Emperors' in Cannadine and Price (1987), pp. 56–105.

Prior, Lindsay (1989) *The Social Organisation of Death*. London: Macmillan.

Prioreschi, P. (1990) *A History of Human Responses to Death: Mythologies, Rituals, and Ethics*. Lewiston, NY: Edwin Mellen Press.

Purnell, N. P. (1993) 'Oriental and Polynesian cemetery traditions in the Hawaiian Islands' in Meyer (1993), pp. 203ff.

Ragon, Michel (1983) *The Space of Death*, trans. Alan Sheridan. Charlottesville, VA: University of Virginia.

Rahner, Karl (1969) *On the Theology of Death*. London: Burns and Oates.

Rambo, L. R. (1993) *Understanding Religious Conversion*. New Haven, CT: Yale University Press.

Ramsey, I. T. (1957) *Religious Language*. London: SCM Press.

Reader, Ian (1994) 'Japanese religions' in Holm with Bowker (eds) (1994b), pp. 169–84.

Reyka, Larry (1996) *A Humanist Memorial Service*. Amherst, NY: American Humanist Association (Internet).

Rhie, M. M. and Thurman, R. H. (1991) *Wisdom and Compassion: The Sacred Art of Tibet*. London: Royal Academy of Arts/New York: H. N. Abrams.

Richardson, Ruth C. (1987) *Death, Dissection and the Destitute*. London: Routledge and Kegan Paul.

Ring, Kenneth (1996) 'Near-death experiences' in Bailey, L. W. and Yates, J. (eds) (1996) *The Near-Death Experience*. London and New York: Routtedge.

Rinpoche, Sogyal (1992) *The Tibetan Book of Living and Dying*. London: Rider/Random House.

Rivière, Peter (1972) *The Forgotten Frontier: Ranchers of Northern Brazil*. New York: Holt, Rinehart and Winston.

Robinson, Jane (1987) 'A casket instead of a crib', *Senior Nurse*, 7 (2), pp. 16–18.

Robinson, Jane (1989) 'Perinatal mortality', *International Journal of Health Care Quality Assurance*, 2 (2), pp. 13–19.

Robinson, W. (1880) *God's Acre Beautiful, or the Cemeteries of the Future*. London: The 'Garden' Office.

Rohner, R. P. and Rohner, E. C. (1970) *The Kwakiutl Indians of British Columbia*. New York: Holt, Rinehart and Winston.

Rosaldo, M. Z. (1980) *Knowledge and Passion: Ilongot Notions of Self and Social Life*. Cambridge, UK: Cambridge University Press.

Rosaldo, M. Z. (1984) 'Grief and a headhunter's rage: on the cultural force of emotions' in Bruner, E. (ed.) (1984) *Text, Play and Story: The Construction and Reconstruction of Self and Society, Proceedings of the American Ethnological Society*, pp. 178–95.

Rosenblatt, P., Walsh, R. P. and Jackson, D. A. (1976) *Grief and Mourning in Cross Cultural Perspective*. New Haven, CT: Human Relations Area File Press.

Rosengren, D. (1988) 'Suicide, Durkheim and the Matsigenka' in Cederroth *et al.* (1988), pp. 215–28.

Rowell, Geoffrey (1977) *The Liturgy of Christian Burial*. London: Alcuin Club–SPCK.

Rubin, B., Carlton, R. and Rubin, A. (1979) *L.A. in Instalments*. Forest Lawn, Santa Monica, CA: Westside Publications.

Sanday, P. G. (1986) *Divine Hunger: Cannibalism as a Cultural System*. Cambridge, UK: Cambridge University Press.

Sartre, Jean-Paul (1957) *Being and Nothingness*. London: Methuen.

Schechner, Richard (1988) *Performance Theory*. London: Routledge.

Schulz, R. (1978) *The Psychology of Death, Dying and Bereavement*. London: Addison-Wesley.

Schweder, R. A. and Bourne, E. J. (1991) 'Does the concept of the person vary cross-culturally' in Schweder, R. A. (1991) *Thinking Through Cultures*. Cambridge, MA: Harvard University Press.

Schwimmer, Eric (1966) *The World of the Maori*. Wellington/Auckland: A. H. & A. W. Reed.

Scott Jr, N. H. (ed.) (1967) *The Modern Vision of Death*. Richmond, VA: John Knox Press.

Sellers, J. B. (1992) *The Death of Gods in Ancient Egypt*. London: Penguin Books.

Sharpe, E. J. and Hinnells, J. R. (1973) *Man and His Salvation: Studies in Memory of S. G. F. Brandon*. Manchester: Manchester University Press.

Sherrin, Ned (1996) *Remembrance*. London: Michael Joseph.

Shipps, Jan (1985) *Mormonism: The Story of a New Religious Movement*. Urbana and Chicago: University of Illinois Press.

Simes, Amy (1995) 'Contemporary paganism in the East Midlands'. PhD thesis, University of Nottingham.

Simpson, M. A. (1977) 'Death and modern poetry' in Feifel, H. (ed.) (1977) *New Meanings of Death*. New York: McGraw-Hill.

Skultans, Vieda (1974) *Intimacy and Ritual: A Study of Spiritualism, Mediums and Groups*. London: Routledge and Kegan Paul.

Sloane, D. C. (1991) *The Last Great Necessity: Cemeteries in American History*. Baltimore: Johns Hopkins University Press.

Smale, D. A. (1994) *Davies' Law of Burial Cremation and Exhumation* (6th edn). Crayford, Kent: Shaw and Sons.

Smith, Stevie (1987) in Wain, John (ed.) (1987) *The Oxford Library of English Poetry*. London: Guild Publishing.

Smith, W. R. (1894) *Religion of the Semites*. London: Adam and Charles Black.

Smyth, Newman (1897) *The Place of Death in Evolution*. London: T. Fisher Unwin.

Snodgrass, Adrian (1992) *The Symbolism of the Stupa*. Delhi: Motilal Banarsidas.

Spencer, A. J. (1982) *Death in Ancient Egypt*. London: Penguin Books.

Sperber, Dan (1975) *Rethinking Symbolism*. Cambridge, UK: Cambridge University Press.

Staeglich, Wilhelm (1986) *Auschwitz: A Judge Looks at the Evidence*. Institute for Historical Research.

Steiner, George (1989) *Real Presences*. London: Faber and Faber.

Stotland, E. (1969) *The Psychology of Hope*. San Francisco: Jossey-Bass.

Sullivan, L. E. (1987) *Death, Afterlife and the Soul*. London: Collier-Macmillan.

Tambiah, S. J. (1968) 'The ideology of merit and the social correlates of Buddhism in a Thai village' in Leach, E. (ed.) (1968) *Dialectic in Practical Religion*. Cambridge, UK: Cambridge University Press.

Tambiah, S. J. (1990) *Magic, Science, Religion and the Scope of Rationality*. Cambridge, UK: Cambridge University Press.

Teilhard de Chardin, P. (1974) *Hymn of the Universe*. London: Fontana.

Temple, William (1935) *Nature, Man and God*. London: Macmillan.

Thomas, Dylan (1987) in Wain, John (ed.) (1987) *The Oxford Library of English Poetry*. London: Guild Publishing.

Thomas, Keith (1983) *Man and the Natural World: Changing Attitudes in England 500–1800*. London: Penguin.

Tillich, Paul (1964) *Systematic Theology*. London: Nisbet.

Trigg, E. B. (1975) *Gypsy Demons and Divinities*. London: Sheldon Press.

Turnbull, C. M. (1965) *Wayward Servants: The Two Worlds of the African Pygmies*. London: Eyre and Spottiswoode.

Turner, H. W. (1979) *From Temple to Meeting House: The Phenomenology and Theology of Places of Worship*. The Hague: Mouton.

Turner, V. (1969) *The Ritual Process*. London: Routledge.

Tutu, Desmond (1984) *Hope and Suffering*. London: Collins.

Twitchell, James B. (1981) *The Living Dead: A Study of the Vampire in Romantic Literature*. Durham, NC: Duke University Press.

Tylor, E. B. (1958; 1st pub. 1871) *Primitive Culture*. New York: Harper.

Unterman, Alan (1994) 'Judaism' in Holm with Bowker (1994b), pp. 113–37.

Van Gennep, Arnold (1960) *The Rites of Passage*. Chicago: University of Chicago Press.

Vitebsky, Piers (1993) *Dialogues with the Dead*. Cambridge, UK: Cambridge University Press.

Voelker, R. (1987) *As Old As Fire Itself*. Springfield, MA: Notre Dame University Press.

Vovelle, M. (1993) 'La crise des rituels funèbres dans le monde contemporain, et son impact sur les cimetières' in *Una Arquitectura para la Muerte*. Seville: Junta de Andalucia.

Vulliamy, C. E. (1926) *Immortal Man: Funeral Customs and Beliefs in Regard of the Nature and Fate of the Soul*. London: Methuen.

Waite, A. E. (1994) *A New Encyclopaedia of Freemasonry*. New York: Wings Books.

Wakeman, Frederick (1988) 'Moa's remains' in Watson and Rawski (1988).

Wallis Budge, E. A. (1967; 1st pub. 1895) *The Egyptian Book of the Dead*. New York: Dover Publications.

Walter, T. (1990) *Funerals and How to Improve Them*. London: Hodder and Stoughton.

Walter, T. (1996) *The Revival of Death*. London: Routledge.

Warner, W. L. (1980) *The Living and the Dead: A Study of the Symbolic Life of Americans*. New Haven, CT: Yale University Press.

Watson, James L. and Rawski, Evelyn S. (1988) *Death Ritual in Late Imperial and Modern China*. Berkeley and London: University of California Press.

Watson, R. S. (1988) 'Remembering the dead: graves and politics in Southeastern China' in Watson and Rawski (1988).

Waugh, E. (1948) *The Loved One*. New York: Dell.

Weber, Max (1930) *The Protestant Ethic and the Spirit of Capitalism*. London: Allen and Unwin.

Weir, R. F. (ed.) (1980) *Death in Literature*. New York: Columbia University Press.

Welfle, R. A. (1935) *Our Precious Bodies: Why The Church Forbids Cremation*. St Louis, MO.

Werner, K. (1991) *Symbols in Art and Religion: The Indian and the Comparative Perspective*. Delhi: Motilal Banarsidas.

Wilder, A. N. (1967) 'Mortality in contemporary literature' in Scott (ed.) (1967).

Williams, R. (1990) *A Protestant Legacy*. Oxford: Clarendon Press.

Wilson, B. R. (1970) *Religious Sects*. London: Weidenfeld and Nicolson.

Wowk, Brian and Darwin, Michael (1991) *Cryonics: Reaching for Tomorrow*. California: Alcor Life Extension Foundation.

Wunderlich, H. G. (1983) *The Secret of Crete*. London: Souvenir Press.

Yoder, Lonnie (1986) 'The funeral meal: a significant funerary rite', *Journal of Religion and Health*, 25 (2).

Zaehner, R. C. (1956) *The Teachings of the Magi*. London: Sheldon Press.

# Index